The Struggle for Water

LANGUAGE AND LEGAL DISCOURSE
A series edited by William M. O'Barr and John M. Conley

THE
Struggle
FOR
Water

Politics, Rationality, and Identity
in the American Southwest

Wendy Nelson Espeland

THE UNIVERSITY OF CHICAGO PRESS
CHICAGO AND LONDON

Wendy Nelson Espeland is an associate professor of sociology at Northwestern University.

The University of Chicago Press, Chicago 60637
The University of Chicago Press, Ltd., London
© 1998 by The University of Chicago
All rights reserved. Published 1998
Printed in the United States of America

07 06 05 04 03 02 01 00 99 98   1 2 3 4 5

ISBN 0-226-21793-0 (cloth)
      0-226-21794-9 (paper)

Library of Congress Cataloging-in-Publication Data

Espeland, Wendy Nelson.
     The struggle for water: Politics, rationality, and identity in the American
   Southwest / Wendy Nelson Espeland.
         p.   cm. — (Language and legal discourse)
     Includes bibliographical references and index.
     ISBN 0-226-21793-0 (alk. paper). — ISBN 0-226-21794-9 (pbk: alk. paper)
     1. Water-supply—Government policy—Southwestern States. 2. Water rights—
   Southwestern States.   I. Title. II. Series.
   HD1695.S664E85   1998
   333.91′15′0979—dc21   98-4863
                                                                                      CIP

For my mother,
Esther Marie Nelson Espeland

and for her mother,
Carolina Christina Fredrikka Christensen Nelson

≋≋ **Contents** ≋≋

~~~~~ **Preface and Acknowledgments** ~~~~~

In 1981, a carful of bureaucrats drove the thirty miles northeast of Phoenix to the Fort McDowell Indian Reservation. They came to offer the 400 mostly Yavapai residents $40 million for a large parcel of their land. Although convinced of the propriety and generosity of their offer, they were worried about their reception. The stakes were high, time was short, and Indians made them nervous.

The bureaucrats represented the Bureau of Reclamation, a water-development agency in the Department of the Interior. They wanted to build a dam, best known as Orme Dam, at the confluence of two rivers bordering the reservation. The lake created by the dam would inundate most of the Fort McDowell reservation. The dam was part of the Central Arizona Project (CAP), a plan for bringing Colorado River water to the deserts of central Arizona. CAP was the biggest, most expensive, most controversial water project ever undertaken by the agency, and Orme was one of its crucial components. Orme Dam was needed, these bureaucrats believed, to regulate and store water, generate hydropower, and protect Phoenix from floods.

The Yavapai saw things differently. They did not understand why they should bear the costs of others' mistakes: of building houses in the floodplain; of growing thirsty cotton in the desert; of stopping rivers so that Phoenix could continue its unplanned, ugly sprawl and residents could keep watering into oblivion the desert that first drew them there. Nor did the Yavapai believe that it was their right to sell the land, the last bit linking them to their ancestors, land they believed was sacred. With more than 40 percent of its residents unemployed, and two-thirds of those with jobs making less than $5,000 annually, this was hardly a wealthy tribe. Nevertheless, Yavapai leaders rejected the agency's "generous" offer, saying that they would never sell their land, no matter the price. It was a response the bureaucrats found baffling.

Yavapai leaders were annoyed that these engineers had even bothered to make the trip. They did not understand the bureaucrats' obvi-

ous disappointment at their refusal. After decades of steadfastly opposing forced relocation, why did these engineers think they would
change their minds now? They were offended that the long, costly efforts to defend their land were interpreted as bargaining. Yet, despite
their hard work—the trips to Washington to testify, the endless public
meetings, all the interviews by other bureaucrats—in private moments
it was hard to forestall despair. After all, how many Indian communities have taken on the federal government, the water lobbies, and the
politicians, and won?

This is the story of a dam that was not built. The decision not to
build Orme surprised a large number of people, including me, and my
sometimes obsessive urge to make sense of this unpredictable outcome
gradually turned into this book. The effort is warranted, I think, because of the importance of the decision, its irrevocability, its significance for the people whose lives it touched, and for the fascinating
glimpse it affords of the fractious, fateful world of water politics in
arid regions. But close scrutiny is also rewarded for what this decision
can teach us about some very basic features of modern politics: the
nature and shape of bureaucratic power, the inertia of bureaucracies
and their capacity to change, the effect of organizational ideology for
how members attend to the world and construct their constituencies,
and the fate of social movements that have become institutionalized
in law and organizations. This story also provides a contemporary
twist on the politics of colonization and the extent to which state power
is now dispersed in bureaucracies, disseminated through documents,
obscured by technology, and resisted through the mobilization of culture and identity as political categories. Like earlier efforts to colonize,
this encounter between parties of disparate backgrounds, resources,
and motives demanded mutual interpretation and reappraisal, the effects of which are still being felt.

Naively, I began this project with what I thought was a simple, direct, and eminently empirical question: What happened? Having once
participated in the decision, I wanted to find an explanation that made
sense of it, one that captured its complexity and dynamism, the commitments of its participants, the shifting expectations of those who
worked at it and watched it, and the subtle, dramatic, and often banal
expressions of power that it evoked. But my efforts to sort out what I
had originally understood as interests generated bigger questions and
more complex sets of entanglements. It soon became clear that casting
the decision as a contest of interests left out too much that was interesting, took for granted what required explaining, and, as an account,
arrived too late on the scene. To understand the outcome, one needed
to appreciate interests as accomplishments that may be elicited, im-

posed, imputed, or resisted. Such an emphasis is sacrificed when interests are assumed or rendered static. More fundamentally, the process of constructing interests was also, simultaneously, a process of constructing the subjects who hold those interests: apprehending interests entails acknowledging their ties to participants' understanding of their identities, identities that were negotiated, suppressed, and mobilized in the course of this decision.

But I also came to see that my too narrow lens of interest politics distorted in another way: as an account, it reproduced a logic that some saw as deeply ideological. Some participants believed that having their relationship to this decision cast as an interest belittled them and misconstrued its stakes for them. If I framed this decision as a contest over interests, then parties were granted a standing that conveyed a formal, categorical equality among all those with a stake in its outcome. Cast this way, the consequences of this decision were represented as if differences were a matter of magnitude, of how much something matters, or of whose interests were served, rather than as disparate modes of investment in the decision.

Our tendency to see others as having interests where we have commitments suggests that "interests," as a mode of categorizing politics, detaches while it conveys, an effect that may distort more for some groups than others, and one that may itself become politicized. I began to see that assumptions, including my own, about how to "do" politics and how to make decisions were deeply cultural and that some of our most neutral and universal assumptions about choice are neither.

That is why, in trying to analyze the complex set of conditions that produced this outcome, I came to reengage some old and formidable questions: the uneasy, and sometimes volatile, relation between instrumental reason and substantive values; the conditions that propel commensuration—the transformation of qualities into quantities—and the difference that this makes for how we create and unmake boundaries, attach our selves to categories, and negotiate identities; the consequences attendant on different modes of valuing; and the capacity of ordinary citizens to participate in decisions that affect their lives, especially when these are brokered by powerful bureaucracies. In the end, I came to see this decision as a forum for analyzing competing conceptions of rationality and how these shape our understanding of political participation. The debate about a dam site became, for me, a theoretical site to consider the politics of rationality in relation to democratic practice; it offered a place to examine relations between our ideas for how to be rational, how to do politics, and what sort of people count as political actors.

These are, of course, weighty questions, concerns that are central to much classical social thought. Max Weber, in his efforts to explain the uneven path of Western rationalism, provides penetrating, influential, and sometimes elusive analyses. Characteristically, he never systematizes the relations between varieties of rationality and democracy, but in his discussions of bureaucracy, law, economy, and religion, he describes the uneasy, dynamic relation between them: how the expansion of democracy can propel forms of rationality, especially bureaucratic rationality, the "leveling" effects of democracy that can bolster or threaten bureaucratic authority, or how the technical hegemony and secrecy of bureaucracies can create monopolies of expertise that impede democratic politics. One enduring characteristic of the relation between forms of rationality and democracy, however, is the tension that eventually arises between their opposing tendencies. The impetus for bureaucratic and democratic forms may have derived from the same efforts to eliminate aristocratic privilege; nonetheless, efforts to expand elections, curtail discretion, and remove the barriers that often accompany democratic reform will be resisted by bureaucrats whose technical knowledge and administrative expertise these policies challenge.

Weber believed that the most fateful and profound tensions in modern life exist between forms of rationality. Accounting for the tensions, contradictions, or affinities that result when different forms of rationality clash is fundamental to Weber's analysis of rationalization and to his critique of modernity. It has also become the touchstone of my investigation. Rationality, in my account, is a practical, organizational, and political accomplishment. Rather than presupposing or prescribing rationality, as do many rational choice theorists, I was able to observe rationality as it is practiced, resisted, and institutionalized in the course of a complex and controversial environmental decision. In taking seriously, and trying to answer empirically, the question of what motivates some people to want to "be" rational, what this means to them, and what they do when they are trying to be rational, it was possible for me to appreciate how versions of rationality become powerful frameworks for interpreting the world.

One source of interpretive power attending forms of rationality is their often implicit assumptions about how and which people can become involved in decisions. Rationality, in this decision, required that participants be transformed into interest groups with preferences. How we "do" rationality shapes how we define and interpret our own and others' interests, which, in turn, shape how we assess and assert collective identities. The linkages between rationality, interests, and identity are dynamic, interactive, and politically consequential. And they are far too important to ignore, conflate, or assume.

Interests and identity are mutual constructions that cannot easily or automatically be read from material conditions. A strict materialist rendering obscures the cultural practices that mediate both. To conceive of interests (or implicitly of identity) as stable, ordered preferences that exist prior to choice, as do some versions of rational choice theory, assumes what needs to be explained and misrepresents a lot of interesting politics. It also misses the opportunity to investigate such basic questions as where values or preferences come from, how they change, by what political and cultural processes people come to define their interests, and how these are linked to conceptions of self and other.

Assumptions about how to integrate information is another way that conceptions of rationality shape how we interpret the world. Rationality in this decision also required that alternatives be commensurated. Unless disparate attributes and values are integrated as utility, price, or some other measure of value, it is impossible to make formal trade-offs among different outcomes. But the issue of how and whether to make the components of the decision commensurable was controversial for participants; at stake was not only how best to represent their values and interests but also how to represent them, as individuals and as members of groups. Value made commensurate is a relativistic form of value that precludes the expression of things people believe are incommensurable or intrinsically valuable. Defining something as incommensurable can be an important social boundary, one that is closely linked to people's understanding of themselves, and one that commensuration violates. The assumption that disparate values and impacts can be made commensurate is one that may distort the stakes of a decision for different groups.

Commensuration in public choice is a political act, since it transforms the categories that people use to value and represent what is meaningful to them. Since commensuration is closely associated with rationality, and since it is so pervasive in modern society, it is especially important to understand its consequences. It is not only *what* we value or *how much* we value that matters; *how* we value can be an important cultural form. Changing the form of decision making involves redefining the terms of the debate, what can be talked about and what cannot. Valuing, even when done as "scientifically" or as "rationally" as possible, is ultimately a political process.

Literally hundreds of groups and organizations were involved in this decision, ranging from environmental activists to flood victims to wealthy developers. My account will focus on just three groups with deep investments in the outcome: the Yavapai community , which mobilized to defend their land; a group of loyal bureau engineers, dedicated to their agency and to the dam they had spent years designing and defending; and a group of younger, unconventional bureau employers who were charged with devising a study that would produce what forty years of politics had not—a decision that would resolve the Orme Dam controversy, a decision that would stick.

These groups, with different backgrounds, expertise, and worldviews, were compelled to confront one another, on very uneven terms, in order to interpret their own and one another's interests, actions, and goals. In the process, they encountered different versions of rationality which propelled and framed their actions and which some tried, futilely, to reconcile. What the decision came to mean for each group varied: for one, the dispute reflected their power, their professional identity, their ties to an organization they loved, the value of their work and its place in the world; for another, it was their chance to enact a vision of public service that made government more responsive to its citizens—the decision provided a forum for considering the role of science and reason in public life and the chance to create and practice a new form of democracy, one rooted in a procedural rationality; and, finally, for one group the decision became a referendum on their right to be.

Members of each group were transformed by this experience, as it elicited a more articulate defense of who they were, what they stood for, and the contours of their difference. And I have come to see that rationality is a deeply hermeneutic enterprise, one that changes how we value, our relationship to what we value, and the way in which we construct identities that make sense of our lives. Appreciating this side of rationality is essential for understanding its power and importance, and the practical ways that it affects people's lives.

Books, and their authors, require tending. One of the nicest things about finishing this book is the chance to acknowledge the people and institutions that sustained it and me. I am deeply grateful for the bountiful and often creative support I have received. First, I must thank the many people who kindly agreed to share with me their expertise and stories. I promised not to name them, but I hope they know how I grateful I am for what they taught me. Wendy Griswold, John Padgett, and Paul Hirsch, as my advisers at the University of Chicago, helped launch this book. Their high standards were inspiring; their careful advice, central.

Michael Burawoy generously offered to read my dissertation and then provided me with pages of wise comments about how to revise it. His friendship and support were pivotal. Others who read the whole thing (sometimes in small pieces) and offered thoughtful advice include Bruce Carruthers, Mark Granovetter, Carol Heimer, Charlie Moscos, Robert Nelson, Art Stinchcombe, John Walton, and the anonymous reviewers for the Press.

I am grateful for the influence of some remarkable teachers. Richard Nagasawa's enthusiasm and careful mentoring made me want to become a sociologist. Courses taken from David Greenstone, Morris Janowitz, Hans Joas, Donald Levine, John Padgett, and John Peel showed me that inspired classes endure in the work and imaginations of their students. Friendships forged while at the University of Chicago continue to sustain me: Thanks to Edwin Amenta, Michael Camille, Elisabeth Clemens, Billie Crawford, Ingrid Crepel, Alfred Darnell, Lisa Douglass, Tom Durkin, Blair Gifford, Kathy Hall, Tom Hoffer, Polly Hoover, Fred Kniss, Mark Jacobs, Gayle Janowitz, Maureen Kelly, Mindie Lazarus-Black, Stuart Michels, Kathy Neckerman, Mary Jane Osa, and Kimberly Stanton for your loyalty over the years. I also profited greatly from the Workshop on Culture and the Workshop on Organizations and Politics, led by Wendy Griswold and John Padgett.

The American Bar Foundation has proven itself a wonderful place to begin a dissertation and complete a book. I am grateful to William L. F. Felstiner, its former director, and to Bryant Garth, its current director, for their financial and intellectual support. Thanks to Roz Caldwell, Terry Halliday, Beth Mertz, Susan Shapiro, Peter Siegelman, Brenda Smith, Chris Tomlins, Tom Tyler, and Victoria Woeste for helping to make my time there so enjoyable and valuable. John Comaroff's generous help was especially fateful.

The Center for Dispute Resolution and the Institute for Policy Research at Northwestern University, and a University Research Grant, generously supported this work. Librarians at Special Collections and the Arizona Room at Arizona State University, especially Steven Phalen, were cordial and helpful. Working with John Tryneski and Kathryn Kraynik of the University of Chicago Press has been a pleasure. Mark Jacobs's thoughtful efforts to improve both my prose and my argument are greatly appreciated.

The Department of Sociology at Northwestern University has collectively created a stimulating and supportive community. Being part of a department that values both scholarship and civility has been wonderful. At Northwestern, I am especially grateful to Vilna Bashi, Nicola Beisel, Beth Clifford, Mary Driscol, Brian Gran, Julia Harris-Sacony, Sandy Jencks, Cathy O'Leary, Orville Lee, Stephanie Leonard, Mary Lopez, Tessie Liu, Aldon Morris, Charles Ragin, Paul Schnorr, David Shulman, Lisa Staffen, Mitchell Stevens, Michelle Van Natta, Marc Ventresca, and Chris Winship for their support.

Carmen Cranston, Heather Jones, Nadya Popovich, and Elena Voronova offered friendship and loving, attentive care of my children. As every working mother knows, nothing matters more. Friendships with Sandra Morris Webster, Alicia Palacio, and Natalie Waugh, despite time and distance, still sustain me. Carol Heimer let me interrupt her work anytime to help with mine. In offering friendship without limits, she, along with Art, Kai, and Per, became family. Janet Wilson Greenhow, Elspeth Carruthers, Andrew Carruthers, Bruce and Maureen Carruthers, Mary Carruthers, and Erika Rosenfeld have also become my family during the course of this work, offering their encouragement and love.

My sister, Anne Mitchell, her husband, John, and their children, Scott, Wendy, and Amanda, and my brother, Mark Espeland, his wife, Anne Boyle, and their son, Amos, have been crucial sources of love, support, and phone calls. My parents, Obert L. Espeland and Esther Marie Nelson Espeland, never lost faith in me. My son, Samuel Nelson, and my daughter, Esther Jane, taught me about priorities and unconditional love. My partner, Bruce, loved me through it all with "no weighing of circumstances." Who could ask for more?

Parts of chapter 5 were originally published as "Legally Mediated Identities: The National Environmental Policy Act and the Bureaucratic Construction of Interests," *Law and Society Review* 28, no. 5 (1994), reprinted by permission of the Law and Society Association. Parts of the preface and chapter 1 are reprinted from "Legal Structure in Colonial Encounters: Bureaucratizing Culture, Environment, and Identity in the American Southwest," *Law and Social Inquiry* 20 (1998), copyright 1998 by the American Bar Foundation, all rights reserved. The cartoon in chapter 3 by Reg Manning is reproduced by permission of Mrs. Ruth Manning and Mr. David C. Manning.

 **One**

Contested Rationalities

The fate of our times is characterized by rationalization and intellectualization and, above all, by the 'disenchantment of the world.'

Max Weber

The history of man's efforts to subjugate nature is also the history of man's subjugation by man.

Max Horkheimer

On a cool November weekend in 1991, a group of friends met at the Fort McDowell Reservation in central Arizona to attend a pow-wow. It promised to be a splendid evening, filled with drumming, dancing, speeches, and joy. It was a homecoming, as people who had been apart for years caught up with one another's lives, enjoyed the distinctive Sonoran Desert scenery, and chatted expectantly about the night's festivities. For some, simply returning to the reservation, after many years, was deeply satisfying. It was still beautiful, it was still there.

The Yavapai Community at Fort McDowell

The reservation had been home to the Yavapai community since Teddy Roosevelt created it in 1903. Long before that, when Spanish explorers first arrived in the late sixteenth century, they found Yavapai ascendants living in the same area. The Spanish referred to them in their diaries as Seronos, Mountain People, or Cruzatos (for the crosses they wore). Small by Arizona standards, the reservation encompasses about twenty-five square miles, with currently about 750 residents. At the height of the Orme controversy, about 400 people lived there. It is a peaceful place, bisected by the Verde River, which converges with the Salt River just past the reservation boundary. That the Verde River still flows is cause for celebration, the reason for the Yavapai's pow-wow and for the reunion of those attending it. Both are commemorating the defeat of the dam that would have stopped the Verde, inundated the reservation, and forced the Yavapai from the last bit of their ancestral land.

This was the anniversary of what some believe was the only good decision ever made by James Watt, Ronald Reagan's controversial secretary of the interior. Ten years before, instead of electing to build Orme Dam, he endorsed a plan that, for about the same cost, would provide comparable amounts of water, flood protection, and water-storage capacity without affecting the Verde River or the Yavapai reservation. Watt's decision, and the defeat of Orme Dam that it signaled, were a landmark event for the Yavapai community, the culmination of the long struggle to retain their land that began in the mid–nineteenth century, when the miners, then the soldiers, arrived. The difficulty in conveying to outsiders what the land means to them had made their struggle deeply frustrating. How do you explain to developers that the land is part of you, that, as one young man put it, "there's no real dividing line that separates you from it." How do you rationally defend what is sacred?

Land is central to how the Yavapai understand themselves and is the basis of a complex relationship they describe as "participating with the land." They believe that their capacity to be Yavapai depends on their having a relationship with *this* land, the same land that sustained their ancestors and that they, too, had struggled to preserve. Since this threat to their land quite literally threatened them, their collective future hinged on this decision. They drew analogies between Orme's threat to them, to their culture, and to the endangered species that lived near the Verde River. "Why can't we be left alone?" one woman asked me during the middle of the controversy. "Do they want us to go away, to make us extinct?"

It was the Yavapai's misfortune to live just below an ideal dam site. A confluence dam was an old idea, one first proposed by the Bureau of Reclamation in 1944. The bureau was founded in 1902 to help "reclaim the West." It was, for decades, a premier engineering organization that defined western settlement as a technological problem that dams could solve. The agency (I shall use "agency" and "bureau" interchangeably) has been so successful in finding places and reasons to build dams that few empty dam sites now exist, a condition that both threatened its future and enhanced Orme Dam's appeal. Its location was the reason why the dam was both so efficient and controversial. The confluence site gave the facility tremendous flexibility, allowing one structure to control the flows of four rivers (the Salt, Verde, Agua Fria, and Gila Rivers, the first three being tributaries to the last). But in damming the Verde River, Orme would destroy miles of cottonwood, mesquite, and willow trees, a unique riparian habitat that was home to diverse animals and plants and to a dozen threatened species of plant and wildlife, including the bald eagle, Gila topminnow, hedgehog cactus, river otter, and Gila monster.[1] And Orme would flood most of the Fort McDowell Reservation.

---

1. U.S. Dept. of the Interior, Bureau of Reclamation (hereafter USBR) (1982b) provides the complete list.

Even six months before Watt's decision, few would have predicted the defeat of Orme Dam. The Bureau of Reclamation, historically an extremely powerful agency, had invested some forty years in the project. Those with direct material stakes in the dam included a long and influential list: local farmers and ranchers, the copper mines, and two major utilities all wanted the water; most business leaders backed the project, as did municipal governments, the state's major newspapers, and nearly every politician ever elected to anything in Arizona. The flood protection Orme Dam offered would give developers access to real estate currently located in the floodplains, land that was worth billions.

In 1978 and 1979, Phoenix endured three devastating floods that instantly made flood control the hot political issue. These floods nearly destroyed a blue-collar neighborhood that, for reasons never fully explained, had been zoned residential despite its location in the floodplain. In washing out bridges and crossings, the floods bifurcated the Phoenix metropolitan area, making commuting a nightmare. Local businesses lost over $200 million of revenue, and seven people died. The last, largest flood prompted the state's biggest newspaper, the *Arizona Republic,* to publish coupons demanding Orme Dam, which residents dutifully filled out and sent to Washington by the truckload. Since water and what happens to it are the most tangible expression of power in the arid West, it was almost unthinkable that the tiny Yavapai community and their supporters could influence the shape of water development in the face of so many powerful lobbies.[2] All this made the Orme Dam Victory Celebration, as it is inscribed on the T-shirts that are sold on the reservation, all the more improbable and poignant for the Yavapai.

This extraordinary political victory is commemorated in an annual tribal holiday and a growing array of festivities that includes pageants, parades, races, dinners, tournaments, and a pow-wow. Leaders in the struggle are honored, supporters are thanked, prayers and tributes are offered, visitors are welcomed, participants are fed, and friends join in a celebration that lasts for days. In addition to commemorating their political victory, these festivities celebrate, very directly, what it means to be Yavapai. And after the Orme struggle, this means being effective political actors.

---

2. Other Orme opponents included a group of taxpayers convinced that the Central Arizona Project (see below), of which Orme would be a part, was a waste of money, archaeologists concerned with the inundation of many valuable prehistoric sites, devotees of river tubing who would lose their favored recreational site, and environmental groups worried about Orme's devastating ecological consequences.

The New Guard

Although its consequences were less dramatic and public, Watt's decision was a landmark event for other groups as well. Some of the friends attending the Yavapai's pow-wow were celebrating a victory of their own, and their willingness to travel across the country to commemorate its tenth anniversary testified to its hold on them. They were planners, biologists, social scientists, and engineers, a group I have named the New Guard, all veterans of an elaborate investigation known as the Central Arizona Water Control Study (CAWCS). Officially, CAWCS was launched by the Bureau of Reclamation (with important assistance from the Army Corps of Engineers) to create, investigate, and evaluate a range of alternative plans for improving Arizona's water supply and for providing better flood protection.

The result of a political compromise with Jimmy Carter over water development, the investigation was the most complex and expensive study ever conducted by the Bureau of Reclamation, lasting five years, costing more than $15 million, and involving over twenty state and federal agencies and a small army of employees. CAWCS created special advisory boards, and it included endless meetings with groups ranging from Rotarians to U.S. senators, where investigators explained the study, described the alternatives, and solicited feedback. Its newsletters and "fact books" were sent to over 4,400 individuals and organizations who had requested them (USBR 1982c:8).

But for members of the New Guard, CAWCS was more than just another bureaucratic study, memorable for its publicity, complexity, and the emergence of a notable compromise. CAWCS was their political and organizational coming-of-age, their chance to create a meaningful place for themselves within the agency, to impose a rigorous rationality on agency decision making, and to devise procedures for making decisions more open and responsive. A chance to institutionalize their values, CAWCS was their triumph.

Water and Power

The high-stakes world of western water politics offers a superb venue for studying power, for in the arid West, water is power, literally and figuratively. Its distribution arouses passions that are hard for non-desert dwellers to appreciate, passions which former Arizona Senator Barry Goldwater reportedly summarized as the "three things a western man cares about: water, land, and women. In that order." Water is the basis of all subsequent development; all profit depends on water supply. Westerners' response to aridity has typically been to understand it not as the natural state of a desert but as a mistake to be rectified with big, federally funded water projects. Places like Los Angeles, Phoenix, Denver, and Las Vegas testify to their capacity to transform landscapes, politics, and cultures. The extent to which water politics have defined all politics exemplifies the material and symbolic weight of dam building out West. For years, the most coveted assignments for western legislators involved water and public works: the Interior and Insular Affairs Committees, Subcommittees on Irrigation and Reclamation and Public Works, and the biggest prize, the powerful Appropriations Committees.

Water is a potent symbol in the desert, and this fuels the passion of water politics. For a western politician, delivering the water is like the late Chicago Mayor Richard J. Daley delivering the vote for favored Democratic candidates: it is a pure, dramatic expression of clout. As Helen Ingram (1990:5) points out, people's attachments to water extend far beyond its financial benefits; water symbolizes security, opportunity, and self-determination. In the desert, it is associated with life, power, and status. It is a first principle, the basis of everything, and water projects are sold by politicians, bureaucrats, and editors as necessary to "save life as we know it." Tied to wealth and status, conspicuous water consumption often signals affluence. Central Arizona boasts some of the most opulent golf courses in the world, and a large proportion of its residents own swimming pools and motor boats. The ability to remake the natural landscape has long been a symbol of wealth and privilege. Until quite recently, the most expensive real estate was often that which best disguised its desert location, with irrigated lawns and gardens, imported trees and vegetation, and artificial lakes and streams. Immediately adjacent to the Yavapai reservation, an expensive residential development was built, perhaps encouraged by the prospect of the nearby lake that Orme Dam would create. Its signature is a 500-foot-high fountain, the world's tallest, which reassures prospective buyers and residents alike that water in this desert development is abundant.

Water's link to prosperity and power makes it emotionally potent. This helps explain why, according to Helen Ingram, water "appeals powerfully to local sentiment. Water is seen as wealth: A boom is bound to occur if an area has water and can develop it. A locality sees benefits in water beyond any specific uses; water carries a guarantee of a prosperous future. Even when it would seem that an area has more water than it could possibly put to use, local people are loath to part with or even to share its riches. . . . Even a preliminary study of a water project can create a local boom. Merchants increase their stock, and land values go up. Strong local pressure then exists to go on and build the project" (Ingram 1990:32). Sometimes this has little to do with economic gain. Helen Ingram points out that "people's attachments to water goes well beyond expectations of financial return . . . Water still symbolizes such values as opportunity, security, and self-determination." This meaning is less a function of its economic value than an expression of organizational and political control. Controlling water signals efficacy; failing to do so signals impotence. Ingram says that "a sense of lineage and inheritance are among the emotions stirred by control over water. Strong communities are able to hold on to their water. . . . Communities that lose control over their water probably will fail in trying to control much else of importance" (1990: 5).

Water's social and political significance does not mean that people haven't taken it for granted, often so much so that new arrivals to Arizona are surprised at the cavalier uses of such a "precious" resource. Decades of federal water projects have made water much cheaper and more reliable in arid climates than it is for most eastern cities. Among desert dwellers, there is often a collective unwillingness to acknowledge that the water supply is finite and to confront the hard choices and the head-to-head conflict that doing so would bring. People prefer to find new water, or to assume that new sources of water will found, rather than to learn to live with limits. Water's scarcity scarcely permeates most individual's consciousness most of the time, and does little to inconvenience or alter their lives.

While quotidian life in arid climates involves denying the fundamental scarcity of water and the paradoxes of its seeming abundance, there is, at times, a palpable anxiety surrounding its use. Cecil Andrus, Jimmy Carter's embattled secretary of interior, described it as "an underlying fear . . . that some unforeseen hand is going to reach out and turn off the valve" (Fradkin 1981:13). This usually repressed fear of scarcity can be manipulated to spur political action, but this anxiety is also deeply felt, especially among long-time residents, lending a Freudian quality to water politics. The contradictions between the rhetoric of scarcity and crisis, the apparent but "false" plenitude of water, and the persistent unwillingness to acknowledge the limits of the supply make water a paradoxical political and cultural issue in Arizona. As a result, water politics are conducted on highly politicized and mystifying terrain that features an enormous array of institutions dedicated to developing water supplies, monitoring their use, and jockeying for influence over their distribution.

The Central Arizona Project

The Central Arizona Water Control Study was the culmination of a political crisis, one precipitated by recent environmental legislation, by agency arrogance, and by Jimmy Carter's inept foray into water politics. On January 1, 1970, Richard Nixon, of all people, had signed the National Environmental Policy Act into law. An innovative piece of legislation, NEPA required the federal government to prepare an environmental impact statement (EIS) in advance of federal policy in order to determine its environmental consequences. Very specific guidelines regulate how an EIS should be prepared, procedures that amount to a rough approximation of rational decision-making models where the "costs" and "benefits" of policy are articulated and compared for a range of alternatives. Perhaps most controversial was NEPA's requirement that agencies devise procedures for including the public in the EIS process.

The Bureau of Reclamation only belatedly and begrudgingly implemented this new law, which was designed to change the kinds of information that agencies collected and the way they made decisions. The first EIS (1976) on Orme Dam reflected bureaucrats' zeal for compliance. Written by engineers devoted to Orme Dam, it was a blatantly partisan document that failed to mention the forced relocation of the Yavapai. When this EIS was formally presented to the public, as NEPA required, it became a public relations nightmare, succeeding mainly in galvanizing opposition to the dam. Opposition to Orme Dam was both baffling and threatening to many bureau engineers, who found it hard to acknowledge that their "consensus" over water development had evaporated. Almost inconceivable was the prospect of having this long-planned-for project stymied by those they considered irrelevant. What they had not imagined was that the biggest threat to Orme would emerge from within their agency.

An early effect of NEPA had been to insert a few nontraditional employees into the bureau, people with expertise in biological or social sciences whose role was to help write impact statements. Following the Orme EIS debacle, their visibility and numbers increased. These nonengineers were linked by their marginality, the uncertainty surrounding their jobs, and by their concern to produce EISs that were valid documents that contributed to decisions rather than affirmed made decisions. They understood that their power within the agency depended on their ability to influence decisions. They faced the formidable challenge of helping to restore public confidence in the bureau's credibility; they simultaneously needed to demonstrate their professional autonomy to skeptics and establish their authority in an agency of engineers who were hostile to their mission. Their task was made all the harder by its revolving around Orme Dam.

Orme's sanctity derived from its association with the Central Arizona Project. CAP was the bureau's plan to deliver water from the

Colorado River via an intricate system of dams, power plants, pumps, and aqueducts to the central Arizona desert. Water from Lake Havasu, the by-product of Parker Dam, would be pumped 900 feet up in order to travel via aqueduct through a series of dams and reservoirs to central Arizona, and eventually down to Tucson. Marc Reisner (1986:304) calls it "as incongruous a spectacle as any on earth: a man-made river flowing uphill in a place of almost no rain."

The idea of bringing Colorado River water to the Arizona desert dates back to the nineteenth century, and for much of the twentieth century, CAP was the paramount political issue in Arizona, what some have called Arizona's most sacred cow. As with any legislation affecting the distribution of Colorado River water, CAP was an important regional issue for states composing the upper Colorado River Basin. The agency and its supporters expended an enormous amount of time, attention, and resources on CAP. CAP's congressional authorization, the stuff of legends, took some twenty years. Besides absorbing much of the political careers of men like John Rhodes, Barry Goldwater, and the venerated Carl Hayden, authorizing CAP had initiated a bitter twelve-year lawsuit between Arizona and California over Colorado River water rights; it had required the cultivation of a powerful, well-funded state water lobby; and as for political logrolling, it engendered unprecedented water projects given to recalcitrant supporters in locations dictated more by clout than efficacy. In its final form, CAP was authorized along with nine other water projects in a gargantuan bill costing $1.3 billion, of which $779 million was devoted to CAP. When Lyndon Baines Johnson signed the bill in 1968, it was the single most expensive authorization in U.S. history.[3]

While the specific features of CAP changed over time, the proposed Orme Dam was central. CAP's cost and the controversy surrounding Orme were two reasons that Jimmy Carter gave when he placed the Central Arizona Project on a list of nineteen water projects that he wanted deleted from the federal budget. CAP was about one-quarter completed at the time. Carter hoped to save about $9 billion by eliminating these projects. Because they had been authorized years before on the basis of partisan calculations and absurdly low interest rates, he thought the projects made poor economic sense. Unbiased calculations would demonstrate their status as boondoggles, and further investiga-

---

3. Helen Ingram (1990) has written the definitive account of this legislation, known as the Colorado River Basin Project Act (Public Law 90-537). President Johnson called it a "landmark bill, a proud companion to the other 250 separate conservation measures I have signed" (WHPS 1968).

tion would document their harmful social and environmental consequences.

However credible his economics and courageous his environmentalism, Carter blundered in announcing his "hit list" during a serious drought without consulting or warning the members of Congress whose districts contained the aborted water projects or the federal agencies in charge of building them; nor did Carter even warn his own secretary of the interior, Cecil Andrus, of the timing of his planned announcement (Reisner 1986:325). He simply did not appreciate the political and symbolic significance of water projects, which one journalist has described: "With the possible exception of motherhood, there is nothing more sacred to many members of Congress than the physical evidences of the power that Carter is trying to limit: gigantic dams, huge reservoirs, aqueducts than run for hundreds of miles, all proof—cast in concrete—of the legislators' concern for the folks back home" (*Time* 1977).

Nor did Carter appreciate the function of water projects as what Marc Reisner terms the currency of Congress: "Water projects are the grease gun that lubricates the nation's legislative machinery. Congress without water projects would be like an engine without oil; it would simply seize up" (Reisner 1986:319).[4] Even those who understand the crucial role of water projects as conduits of power often fail to grasp their broad significance for seemingly unrelated domestic policy. Water projects create passionate alliances both locally and in Congress and were for years prime timber for congressional logrolling. The water project expunged in Arizona could also compromise the airport in Maine, the highway in Florida, or the museum in Indianapolis. As fundable, fungible legislation well suited for targeting dollars and jobs, water projects have long been favored forms for creating and expressing domestic agendas. Dams were the infrastructure for both Progressive politics and New Deal reforms. LBJ's noted capacity to twist southern congressional arms in his pursuit of a good society relied heavily on his willingness to hold pet water projects hostage.[5] As someone whose political career began with a dam, LBJ understood their political potency. But all this seemed lost on Jimmy Carter.

In this public display of stunning naïveté, Carter quickly revealed

4. John Ferejohn makes a similar point in explaining why, given the structure of Congress, the attractive features of local benefits and dispersed costs make water projects useful for enhancing the discretion of powerful congressional leaders and channeling funds to their own and to their allies' districts (Ferejohn 1974:235–52).

5. It is reported that LBJ would sometimes end political discussions with a member of Congress by saying, "Now about that dam" (*New York Times* 1977, p. A13).

himself as a political outsider who did not understand how Congress worked. Instantly, his relationship with Congress was permanently damaged, and he became one of its most-vilified, least-effective executives. His actions were taken as a declaration of war by many western politicians, who nearly tripped over one another at news conferences to express their outrage. Arizona Congressman Morris Udall claimed that without CAP water, Tucson and Phoenix "are going to dry up and blow away." Senator Henry Jackson, a noted environmentalist, pronounced it an "absurd mistake." Among the milder rebukes was that of Ellis Armstrong, former commissioner of reclamation, the agency with the most water projects on Carter's list, who called the Carter administration "uninformed amateurs" (*Time* 1977:16; Fradkin 1981:9). Unprepared for the response, Carter quickly arranged for what was supposed to be a conciliatory meeting with congressional leaders. Jim Free, Carter's congressional lobbyist, characterized the meeting as a "lynch mob" composed mostly of table-pounding Democrats (Reisner 1986:327).

The annual appropriations hearings that followed Carter's hit list generated impassioned speeches in defense of the threatened projects. In a special appearance, Majority Leader Jim Wright, quoting the Bible, condemned Carter's advisers and invoked the classic themes of water development: water "is man's most indispensable commodity and man's most useful servant. Trapped, harnessed and directed by human intelligence, it runs our mills and grows our crops; it powers our machinery and lights our homes; cleanses our waste and moves our commerce. Unharnessed and left to rampage, it can inundate our cities and our farms, destroy our homes and our hopes, afflict us with disease and death, and carry away to the seas the fertile topsoil upon which our vaunted civilization rests" (U.S. Congress 1977:5). Not only were Carter's methods inappropriate for capturing the important benefits of water development, Wright argued, but existing criteria were already too stringent, systematically understating the true value. He noted it was "hard to put a dollar sign on benefits like these." Jim Wright's partisan remarks hint at what I believe are perplexing and perennial problems for those who make public policy. What are appropriate ways of representing what we value when making public policy decisions? Just what is at stake in "putting a dollar value" on the things we care about?

The process of transforming different values or units into a common metric is called commensuration. Given that, as Wright suggests, commensuration is hard to do, why do we keep doing it? Commensuration is considered crucial for rational decision making by many decision analysts. What is at stake in making commensuration a prerequisite for rationality? I believe that efforts to understand commensuration and its link to rationality are especially important for understanding modern politics. Commensuration is a deceptively radical process, but one that requires vast resources and discipline. Commensuration is also ubiquitous, with many disparate forms. Understanding the variety of its forms and audiences seems crucial for appreciating its consequences. The Central Arizona Water Control Study presents an arena where Wright's questions can be interrogated, and where the motives behind commensuration can be reconstructed. It provides a vantage point from which to assess both the costs and virtues of commensuration.

Commensuration in water politics took place in many arenas and in varied forms. Legislators who voted on water policy were crudely commensurating what they imagined their constituents' interests to be, or at least the interests of those who mattered to them. Water projects, as the "currency" of Congress, were themselves an often-opaque form of commensuration. What explains the changing forms of commensuration? Who profits from these? What difference does it make to politics if policy is evaluated in terms of performance measures constructed by engineers or the utility functions of citizens or as prices generated by markets? When is commensuration made explicitly and when does it remain obscure? As Theodore Porter (1995:148–89) has argued, quantitative technologies such as cost-benefit analyses are often responses to conflict, distrust, and scrutiny. But the authority of numbers can threaten or limit other forms of authority, such as personal discretion, character, informal knowledge, and expert judgment. Understanding why this occurs is crucial for appreciating their power.

The Central Arizona Water Control Study

In Arizona, Carter's hit list created a staggering political crisis. After investing twenty-five years in its authorization, Arizonans' sense of entitlement ran deep. That Carter could so cavalierly dismiss what many politicians had spent careers securing seemed outrageous. After a period of uncertainty, a deal was finally brokered by Arizona's congressional delegation. To preserve CAP, they agreed to eliminate three dams, including the controversial Orme Dam; in return, Carter agreed to fund a study to investigate "suitable alternatives" to Orme Dam, a by-product of which would be an environmental impact statement that would pass muster. This study became the Central Arizona Water Control Study.

Not surprisingly, an investigation of this magnitude came to mean different things to different groups. Some viewed CAWCS as a way to buy time before having to make a difficult policy decision; others saw it mainly as a device for resurrecting Orme Dam. Some believed the study was an intellectually useless, but politically and legally necessary justification of the dam. Some of Orme's supporters reasoned that a procedurally scrupulous EIS would leave the agency impervious to lawsuits. Opposing groups, including a number of environmental groups, were suspicious that the study would turn out to be another biased vindication of the dam that everyone knew the agency wanted to build. What everyone acknowledged about CAWCS was that because of the publicity and controversy surrounding Orme Dam, it would become one of the most highly scrutinized and politically volatile investigations ever conducted by the Bureau of Reclamation. And no one truly believed that Orme was dead.

Participating in such a demanding and controversial investigation was a heady, and sometimes terrifying, experience for members of the New Guard, who tended to be younger employees with shorter tenure in the agency. Since CAWCS was so important to the agency, it attracted unusually talented and ambitious people from throughout the agency. Over time, its ranks expanded from the group of pioneering EIS writers to include less traditional bureau engineers, who were intimately involved in designing and managing CAWCS, and the external consultants contracted to supplement their own expertise. For a time, I was one of them. Hired as a consultant during graduate school to do fieldwork and conduct interviews on the Fort McDowell Reservation, I eventually helped write the reports that analyzed the social impacts associated with the various plans, including parts of the EIS.

Clearly careers were on the line with CAWCS, but as members became more involved with the issues and with one another, many came to see its stakes in broader terms. One intriguing intellectual puzzle that these people confronted revolved around how to organize and integrate the information NEPA now required agencies to collect. Assessing the social and environmental effects attending the alternative plans for a study like CAWCS meant including, along with the traditional engineering and economic data, data drawn from archaeological, anthropological, sociological, biological, meteorological, recreational, and historical analyses, among others. NEPA also required that some means be found for incorporating and documenting the opinions and values of the public. How to reconcile such disparate forms of information?

Some members began to see the problem of commensuration as linked to their concern with devising an investigation that would restore the credibility of the agency. A rigorous technique for measuring and integrating disparate information and for enlisting public participation would assure people that reliable information addressing their concerns and preferences was systematically included in the investigation, that appropriate methods were employed, and that the study was, therefore, balanced and unbiased. The legitimation crisis prompted by the botched EIS, and the problem of integrating disparate information, could be resolved by the same means, through recourse to a rigorous, retrievable rationality.

To solve their dilemma, members of the New Guard turned to science, adapting models of rational decision making drawn from economics and cognitive psychology. A key assumption underlying the conception of rationality used in most economic theory and much decision analysis is that different values and entities should be made commensurable; in order to make rational decisions, this theory holds, precise comparisons must be made between alternatives, and this requires that values be expressed in accordance with some common scale. Members of the New Guard believed these models had much to offer: guidance in how to break down complex decisions into their component parts, strategies for integrating information, and flexibility that would allow new information to be easily incorporated as it became available. Furthermore, the models were based on public, defensible procedures that can easily be reproduced and defended if their credibility were challenged. Those who were in charge of devising the framework for the study were taking rational choice models of decision making very seriously as their guide for how to be rational. CAWCS became the forum for devising and testing procedures, for trying to accomplish practically what many decision theorists were advocating theoretically, and for trying to change the decision-making routines deployed by people within this organization.

For some members of the New Guard, then, CAWCS became their chance to fuse their intellectual and political commitments, to enlist rationality in the service of democracy. CAWCS permitted them to create procedures that allowed more people to participate in decisions and to improve the quality of information used in making them. These procedures could vindicate the quality of decisions made more democratically. For these bureaucrats, CAWCS offered the opportunity to act on their long-suppressed idealism about what government should be and what it could do. It was a place where their values and expertise as scientists could shape policy.

And that is why Watt's decision was more than just a successful solution to an urgent political and organizational problem. It was that, and the New Guard's role in helping to broker this outcome for one of Arizona's pressing political problems propelled successful careers for many members. But the meaning of this event enveloped more than their careers. For some, what mattered most was that the Yavapai community and the Verde River had been spared. Equally satisfying to many was their sense of having worked on something important, on having made a difference to people's lives. As marginal members of what had long been an engineering organization, the outcome vindicated their expertise, their value to an organization that was reluctant to embrace them. For other members of the New Guard, this outcome was an endorsement of the process they had created, of their vision of rational, responsive government. It was only long after the event was over that most realized how much it had meant to them, how singular it had been. As one woman put it, "It was the best thing I'll ever do. Too bad I was so young."

The Old Guard

Not everyone saw CAWCS as a triumph of rational planning or felt like celebrating the demise of Orme Dam. For a small group of older bureau engineers, the decision not to build the dam felt like a betrayal. More than fifteen years later after the 1981 decision, their bitterness remains palpable as they describe how millions more dollars had been spent to build an inferior compromise project, how emotions, politics, and tree huggers had conspired to destroy the best plan, how the agency had abandoned its true constituents.

At first I was puzzled by these men's reactions, a group I subsequently named the Old Guard. The alternative that Watt selected seemed an ideal solution to a vexing controversy. Plan 6, as it was known, called for raising the existing Roosevelt Dam, replacing an old dam with a new one on the same site, and building one new dam, Cliff Dam.[6] It provided comparable amounts of flood protection, stored and delivered the same amount of water, generated the same amount of power, and cost about the same as Orme would have. And it did so without affecting the Yavapai community and without the most potentially devastating environmental effects. So why weren't these men happy that the conflict had been resolved? Why weren't they pleased that CAP could now be competed?

Members of the Old Guard held powerful, visible positions within the agency. Where members of the New Guard were social or environmental analysts, planners, or managers of studies, members of the Old Guard were heads of local and regional offices, or division managers. Since their jobs often involved overseeing many subordinates, they

---

6. Cliff Dam was later eliminated from the plan in exchange for environmental groups' agreement to drop their lawsuit.

were more removed from the day-to-day concerns of CAWCS. Although they might not have recognized themselves as a group, this fact says more about what they took for granted than it does about their similarities. Members shared many characteristics: they were male, older (many are now retired), experienced employees, and most were engineers; they were intensely loyal to the agency; and its members were suspicious of NEPA, unconvinced of its usefulness and reluctant to abandon a system that had produced such fine decisions and so many great projects. Most important, members were long-time supporters of Orme Dam, some of whom had devoted twenty years to developing or promoting CAP and Orme Dam.

Their attachment to Orme Dam was no simple expression of their material interests as members of this agency. The organization clearly needed and wanted to secure this large water project at a time when most rivers were already overbuilt and when the flow of tax dollars was getting smaller. This goal does not, however, distinguish Orme from its alternative. In order to secure the necessary funding, it was even more imperative that the controversy be resolved so that the agency could arrive at a permanent decision and allow them to get on with construction. This seemed more likely with the Orme alternative, since opposition to Orme Dam was firmly entrenched and litigiously inclined. One could argue that from the point of view of the broader agency, the Orme alternative was politically superior to Orme, since it generated the same amount of money for the agency and was more likely to be implemented.

The short, if unacknowledged, answer to why these men could not embrace the Orme alternative is that over time, their investment had become deeply personal. At first glance, this hardly seems noteworthy. Many of us would feel bad if our projects went unrealized, and, as engineers, with their emphasis on solving problems and getting things built, the Old Guard felt this even more keenly than most. But the disappointment went deeper than this. The better, longer answer to this puzzle required me to disentangle their investment, to try and discern what motivated and sustained it, and to disclose a significance that was simultaneously personal, professional, and organizational.

I came to appreciate how much the Old Guard's commitment to Orme Dam was an organizational accomplishment, one shaped by a powerful ethos that fostered investments in particular projects and structures and magnified by the importance and duration of CAP. Derived and adapted from Christian theology, this ideology was informed by the Christian precept that celebrated man's dominion over nature. Progressive politics, the federal irrigation movement that gave rise to the agency, and the professionalization projects of its early engineers fed the ethos that infused the agency. It was displayed on the bureau's walls, reproduced in its budgets, celebrated in its rituals, and evinced in its career tracks. In promoting technical solutions to social problems, a vision of nature as God's unfinished handiwork, a resource to be tamed according to man's will, and an aesthetic celebrating dams as both useful and beautiful, this ideology rendered dams distinctive, their designers immortal.

For members of the Old Guard, Orme's status had shifted over time from a significant structure to a structured signifier. Where once it had been a technical solution to a water-supply problem, it had become a referendum on water development, an expression of professional identities. Orme Dam had come to symbolize their work, their power, and their era, evoking that glorious but receding past when vacant dam sites were plentiful, when big budgets and big water projects were normal, when politicians cultivated the bureau, when "development" wasn't a dirty word, when engineers were trusted and technology seemed more promising than threatening, a time when dams were feats the whole country celebrated. To abandon Orme Dam was to admit having wasted much of their careers. It meant acknowledging that their engineering ideals were controversial, their agency was a relic, their power had eroded. The fight for Orme Dam was their struggle to preserve the past.

The relations between the New Guard, the Old Guard, and the Yavapai community reveal the tensions, contradictions, and ambivalences that arise when modes of rationality collide. The rigorous instrumental rationality of the New Guard's models could not accommodate the substantive rationality that made incommensurable land and culture for the Yavapai, and dams for the Old Guard. Rationality is a highly contingent accomplishment, a potential that is enacted and propelled by people in contexts with disparate motives, constraints, and levels of self-consciousness. Making sense of the decision not to build Orme Dam has forced me to ascertain just what being rational meant to these groups, and what were the political, organizational, and cultural consequences stemming from their efforts to impose or resist new forms of rationality.

Why did this decision become a contest over rationality? While I believe that a book is required to provide a satisfying answer, a more expedient answer points to a complex set of conditions, some general, some particular. The duration and profile of the decision, the conflict it generated, its disparate audiences, and the introduction of new law that required interpretation and implementation are all factors shaping this process. Also relevant is the bureaucratic politicking that took place within an agency in need of reinventing itself. What emerged from all this was an encounter between disparate groups who were forced, by politics, to define and defend themselves to one another publicly, to try to interpret each other's motives and meanings. And in the process of doing so, each group was transformed.

With alternative visions of what it meant to be rational and of the terms under which groups should participate in their fates, the result of this encounter was a sociologist's dream: the rare situation where actors are made self-conscious and articulate about what had formerly been tacit, where participants must state and defend the obvious, where normal bureaucratic routine is upended and made public, when outsiders can glimpse bureaucracies processing the world. What this decision offers, then, is a chance to watch actors create and revise interpretations and to observe hegemonic forms of power as these are practiced and challenged.   .

Theorizing from a Case: Methods, Data, and Linkages

My analysis is based on evidence collected from three main sources: fieldwork conducted in the Bureau of Reclamation (BR) and on the Fort McDowell Reservation, where my roles ranged from full participant to pure observer; formal interviews conducted during and after CAWCS; government documents, media accounts, archived papers, organizational records, and personal records that some participants generously shared with me. My formal role as a participant was as a consultant for the social impact assessment that analyzed how various plans would affect people and communities in the area. I conducted interviews on the Yavapai reservation and observed community events such as council meetings, pow-wows, and political activities associated with Orme Dam for about three months. I helped write parts of, and briefly supervised, the social impact assessment which incorporated a broad range of data, including over seventy interviews with people affected by the Orme decision.

After CAWCS, I did fieldwork at one of the branches of the Bureau of Reclamation for about four months; my formal (paid) role was to examine other BR analyses and review their guidelines for social assessment and public involvement. This broadened my understanding of agency decision making. During this time, I also observed meetings, read documents, toured departments, and interviewed a wide range of agency employees. I was also a paid consultant to the bureau on two other, unrelated projects. These experiences allowed me to compare how policies developed in one context were applied in others, which deepened my understanding of how bureaucratic procedures were actually used.

To complement my fieldwork, I conducted formal interviews with over fifty people affiliated with or affected by the Orme decision.[7] My participation both eased and complicated my research. It has made me more cautious in interpreting people's views. Had I not first participated in CAWCS, I never would have been granted access to much of the information I received. Sometimes this was simply knowing what to ask for and whom to ask. My former affiliation usually made people more willing to talk to me, but, for some, it made me more suspect.

Concerned as I am with analyzing the relations between rationality, power, and meaning, it is important to explain why this decision is a good case to investigate these questions.[8] The New Guard's efforts to adopt rational choice decision procedures allows me to analyze both the conditions that prompt some groups to become advocates of rationality and the practical and political consequences of doing so. Their application of these procedures to a visible, fateful decision reveals how these procedures influenced the political process, including how participants understood their interests and their relations to one another. CAWCS and the water politics that preceded and succeeded it offer a before-during-after scenario that is analytically useful for understanding how the adoption of the New Guard's rational decision framework shaped people's identities and political power.

My analysis is devoted mainly to three groups. For a decision that involved so many other groups, this requires some justification. First, there are limits to what can be accomplished by a book. Other groups and individuals were clearly important political players, but their participation was often less sustained, their investments less deep, and their influence on the decision framework less pronounced than that of the Old Guard, the New Guard, and the Yavapai community.[9]

7. I promised the people I interviewed not to reveal their names. If someone is quoted more than once, I use pseudonyms so that readers can track this; otherwise, I rely on general characteristics to describe people. Quoted statements are literal records of someone's comments; paraphrased statements do not appear as quotations. Several times I omitted or slightly altered distinctive biographical information to make it harder to identify the speaker. Where labels are my invention, I note this; otherwise, the language and categories used by people I interviewed are their own. When I quote excerpts of interviews that were conducted during CAWCS and appear in BR documents, I cite these documents. Other interviews conducted later are not referenced.

8. John Walton (1992) observes that cases are made for theoretical reasons. Both the designation and justification of a case depends on the theoretical purpose it serves, which, in turn, explains the close tie between case studies and theoretical advances and why new theory recreates old cases.

9. Some were long-established groups like the Maricopa Audubon Society (led by Robert Weisman), the Sierra Club, the Central Arizona Project Association—a pro-CAP lobby directed for many years by Rich Johnson, and the Salt River Project, a large utility that conducted its own investigation of Orme and its alternatives. Others were smaller

Besides their centrality, my emphasis on these groups was guided by my theoretical and methodological concerns. Understanding rationality as a practical and political accomplishment required that I attend to those people and sites that best highlight the motivations for and consequences of adopting new forms of rationality. The existence of these groups, their understanding of their ties to one another, and how they defined and expressed their interests were shaped by a rational decision framework and by their engagement with one another. Interpreting these dynamic processes demands a close attention to detail that necessarily limits the scope of analysis. In the trade-off between scope and depth of interpretation, I have opted for depth.

But this does not signal an unwillingness to generalize, first, because there are many empirical examples of the phenomena I am analyzing. The sorts of rational decision models I analyze are widely used to make decisions. These models diffused broadly within the BR and were exported to other agencies. Although they were adapted here to NEPA and the specific needs of the BR, they are theoretically faithful to more general models of rational choice theory. Finally, I believe that the commensuration that is required of these models is a very general and important social phenomenon whose influence is even broader than the use of these models.

Second, although there were interesting variations, some of the patterns that emerged applied to each of these quite different groups. For example, all found that there were limits to what could be "commensurated," although it took longer for some to understand this and the groups varied in their ability to explain these limits. That some of the same effects were experienced by both seasoned bureaucrats and Yavapai residents suggests that consequences of these forms are not felt only by "traditional" or otherwise marginalized groups.[10] Other scholarship also suggests that my findings are not idiosyncratic.

Theodore Porter (1995:148–89) shows how politics, controversy, and a precarious authority has propelled cost-benefit analysis, a now widely diffused form of commensuration, for harried bureaucrats. Quantitative decision techniques are the province of weak elites who are accountable to powerful outsiders. These characteristics apply to members of the New Guard and help explain their promotion of com-

---

groups or coalitions created in response to the current Orme crisis, such as the Committee to Save Fort McDowell, founded by Carolina Butler, or Citizens Concerned about the Project, led by Frank Welsh. For a more exhaustive list of both invited and actual participants, see USBR (1981b), or Welsh (1985:166) for Orme opponents.

10. Michael Lawson (1994), Patricia Mariella (1983:255–308), and Bernard Shanks (1974) have analyzed comparable difficulties with valuing and compensating Native Americans for land destroyed by water projects.

mensuration in rational decision making. Viviana Zelizer (1985) describes the paradoxical effects of affixing prices, in insurance, law, and labor, to priceless children as the terms of their value shifted from primarily economic to emotional and moral. Her later work analyzes the ingenious ways that people have devised to subvert the commensurability of money (1989, 1994). Yavapai residents, too, were effective in rejecting the commensuration of their land and culture, which in turn, reaffirmed the importance of incommensurable categories in defining their identities. Cass Sunstein (1992) discloses the hazards associated with efforts to commensurate plural, diverse values in law, arguing that how we value matters, and that the commensuration of human goods weakens rather improves reasoning. My analysis of the Orme decision confirms the salience of pluralistic modes of valuing and reasoning and discloses some of the distortions that emerge from efforts to commensurate the incommensurable.

Third, I believe that theorizing, as a form of generalization, requires detail. Arthur Stinchcombe has forcefully defended this claim, having written a whole book about "how generality can be wrested from facts" (1978:115). I think Stinchcombe is right that it is less productive to test theory with history than it is to "use history to develop theory" (1978: 1); he argues that the way to do this is to develop general concepts that are grounded in detailed, deep analogies between particular causal assertions that help explain historically specific facts.[11] The historically specific facts I want to explain involve why actors adopted particular rational forms in a decision and why these facts affected the three groups as they did. What is or can be made analogous to other contexts is the sorts of motives that propel people to "be rational" and "calculate commensuration," the different strategies for doing so, their relative legitimacy, and how these variations explain differences in effects. For Stinchcombe, social change is caused by "people figuring out what to do." Good historical work requires explaining what "cause[s] people to change their notions of what kind of situation they are in, and to sustain those new notions sufficiently long to build them into institutions that in turn sustain them" (1978:117). That is what I attempt in this book. And finally, my willingness to generalize from this case stems from its relevance for theorizing about identity and interests in other fields like law and social movements—in principle concerned with the emergence, distinctiveness, and ills of modernity—and most concretely for the rational choice theory that inspired members of the New Guard.

11. Stinchcombe's view, endorsed by Walton (1992:9, 289) is similar to that of Weber, who argued that sociologists' job should be to create the general concepts that are used to generate causal explanations of specific historical events.

"Identity" has become a contested term, with recent scholarship emphasizing identities as plural, layered, dynamic relations. In varied fields, attention has focused on understanding when identities are invoked and challenged and how they are mediated by experience and institutions. Sociolegal scholars, for example, now ask how law shapes people's understanding of themselves as individuals and members of groups, how law helps constitute certain types of subjects, rather than presume that law acts on stable, coherent communities or selves (Mertz 1994:972).[12] In my analysis, NEPA created a organizational constituency that became the basis of group identity for the New Guard. In changing the terms of relevancy, NEPA helped disclose as distinctive and controversial what the Old Guard had presumed was universal, as its members were finally forced to confront the relativity of their worldview. In redefining who could participate in this decision and how they could do so, and in prompting the adoption of a more rigorous instrumental rationality, NEPA mediated the encounters between these three groups in ways that caused each to reappraise its identity and to reinterpret its ties to one another and its place in the world.

Recent social movement theory also emphasizes the contingent, dynamic, and often fragile processes of constructing group identities and defining collective interests (Buechler 1995:442). Instead of assuming that class location dictates interests or political units in any mechanical way, scholars have emphasized identities other than class location as sites for mobilizing and the importance of cultural and ideological processes in shaping how people define their interests and their identities.[13] The Orme Dam decision reveals how the mutual construction of interests and identities is often a contingent process. This process is shaped by groups' encounters with one another; these encounters, in turn, are mediated by conceptions of rationality, organizational structures, and the assumptions of bureaucratic actors about the appropriateness of political units and the boundaries that define homogeneous or stable values.

A concern with understanding how rationality has become institu-

12. Law has been analyzed as a venue for producing categories of sameness and difference, for constructing boundaries that distinguish self from other, normal from abnormal, autonomous from dependent (Minnow 1990:9); law may impose or presume some forms of collective identities such as "tribe" (Goldberg-Ambrose 1994), "community" (Levine 1994), and "race" or "ethnicity" (Gooding 1994; Darnell 1990), or be a forum for challenging or negotiating identity claims tied to kin and marriage (Lazarus-Black 1994: 192–220; Felstiner and Sarat 1992; Hopper 1993; Clifford 1988:277–346).

13. For example, the effects of framing (Snow et al. 1986; Snow and Benford 1992; Babb 1996), of cultural scripts and organizational repertoires (Clemens 1993, 1996), of boundary work (Moore 1996), and of legend and historical memory (Walton 1992) have all been identified as important mechanisms that shape the processes by which individuals come to define themselves as collectivities with interests warranting political action.

tionalized and internalized is central to modern social thought. While theorists have emphasized different causes, characteristics, and consequences of different kinds of rationalization, Karl Marx's (1977, 1978) commodification and alienation, Georg Simmel's objectification, Max Weber's (1978) rationalization, Hans-Georg Gadamer's (1985) method, and Georg Lukàcs, Max Horkheimer and Theodor Adorno's (1972) reification share a family resemblance. All argue that processes of rationalization change what is meaningful and how we apprehend meaning. Most wanted to understand what caused rational forms to proliferate, emphasizing what propels the changes in our systems of meaning. My concern is to explain how it is that rational forms change how we interpret meaning. This requires understanding the theory and assumptions that inform the rational decision-making procedure used by the bureau during CAWCS, and how these shaped the expression of people's interests and participants' interpretations of themselves and others.

Rational Choice Theory

There's no accounting for taste.

It is hard to pin down what rational choice theories have in common since their uses are varied and they make different underlying assumptions. Rational choice analyses are formalized in game theory and incorporated into economic and policy analyses, historical explanations, ordinary observation, as well as an increasingly influential body of political and sociological theory.[14] Contemporary rational choice theory derives from modern utility theory, first systematized by von Neumann and Morgenstern (1947) as a model for rational decision making. Modern utility theory is based on a formal analysis of preferences and decision rules, such that an actor who satisfies these can be said to be a utility maximizer. This is accomplished by actors having goals which induce a preference ordering over a set of alternatives, and then selecting that alternative which maximally satisfies their goals, subject to risk and uncertainty. The utility function of the actor involves integrating values, making trade-offs, and assessing expected compensation. The outcomes must be commensurate with respect to some underlying dimension or metric.

When confronted with evidence that people often do not act this way when they decide things, those who hold to this rigorous definition of rationality sometimes reassert the original prescriptive goals of expected

---

14. Green and Shapiro (1994:2–3) document the ascendance of rational choice theory in political science.

utility theory.[15] For those who want the theory to explain or describe behavior, some of these assumptions have to be relaxed, and much interesting work has been devoted to devising alternative conceptions of rationality that modify or eliminate some of the original axioms in ways that bring the formal model more in line with empirical findings.

Rational choice decision making is a way of breaking decisions down into their component parts and systematically aggregating these to derive a decision. Rational choice is instrumental, since it is guided by the outcomes of actions. Actions are not valued or performed for their own sake but for how well they help accomplish some desired end (Elster 1989:22). Rational choice is maximizing, since it involves finding what people believe are the best means for accomplishing some goal. Elster summarizes rational choice theory in a "deceptively simple" sentence: "When faced with several courses of action, people usually do what they believe is likely to have the best overall outcome." Amartya Sen's (1982:182) definition is even simpler: a rational choice is a logically consistent choice.

John Steinbrunner (1974:25–46) summarizes the general characteristics of the rational choice paradigm as deriving from three basic assumptions: First, separate dimensions of values are integrated through trade-offs, in a deliberate balancing of competing claims of values. Integration is accomplished by creating some metric that gives the worth of one value in terms comparable to the other, and this commensuration of values must occur in advance of the final analysis of outcomes. The concept of utility is, at least conceptually, a mechanism for integrating values; it is a measure of absolute value, an ideal measure that would subsume all dimensions of value and provide a basis for making comparisons between choices. Cost-benefit ratios are a common form of value integration in policy decisions. Second, alternative outcomes are evaluated and analyzed; outcomes are calculated on the basis of predictions about the consequences of a given course of action. Third, people's expectations are adjusted as more is known about how alternatives will perform, but the new expected outcomes are evaluated by the same metric.

As the premises of rationality, these assumptions provided the intellectual foundation for CAWCS. NEPA provided legal motivation for enacting the second assumption, since EISs were required to construct alternative plans and evaluate their consequences. This was no small

15. As Thomas Schelling (1986:191) describes the predicament: "The human mind is something of an embarrassment to certain disciplines, notably economics, decision theory and others that have found the model of the rational consumer to be a powerfully productive one."

breakthrough for an agency that had in the past narrowly construed alternatives as variations in a dam's dimensions. The first assumption, that values be integrated in advance of deciding, was not required by NEPA; nevertheless, members of the New Guard believed that the success of CAWCS depended upon commensuration. After describing what commensuration entails, I will explain why I think this is such a provocative and important assumption.

Defining Commensuration

Commensuration is concerned with measuring different properties normally represented by different units with a single, common standard or unit. The commensurability assumption in many rational choice models has important implications for how value is derived and represented. The basic structure of value in these models is that of an analogy; its unity is based on the common relationship that the two things share with a third metric. Among commensurate relations, difference is expressed quantitatively as magnitude.

Relativity is fundamental to commensuration. Commensuration creates a relation between two attributes or dimensions where value is revealed in comparison, in the trade-offs that are made among different components in a choice. Value concerns how much of one thing is required to compensate for another. So, for example, the value of a change in wildlife caused by a new dam might be expressed as how many additional cranes or ducks it would take to compensate for the loss of ten bald eagles. Commensurated value is a special form of reducing quality to quantity. In representing value in this way, these models do not permit the expression of incommensurate values, things which people believe have some intrinsic, incomparable worth.

Commensuration culminates in a common metric, which distinguishes commensuration from other forms of standardization but cannot be reduced to just this feature.[16] Our urges to impose order, exert control, or manage uncertainty have generated an almost infinite variety of techniques of standardization. Commensuration may be considered a particular kind of standardization. One key difference is that even though standardization can occur in discrete, unconnected steps, commensuration is always a process.

The steps that must precede commensuration help explain its effects

---

16. There are many types of standardization. A common method requires that information be accumulated and stored on standardized forms like those used by census takers, the IRS, or sociologists. Standardization is also accomplished by teaching people interactive scripts, like those delivered by McDonald's employees or flight attendants. Robin Leidner (1993) and Arlie Hochschild (1983) provide astute analyses of these types of standardization.

on decision making. Commensuration reduces large amounts of information to a single number, which can then be easily compared with another number. A growing appreciation of people's cognitive limitations is one factor promoting commensuration in choice, since commensuration condenses and limits the amount of information we have to process when making comparisons. When commensuration is motivated by choice, the procedure for deriving this single number is basically a series of aggregations, which may involve making many disparate qualities commensurate. In complex choices, commensuration will often occur at several levels of analysis.

During CAWCS, for example, investigators needed to know how the proposed plans would influence water quality. Various indicators of water quality (e.g., changes in pH, turbidity, temperature, and total dissolved solids) are measured using different scales. These scales can be made commensurate by aggregating them as attributes of some broader category (e.g., water quality) that is then calculated for each alternative. This characteristic may then be combined with other categories of impacts to create an even more general component (e.g., environmental degradation) that is also weighted. This aggregation was needed to derive a single measure for each alternative. Further aggregation is required in order to incorporate people's preferences about how good or bad a particular impact, "environmental degradation," say, is for different groups.

Another way to think about commensuration is to conceive of it as a system for throwing away information. Commensuration creates new forms of information for decision makers. It is largely a process of abstracting and reducing what is known and often obscures the link between what is represented and the empirical world. For example, a commensurated value of "7" on an income scale may represent to a decision maker how important an impact on family incomes some policy will have relative to other impacts measured along other dimensions. Yet a dollar figure (e.g., $8,000) will be more accessible, more meaningful in relation to the decision maker's personal experience. Unless a deliberate attempt is made to leave enough information (what is known as an "audit trail") to allow the decision maker to evaluate the commensuration process independently, commensuration may preclude relying on more routine ways of evaluation. Everyday experience, practical reasoning, and empathetic identification become an increasingly irrelevant basis for judgment as context is stripped away and relationships become more abstractly represented by numbers.

Regardless of the complexity of choice, systematic commensuration minimally requires that the impacts of various alternatives be determined and that values or preferences about these projected impacts be described in a common scale. These two types of judgments, those

pertaining to "facts" (often called technical judgments) and those pertaining to values (preferences), are essential to rational choice. Market-
based models, developed mainly by economists, offer one general
strategy for making public values commensurate.[17] Judgment-based
models, developed mainly by decision theorists, often trained in cognitive psychology, offer another strategy for commensurating values.[18]
Both methods quantify diverse impacts or attributes according to a
common scale; they differ in how that scale is derived.

Members of the New Guard used both models to assess value during
CAWCS. In the economic analysis, cost-benefit analyses were used to
measure economic impacts. In most cases, it was fairly easy to attach
prices to economic impacts since most were ones that the BR had established routines for doing so. In cases where it was impossible to make
price projections, "willingness-to-pay" models were used, not always
successfully. In the public involvement portion of the study, a user-
friendly judgment-based model was devised in order to commensurate
public preferences about the various plans. The social analysis more
loosely adopted the logic of the various models. What was constant
across each component of the investigation was that a sharp analytic
distinction was made between factual judgments about expected impacts by the "experts" and the evaluations of those facts, for example,
whether or not these impacts were a good thing.

Why Commensuration Is a Powerful Idea

That values can be made commensurate is a radical idea. Embedded
in it is the assumption that disparate or even idiosyncratic values can

17. Market-based models measure values as the estimated amount of money people
are willing to pay for things on an open market. The value of a certain habitat might
be measured, e.g., as how much people would pay visit a particular area. Cost-benefit
analyses are an example of a market-based model. One virtue of this approach is that
decisions are analyzed in naturally occurring settings; however, its scope is limited to
things for which a market price exists or can be reasonably projected. One troublesome
assumption made in most of these models is that a fixed sum of money, or "price," is
valued equally by all people. Price is less anonymous than this.

18. Judgment-based models measure values according to a common scale that is constructed by having people judge the importance of units of change on different scales
of measurement. For example, the relative value of additional flood protection and the
loss of riparian habitat might be assessed by having people judge how much value associated with an increase in flood protection is needed to offset the value of lost habitat.
Judgment-based models can be applied to any decision. They allow analysts to isolate
precisely the factors that most influence the decision, measure how robust these are, and
measure preferences precisely. Since they rely on individuals' subjective assessments in
hypothetical situations, people may respond differently in hypothetical situations than
in contexts that are more real to them.

be expressed in standardized forms and that doing so does not fundamentally change their meaning. Put another way, the "contents" of values, preferences, or beliefs are malleable and autonomous enough to be translated into different forms without distortion that harms decision making.

The assumption that changes in form do not significantly alter meaning is at odds with much literary, linguistic, and anthropological theory. What this view denies is that meaning is intimately linked to form and that to express meaning in ways divorced from cultural form and context is to transform value, to re-create it. Sometimes this transformation misrepresents what it purports to measure neutrally. Because commensuration is linked with our notions of rationality and objectivity, it is a pervasive and powerful social form.[19]

Commensuration is also an old idea, one long associated with living a good, reasoned life. Seldom the primary or explicit focus of social theorizing, commensuration has often been incorporated into theories about the emergence of capitalism and into explanations of the development of Western rationality. The associations between commensuration and rationality, and incommensurability and irrationality, are not Enlightenment inventions. According to Martha Nussbaum (1984:56–57), the linking of enumeration, measurement, and commensuration with order and comprehension and, obversely, the linking of incommensurability with chaos and anxiety characterize Greek writing in the fifth and early fourth centuries B.C. Nussbaum argues that commensuration was crucial to Plato's understanding of the good, since he believed that we need to make our ethical values commensurate to order and grant priority to them. Commensuration represented the only way to overcome conflicting and complex ethical concerns that, if left incommensurate, would create conflict, confusion, and pain.[20]

19. My understanding of commensuration as a social form is informed by Georg Simmel (1971), who saw social forms as organizing principles of selection that confer unity and coherence to social life, that make it meaningful and comprehensible. We collectively construct, reproduce, and objectify social forms. Our interactions with them shape our perceptions and change us. Explaining the prevalence, use, and consequence of social forms motivates Simmel's sociology (see Levine 1971:xxxiii–xxxvi).

20. Plato believed, as Karl Marx, Max Weber, and Georg Simmel would believe much later, that commensuration was a mode of perceiving the world that changed those who used it. Commensuration improves self-control by structuring our choices in ways that make it obvious what we should do. By deliberately eliminating the heterogeneity of our values, we temper our emotions and attachments by removing motives for irrational behavior. A general concept of value allows us to frame choices as being between more or less of the same quantity, which changes our investment in things. Commensuration makes us more stable, less passionate. Plato understood that this idea was both appealing and frightening. Aristotle judged the prospect of eliminating our vulnerability and pas-

Commensuration and the homogeneity it produces simultaneously diminish risk and threaten the intensity and integrity of what we value. These themes inform our most compelling critiques of modernity: in Marx's critique of capitalism, commodification distorts our relations with each other by turning people into means and things into ends; in Simmel's analysis of money, where the objectification of value inserts distance between us and what is valued, fostering intellectualization and detachment; and in Weber's conception of the iron cage and the disenchantment attending rationalization. Commensuration makes the world more predictable, but at what cost? One consequence of commensuration is its potential to change our relations to what we value, to alter the way we invest in things and people. Comparing lovers is demeaning, calibrating friendship dehumanizes. Yavapai residents who spoke bitterly about bureaucrats attaching a price to their culture, quantifying their right to exist, were expressing a similar objection.

Another distinctive characteristic of commensuration is its radical inclusiveness. Commensuration creates an abstract form of unity that is capable of encompassing any valued thing. In doing so, commensuration creates relationships among extraordinarily diverse and remote things. Whether commensuration is accomplished in a price, utility curve, cost-benefit ratio, or a multiattribute trade-off scheme, at least as it is conceptualized in rational choice theory, any value or preference can be made commensurate with any other, and all choice can be transformed into a quantitative relationship.[21] The capacity to create relationships between virtually any two things is an extraordinary feature, one that simultaneously overcomes distance, by creating ties between things where none before had existed, and imposes distance, by expressing value in such an abstract and remote manner.

But just as commensuration can create new relationships among disparate things, it can also undermine other relationships by transforming and transgressing the important social and cultural boundaries that mark and sustain these relationships. One way it does this is by preventing the expression of incommensurable values. Defining

---

sion as too disturbing. He believed that beauty depends on its ephemeral qualities and our ethics require us to invest in the singularity of others. Investing in something unique is risky, but the loss of vulnerability is riskier still, for goodness depends on its fragility (Nussbaum 1986).

21. Joseph Raz describes this "unrestricted generality" as a "theoretical desideratum." He says, "Theories which provide general recipes for comparing values, when they are not victims of the illusion that revealed preferences provide the clue to their problem, begin by establishing people's actual judgments on the relative value of options, and extrapolate principles which can be applied generally and without restriction to any pair of alternatives" (1986:335).

something as incommensurable is a special form of valuing, a special way of investing something with meaning. Incommensurables preclude trade-offs. An incommensurable category encompasses things, people, or experiences that are defined as socially unique in a specific way: they are not to be expressed in terms of some other category of value. Joseph Raz (1986:328–29) broadly defines an incommensurable as a denial that the value of two options are comparable; it is the "failure of transitivity" which pertains when neither of two valuable options is better than the other and there could exist some other option that is better than one but not the other.

The significance of excluding incommensurable categories, or in rendering these commensurate, will vary, partly because the significance of this symbolic boundary will vary. Not all social categories defined as incommensurable are equally important. The importance of incommensurable categories varies by the passion we attach to them, how central they are for defining our roles and our identities, and how much effort is required to breach them. Raz argues that distinctions between kinds of incommensurables help reveal their social significance (1986: 322–57).

Sometimes something is defined as incommensurable for purely strategic reasons, as a bargaining position. This is how some members of the Old Guard interpreted the Yavapai's reluctance to sell their land.[22] A trivial form of incommensurability occurs if, given a choice between a cup of tea or of coffee, neither is of greater value to me, even if warming the tea to make it taste better still does not make it better or worse than the coffee (Raz 1986:328–29). Sometimes, however, incommensurate categories are vital expressions of some important value and signal to people how they should act toward members of that category. A belief in incommensurability may be a qualification for having certain kinds of relationships. When this type of category becomes important in defining how to "be" with those things, this is a distinctive form of incommensurability that Joseph Raz calls "constitutive incommensurables" (1986:345–57). In confronting a choice that involves a

---

22. Deciding during negotiations whether resistance to compensation is bargaining or something more is difficult. This distinction requires one of three things: that I assume my judgments are good predictors about what others would do (shared values or preferences), that I understand the people involved well enough to interpret their behavior correctly, or that I wait for an outcome that confirms or disconfirms my interpretation. Some engineers could not be convinced that Yavapai residents thought about money differently than they did. They wanted to believe that, as one man put it, "the Indians are sorry now" that Orme was not built. That the community annually celebrates the decision that deprived them of income suggests that they do not regard the Orme outcome as an example of having gambled and lost.

constitutive incommensurable, people will typically refuse to participate in that choice, and their refusal to do so will be meaningful to
them; some may find the very idea of choice abhorrent. Raz notes that
while "there are many gradations of lesser or greater reluctance to un-
dertake such comparisons . . . , for almost every person there are comparisons he will feel indignant if asked to make, and which he will, in
normal circumstances, emphatically refuse to make. . . . The fact that
two options cannot be compared is viewed as an obstacle to trade-offs.
The barrier is not absolute. It is as if trade-offs involve a heavy price.
The very willingness to exchange such incomparables has grave consequences to the life of the agent" (1986:346).

We can all think of things we would define as constitutive incommensurables in our own lives. Two of Raz's examples are children and
friendships. Believing that the value of children cannot be expressed
with money and that the very idea of exchanging a child for money is
abhorrent is fundamental to being a good parent.[23] Similarly, believing
that friendship cannot be bought, or that what we derive from our
friendship with a person is distinctive and cannot be duplicated with
any other person, is basic to what it means to us to be a good friend.
If we thought that our friends were in some way interchangeable with
money, or social esteem, this would preclude us from having genuine
friendships. The pain that some people experience in selling the house
where they or their children grew up, an attachment to a family heir-
loom, the reluctance some feel about selling their blood, our disap-
proval of sex for profit, and even the affront some faculty feel when
they are asked to evaluate subordinates in terms of ranked comparisons with persons defined as "benchmarks" are all examples of people
grappling with incommensurable categories.

Believing in incommensurables is one way of limiting what can be
rationally chosen. The debate over abortion and euthanasia is partly
about disagreements over what can morally and legally be the subject
of choice. The horror of William Styron's novel *Sophie's Choice* is another example of the consequences of having to choose what should
never be chosen. Styron depicts a Nazi doctor who forces a mother to
choose which of her two children will die, and how it became impossible for her to live with the consequences of having made that choice.
For some Jews, the Holocaust is a constitutive incommensurable. Some
regard any comparison made to the Holocaust as immoral and threat-

---

23. Raz notes that this relationship cannot be reduced to a preference order where
not exchanging a child for money is better than having a child, which is better than
having money, since "the value of not exchanging a child derives from the value of
having children" (1986:348).

ening to their understanding of themselves as Jews. Some believe that understanding the Holocaust as an incommensurable evil helps to guide people about what it means to be and act as a Jew. I will argue that land was a constitutive incommensurable for Yavapai residents, and that valuing land as incommensurable was closely connected to what it means to be Yavapai.

It is easy to overemphasize the relation between value and choice. Important investments need not take the form of a deliberate choice. Raz argues that there are many meaningful endeavors and relationships in our lives that we willingly embrace without having deliberately chosen to do so. In some cases, choice seems an inappropriate way to frame some relationships. As he put it, "It is wrong, according to general consensus, to choose whether to be a devoted child by one's chances of success. One should simply do one's best to succeed" (1986:343).

The association of commensuration with rationality and objectivity, the proliferation of techniques for calculating commensuration, and their extensive use in business, administration, and education all suggest how important it is to understand how commensuration shapes how and what we value. Doing so will require that we understand how its meaning interacts with other meanings, with other social forms, including the oppositional category of incommensurables. As commensuration becomes the predominant mode of valuing, does this diminish incommensurable categories, making them increasingly irrelevant or inferior modes of value? Or does the proliferation of commensuration make incommensurable categories more distinctive and precious? The meaning of each deeply depends on the other, so it is important to investigate the relation between these incompatible modes of valuing. Variation in the type, use, and defense of incommensurable categories suggests that basic to understanding the importance of incommensurable categories is empirical explanations of how and when they emerge, and exactly how they inform behavior.

Theoretical Implications: Turning Assumptions into Variables

One general lesson to draw from this book is the importance of explaining what is often assumed.[24] Political explanations often focus on how groups pursue their interests, where groups as collective entities are presumed and interests are given. Such explanations neglect the cultural work involved in constructing the collective "subject" that is capable of "having interests" and the processes by which interests be-

---

24. My subhead paraphrases Art Stinchcombe's (1990:214) admonition that many sociological debates can be advanced by turning disagreements into variables.

come attached or attributed to that subject.[25] The symbolic boundaries that define groups, the categories that are created to represent mutuality, and the reification that turns collectivities into things are themselves cultural and political accomplishments. My analysis reiterates the importance of appreciating the historical specificity and dynamism of interests and identities, and of recovering and explaining the cultural processes involved in constructing and interpreting both.

Our explanations will be better if we treat the creation of interests and identities as empirical questions rather than as assumptions. Doing so will allow us to understand how assumptions (both theoretical and practical) about engaging in politics and being rational shape people's political responses. Rather than take for granted that people organize themselves as interest groups, we need to ask how and when this now common form of politics emerged, what conditions sustain this form of politics, and what its effects are.[26] As I will argue, I believe our ideas about how to be rational can be a powerful mechanism for reproducing this form of politics. In conceiving of politics as decision making, in framing political participation as people's having preferences and values they care about maximizing, and in understanding and creating political units on the basis of models of rational individual actors, where community or "groupness" is defined by assumptions about people's sharing homogeneous, stable values, our conceptions of rationality elicit and reinforce interest-group politics.

Understanding the processes by which interests and identities are constructed will also help us to sort out those conditions that sustain identity politics, that make them persuasive to some audiences and effective in some arenas and not others. This will help us understand both the more tacit forms of power that render some interests invisible and some groups unimaginable and the more explicit power conferred by nationalism and fundamentalism, where entitlements, obligations, and law are premised on the essentialized identities of its subjects.

Assumptions of rationality also warrant unpacking. Where much rational choice theory is dedicated to showing how, given people's preferences and opportunities, outcomes are rational, my questions are somewhat different. I want to understand the conditions under which certain conceptions of rationality are promulgated and contested and the difference this makes for how politics are conducted. I think it is

25. This neglect also characterizes scholarship on professions. For an analysis of these processes as they pertain to the creation of professional identity, see Espeland and Halliday (1994).

26. Elisabeth Clemens (1997) exemplifies the value of this line of inquiry in her comparative analysis of the distinctive interest-group politics that emerged in the United States during the Progressive period.

important to take seriously, and treat empirically, the question of what motivates people to adopt or reject some forms of rationality. We need to better understand when the terms and legitimacy of rationality become controversial, how these shape what people attend to, and how people participate in politics.

Despite my different emphasis, my analysis offers useful lessons for rational choice approaches. First, not all choices can be expressed in terms of the means-ends logic that characterizes rational choice explanations. Efforts to assimilate noninstrumental action into the terms of instrumental action can misrepresent the nature of people's commitments and violate their understanding of themselves. This is because what we value and how we value have implications for who we are.

Second, with few exceptions, rational choice theory does not address the significance of, or benefits from, restricting choice. Constraining choice is a ubiquitous activity that often marks an important social relationship. In some conditions, it helps define for people both how to be and how to act. The comprehensive claims made by some rational choice theorists should be tempered with an appreciation of the multiple ways that we can invest something with value and the incompatibility of disparate modes of valuing.

Third, my analysis calls into question assumptions made by some rational choice theorists. In some versions, preferences, tastes, or interests are conceived of as exogenous, fixed before choice, and stable. Furthermore, some assume that preferences are characteristics of autonomous individuals and that they are independent of outcomes. I argue that understanding where preferences or interests come from is important, because these do change over time, sometimes in ways that are consequential for how people understand themselves as social actors. I show how these shifts, as organizational, cultural, or political accomplishments, are fundamentally social, collective projects. Sometimes preferences change in patterned ways that are theoretically important, as when what was formally a means for accomplishing some goal becomes a valued end. And sometimes, rather than existing before choice, preferences are the product of choice.

Fourth, my analysis can help rational choice theorists better understand the dimensions of choice. I show how cultural processes, organizational structure, and power influence the construction of feasibility sets or alternatives that define the range of outcomes that people attend to when choosing.

And finally, my findings offer a cautionary tale for those who conceive of rational choice models as neutral techniques for improving decisions and integrating values, as did members of the New Guard. When used to represent impacts to different groups and integrate the preferences of different audiences, these models systematically distorted their meanings for some groups. Since these models, and the conception of rationality on which they are premised, are used so pervasively, we need to better understand their use and their influence.

Despite the advances made by rational choice theorists in formalizing and making more rigorous Max Weber's conception of instrumental rationality, his analyses are indispensable to those who want to understand the consequences attending contemporary forms of rationalization, as I do. His conception of instrumental rationality is complemented and contrasted with other forms of rationality, and his emphasis on the tensions and the contradictions that competing forms of rationality can generate, are crucial insights for understanding rationalization.

Rationalization, Instrumental Reason, and Domination

> *This simple proposition, which is often forgotten, should be placed at*
> *the beginning of every study which attempts to deal with rationalism:*
> *one may rationalize life from fundamentally different points of view in*
> *very different directions. Rationalism is a historical concept which*
> *covers a whole world of different things.*
>
> Max Weber

Rationality, as Weber understands it, is a diverse and dynamic set of relations that account for the distinctive character of modernity. Weber defines rationality in a series of distinctions, the most fundamental being that between rational and irrational action, with affective (or expressive) and traditional (habitual) motivations exemplifying the latter.[27] Rational action entails some logical relation between the action and the goals of the action, whether these are some desired end or belief.

Weber further distinguishes (not always explicitly or consistently) between the subjective rationality that may guide an individual's behavior and objectified rationality, an orientation that has become institutionalized as patterns of action regulated by various values, rules, or techniques within spheres such as law, religion, administration, or art. This distinction is important, since people's passionate commitment to substantive values has often dramatically and unintentionally promoted other forms of rationality in other spheres. Profound shifts in

---

27. Alan Sica's (1988) exemplary exegesis shows the ambiguous place of the irrational in Weber's scholarship. Sica argues (vii) that for Weber, influenced by the marginal utility theorists of his day, hypostatizing rational action was theoretically costly, resulting in his "brittle" theory of social action and his relegating crucial features of modern life and the bulk of human behavior to the residual.

other forms of rationality often emanate from people who were systematically pursuing some ultimate value. In Weber's account, rationalization does not develop as some natural, gradual expansion of calculating, self-interested action associated with early forms of capitalism. Traditional forms of authority required more abrupt ruptures than that, ruptures that dramatically changed people's motivations and orientations to the world (Weber 1981:355, 365).[28] Furthermore, the conditions that produce a particular rational form often become increasingly irrelevant as these forms develop, spread, and squeeze out nonconformists. This crucial insight of Weber's is one that neoinstitutional organization theory has vigorously documented and refined.[29]

The two forms of subjective rational action that dominate Weber's analysis are instrumental rationality (*Zweckrationalität*) and substantive or value rationality (*Wertrationalität*). Instrumental rationality is oriented toward evaluating the means for accomplishing some defined end, and value rationality is action concerned with the intrinsic value of some action without regard for its success or consequences (Weber 1978:24–25). These are different and irreconcilable logics, one based on calculating means for ends that are predetermined and formally outside its realm, and the other linked to ways of being and acting that are rooted in deep commitments to values for their own sake.

Weber is less clear when he describes the various forms of objectified rationality. His most basic distinction between substantive rationality and formal rationality parallels his distinction for individual action: substantive rationality is oriented toward some criteria of ultimate ends or values, and formal rationality is oriented toward the calculation of means or procedures; the former is a matter of value, the latter a matter of fact (Brubaker 1984:36). So, for example, economic action is formally rational for Weber when it is based on quantitative calculation, accounting, and deliberate planning; it is substantively rational to the extent that some ultimate value, whether it be hedonistic, utilitarian, egalitarian, or any one of the infinite variety of possible values, provides the criterion for evaluating the results of economic action (Weber 1978:85–86).

28. Weber's most famous example of such a rupture is his analysis of the critical role played by Calvinist notions of "calling" for the accumulation of capital. In what was originally an effort to assure oneself of God's approval, a duty to work became devotion to work for its own sake and not for the results of labor. This ethos honed the discipline needed by capitalists adopting the ceaseless and fundamentally irrational goal of increasing profit. A hallmark of capitalist cultures, this devotion to work no longer has religious underpinnings and is no longer optional. As Weber put it, "The Puritan wanted to work in a calling; we are forced to do so" (1976:181).

29. See, e.g., DiMaggio and Powell 1983; Meyer 1986; Ventresca 1995; Dobbin 1994.

The tensions between modes of formal rationality and value rationality, both in their subjective and objective versions, are fundamental to Weber's historical analyses, methodology, and moral vision: Weber repeatedly demonstrates the hostility of spheres of life or institutions characterized by substantive rationality to formal rationality, as well as the essential role that substantive rationality has played in the emergence of capitalism; his efforts to construct a value-neutral methodology requires the conceptual and political separation of fact and value, means and ends. Weber's prescription for a moral life requires a commitment to fundamental values and the use of reason to guide behavior in light of those values, but these values cannot be defended on rational premises (Brubaker 1984:98).

Nor is there for Weber some Archimedean point from which the rational could always be distinguished from the irrational. As he put it, "A thing is never irrational in itself, but only from a particular rational point of view. For the unbeliever every religious way of life is irrational, for the hedonist every ascetic standard, no matter whether, measured with respect to its particular basic values, that opposing asceticism is a [form of] rationalization" (1976:194). Weber's distinction between substantive and formal rationality is similarly relational. Just as there is no completely objective stance that can determine whether and how action is rational, neither is there a rational basis for defending our choice of substantive values. Rational techniques can illuminate which means are most efficient to achieve some valued end, but they cannot defend that choice of end or adjudicate conflict among disparate values. Today, such a dilemma might be termed an existential choice, but these are harder to abide by since they cannot be defended in the terms of instrumental rationality that dominate bureaucratic and corporate discourse. Paradoxically, the very recognition of the nonrational nature of such choices reflects the limits of rationality, which become increasingly apparent when living in a highly rationalized world.

The relativity of rationality, the irreconcilability of its different forms, the ambiguous place of the irrational, the gap between facts and values, and the incommensurability of what Weber termed value-spheres all suggest a messy, compartmentalized world where difference is both receding and hard to reconcile. We can sense in Weber a nostalgia for the absolute, which, after Nietzsche, could not be recovered for scholars of his era and learning. Weber's distinctions do not permit some easy rapprochement; neither epistemology nor ethics can provide us with the universal truths or technologies needed to stand outside and adjudicate these dilemmas. This is the tragedy and, as I hope to suggest, the vitality of Weber's modernity.

Weber's admonitions on how to study rationalization are worth heeding. He is adamant that rationalization be studied historically, as a complicated series of interrelated processes. Weber knew too much history and was too good a theorist to portray rationalization as some ineluctable, monolithic process. The development of rationalism, he argues, "by no means follows parallel lines in the various departments of life" (1976:76–77). In law, commerce, religion, politics, and administration, he shows how bumpy and erratic its course was, how dependent different forms of rationalization were on the many irrational motivations that gave rise to it, and how many efforts to rationalize a sphere of life were impeded, even thwarted, by those it threatened. Yet Weber believed that the broad trend is clear: encroaching rationalization, embodied most clearly in bureaucracy, is irreversible. It is a formidable force that threatens the personal, the particular, and the passions that impede its progress. Its capacity to remake existing relations of status and dominance can be liberating, but its efforts to standardize, depersonalize, and render calculable wide domains of human action can stifle initiative, creativity, and freedom, detach people from one another, dilute their passions, and make our lives seem less meaningful.

Weber urges scholars to analyze rationalization's particular forms and consequences in the specific contexts in which they emerge in order, as he put it, to "find out whose intellectual child the particular concrete form of rational thought was" (1976:78); he insists that the distinction between motives and effects be appreciated and explained. But rationalization cannot be reduced to a simple story of what agents choose to do, since its coercive effects become objectified in forms and practices that agents do not control. Constraints, opportunity costs, hegemony— whatever your preferred phrasing—things we cannot control become encoded in forms we inherit, forms as fateful as commodities, as taken-for-granted as money, or as literal as the standardized documents that members of bureaucracies routinely process. Such forms shape how actors frame their decisions and conceive of what is rational. Disclosing their influence on how we process the world is central for understanding both the diffusion and consequences of rational forms.

Another lesson to learn from Weber is how crucial it is to account for the antagonisms and reinvigoration that arise when forms of rationality converge. To do so requires finding sites where the terms of rationality are contested, where there are conflicts among its various forms, where its consequences are controversial. Just what is it that makes different forms of rationality irreconcilable? Where precisely do these tensions reside? How do they change the terms of relevancy and participation? Derived, but not always answered, by Weber, these questions motivate this book. As Weber understood, situations where people try to extend or develop rational forms are good places for analyzing their effects.

The controversy over Orme Dam was just such a situation. The decision procedures that were being devised by members of the New Guard were all strategies for evaluating which alternative best accomplished some end. Their models substantiated instrumental rationality. As members of the New Guard emphasized, they were completely neutral about which goals were evaluated or whose values were maximized. The models could be deployed in any decision, regardless of its context or the particularity of its users. A sharp distinction between facts and values is built into these models; goals are formally and discursively outside their purview. Their technology can commensurate any value and quantify any impact. There is no alternative future they cannot calculate.

What was so remarkable in this decision was how refined and universal this rationality had become, how sophisticated and self-conscious members of the New Guard were in trying to institutionalize it. This sophistication prompted the creation of computer programs for constructing utility functions for individuals that would mechanically tell people what they wanted. These models and strategies provided a way to make sure that the public had access to appropriate and accurate information and that it was organized to ensure a reasoned response. In complex decisions, involving difficult technical information that even taxed expert knowledge, these models could structure participation in ways that allowed ordinary citizens to make sophisticated decisions in accordance with their values. Weber, I think, would both marvel and shudder at how far it had all come.

Weber's investigations of instrumental rationality has powerfully influenced critical scholarship, most notably that affiliated with the Frankfurt school and its heirs. Weber concluded from his comparative studies of rationalization that large-scale irrigation played a pivotal role in the emergence of early forms of bureaucratic administration in Egypt, China, and Mesopotamia (1988:84; 1978:972; 1981:56–57). The complexity and scale of the task, and the number of resources required, fostered coercive labor practices and the development of the world's "oldest officialdom."

Intrigued by Weber's argument, Karl Wittfogal (1957) continued to investigate the relationship between water development and political power. Wittfogal famously concluded that in the ancient world, large-scale irrigation gave rise to a distinctive bureaucratic state controlled by technological elites, what he termed "hydraulic society." Wittfogal's claims of the universal link between irrigation and totalitarian forms of power and social inertia has been widely criticized. Yet the historian Donald Worster (1985:30) argues that Wittfogal's lessons can be usefully extended to contemporary societies and that his fundamental question, derived from Marx, remains extremely pertinent: How, in the remaking of nature, do we remake ourselves?

In his analysis of water control and development, Worster (1985:7) describes the American West as a "hydraulic society." Characterized by a vast technological complex dominated by engineering and economic elites, this monolithic empire, devoted to controlling water, as did its predecessors, concentrates wealth and power. It is propelled by our deep commitment to instrumental rationality, the form of reason that, while dedicated to developing increasingly masterful means of dominating nature, is incapable of interrogating or justifying this end (1985:55).[30] It is also incapable of limiting its own domination. By making ends irrelevant, by reducing value to the exogenous preferences of individual "tastes" beyond dispute, only "facts" are relevant, and nature, like reason, is reduced to a tool of the privileged. For Worster, the prospects for disrupting the tyranny of instrumental reason seem bleak.

Understanding the conditions that foster resistance to the domination of instrumental rationality is central to John Walton's (1992) investigation of California's most famous water war, in which he analyzes Owens Valley residents' efforts to control development of the valley. This 130-year struggle began with the Pauite Indians' attempts to resist white conquest and their economic incorporation as wage laborers, and ended with residents' sustained rebellion aimed at preventing Los Angeles from appropriating the Owens River. Instrumental reason is the premise of dependent development, where regions or countries are resources to be manipulated for the advantage of the more powerful. Walton shows how deeply this logic has characterized the development of the American West, including the conflicts over Owens Valley. Unlike most accounts of dependent development, however, his is not the familiar tale of heroic and ultimately doomed efforts to resist incorporation. Rather, his analysis reveals how resistance can be both sustained and effective.

Walton's analysis, like mine, supports many of Worster's central claims: the extensiveness of the hydraulic empire, how fundamentally it has affected western development, how well its policies have served the wealthy and powerful, how crucial the role of both local and federal governments has been in promoting and subsidizing this empire, the incredible power wielded by water-development institutions like the BR or Los Angeles Department of Water and Power, the hubris and folly of water development that fosters uncontrolled and destructive growth, and the failure to contain or even acknowledge the limits of instrumental reason.

But Walton (1985:298) objects to Worster's nearly exclusive focus on instrumental reason, on what he views as Worster's selective bor-

---

30. Worster's critique of instrumental reason is deeply indebted to Max Horkheimer and Theodor Adorno. See Worster (1985:53–60); and Jay (1973:255–61).

rowing of Weber. Walton argues that sometimes substantive values can coexist and compete with instrumental rationality, especially when the terms of instrumental reason are perceived as being illegitimately imposed upon community traditions. Alternative values of community and visions of prosperity, a deep commitment to popular justice, and vibrant traditions of cooperative organizing galvanized the Owens Valley residents' struggle against the efforts of the power and economic elite to expand their hydraulic empire (1985:196–97).

The Orme dispute, as in Walton's analysis, shows how conflict can transform physical locations into social locations. By investing "place" with meanings that are incompatible with and irreducible to instrumental logic, the terms of value can become the terms of struggle. For the Yavapai, the New Guard's decision framework misrepresented not only their interests, but them. The New Guard's procedures required that the dam's consequences for the Yavapai be made commensurate with its other effects. Portraying value as fundamentally relative is at odds with how most Yavapai understand and value their land. Land is unique and intrinsically valuable, just as people are; how one relates to land is intimately bound up with how one is Yavapai, and how one relates to others and to the world as Yavapai. Most believe that it is wrong to value land as a commodity or as commensurate with other things. Doing so betrays its distinctiveness, cheapens it, diminishes oneself.

In Weber's language, land was a substantive value for the Yavapai. Efforts to translate this substantive rationality, which Yavapai people describe as "having [or being] a culture," into the terms of instrumental logic, where land is a means for obtaining some other goal, is not merely futile or distorting. It is an expression of power that harms them; it is wrong. Making sense of and explaining this wrongness shaped their resistance to the dam. It stimulated a reinterpretation of their collective identity and the adoption of political strategies that emphasized and articulated their difference as the source of their authority and power.

Conflict can have a comparable effect on people's commitment to plans as well as to place. While planned-for dams are not tangible in the way that rivers and communities are, they too can become invested with meanings, values, and identities in ways that cannot be contained within, or represented by the logic of, instrumental reason. And these meanings can also acquire constituencies, be sustained in politics and organizations, and develop over time. For members of the Old Guard, Orme Dam was transformed from a means into an end, from instrumental rationality to a substantive value. As such, Orme's status could never simply be that of one alternative among several. Largely an organizational accomplishment, their commitment to this dam left them unable to switch their support easily when a politically superior, organizationally more desirable plan emerged. The efforts of the New Guard to make Orme Dam formally commensurate with other plans, and to document its inferiority in technically commensurate terms, did not jibe with either the Old Guard's beliefs or feelings. Yet they did not possess a legitimate discourse for the expressing this gap. As seasoned bureaucrats, they were fluent in the cool language of efficiency. They could not prove the New Guard's calculations wrong, nor could they claim to love a dam. Rendered mute, they were unable to define or defend its incommensurability.

The decision about the dam became the turning point where members of the Old Guard were forced to confront the relativity of their worldview. Whereas once their power and their ethos had kept them from seeing its distinctiveness, had allowed them to ignore those who disagreed with them, had insulated them from a changing world, they were now finally forced to acknowledge that Orme Dam was dead, that their agency was no longer the place it had been, that they were relics. Fifteen years later, they still mourn Orme and wonder at its demise.

In prompting close scrutiny of the dimensions of decision making, members of the New Guard became convinced that a rigorous, retrievable rationality was warranted. Their efforts to impose a sophisticated version of instrumental rationality created a context where the contours of rationality became part of the debate. The commensuration that their models demanded remade and in some cases subverted the boundaries that people had created around the things and people that gave meaning to their lives. For the Old Guard, Orme Dam was made vulnerable by commensuration and was done in by a rigorous instrumental reason. But another paradoxical effect of this was to generate new defenses, and attribute new significance, to those things which people experienced as incommensurable.

The result, however, might have surprised Weber. In politicizing the terms of rationality, the decision about a dam prompted a critique and generated a political strategy for those who felt threatened by its extension. Had Weber acknowledged that, under some conditions, attempts to impose and objectify instrumental rationality could generate new claims, new strategies, and new interpretations of substantive values, perhaps he'd have been less pessimistic. Perhaps he might have appreciated how a politicized rationality sometimes offer new defenses. And that is my story here.

This book investigates how a political dispute over a dam became a contest over the terms of rationality, the boundaries of bureaucracy, and the contours of culture. Mediated by law, organizational ideology, and historical memory, this decision generated contradictory interpretations and conflicting investments. From the vantage points of three groups with deep but disparate stakes in the decision, I explain how their relation to the decision and to one another transformed the interests and identities of each group, and how these transformations responded to people's conceptions of rationality.

Chapter 2 describes the origins and influence of a powerful organizational ideology within the Bureau of Reclamation. I explain how this engineering ethos shaped the structure of the organization and the way employees did their jobs and invested in its projects, and how they responded to changes both inside and outside the agency. This ethos helped the agency become the world's premier dam builder, but it also fostered an insularity that encouraged members to underestimate the potential of environmentalism and environmental law.

Chapter 3 describes how the agency's engineering ethos and the long political battles to authorize the Central Arizona Project affected the Old Guard's investments in Orme Dam. I explain how what had been a minor structure in a big water-development project became a symbol of their work and the value of their agency's mission, and why its meaning for them was incompatible with a rational decision framework.

Chapter 4 examines the conditions that allowed a marginal group of employees to create an organizational niche for themselves as planners committed to more inclusive and rigorous decision making. I explain how the National Environmental Policy Act and the organizational crisis that Orme Dam grew into provided an opportunity for the New Guard to implement rational decision procedures as a way to resolve the crisis. These procedures and their commitment to broader public participation have become institutionalized in the agency and have helped to redefine its mission.

Chapter 5 examines how the long, bitter struggle to retain some part of their land has shaped Yavapai people's understanding of themselves and their culture. I explain why their investment in their land was incompatible with the assumptions informing the decision framework that was implemented, and how these contradictions influenced the way residents responded to the threat of Orme Dam.

Chapter 6 argues that the terms of instrumental rationality, and the commensuration that it requires, are powerful frameworks for interpreting the world. They can change what we attend to, how people participate in decisions, and how they understand themselves and their interests. Disclosing the mutual and contingent relations between rationality, interests, and identity will help us better understand bureaucratic authority and contemporary politics.

~~~~~ **Two** ~~~~~

Nature by Design: The Bureau of Reclamation's Western Conquest

The wilderness and the solitary place shall be glad for them; and the desert shall rejoice and blossom as the rose.

Isaiah 35:1

Thus sayeth the Lord, Make the Valley full of ditches.

2 Kings 3:16

Bureau of Reclamation engineers have built more than the West: they have built the great works of the American era.

William E. Warne

Ideology structures consciousness. It simultaneously offers a way of seeing and not seeing, an elaboration and defense of some relations that inevitably render others inchoate, invisible. Ideology is part of the struggle to control the cultural terms by which power is legitimated and the world is ordered. Jean Comaroff and John Comaroff (1991:22) characterize ideology as the collective, defined system of meanings, values, or beliefs of a particular social group that expresses a "worldview." It is power expressed by agents, by people with intentions in specific, historical contexts. Among other things, ideology is practical work that people routinely do when they perform their jobs, explain their actions, or describe themselves to themselves or to others.

The project sponsors, employees, and allies of the Bureau of Reclamation collectively created a compelling worldview that defined its role, structured its relations, and legitimated its projects. Rooted in frontier narratives, Progressive ideals, and Christian theology, and nurtured by professional aspirations, their ethos celebrates our rational mastery of nature as redemptive, an act of worship. It makes reclamation synonymous with dam building, the domain of engineers. It transforms technology into God's tool, makes irrigation a symbol and expression of democratic government, and defines dams as both useful and beautiful. Created through myth, rituals, and folk songs and the symbolic power of big dams, as well as cost-benefit ratios and arcane reports, this vision of the world is reproduced in the agency's structure, in the way budgets are allocated and careers organized.

Adapted to new circumstances and appropriated by new audiences with compatible interests, this ethos has endured, with lasting consequences for how BR employees understand its goals, conduct its business, and interpret the world. Both a source and a manifestation of power, this worldview was a means for making the agency coherent, accessible, and meaningful. But in doing so, it also left the agency insular, vulnerable, and unable to apprehend that the consensus surrounding water development, never universal, no longer held sway with some segments of the public.

This long-latent vulnerability was a symptom of success. For when ideology becomes naturalized in forms of life, habitualized and internalized in ways that remove it from debate, power becomes "hidden in orthodoxy" and hegemonic. Consciousness of power, and our capacity to see it and contest it, are what distinguish ideology and hegemony as forms of power for the Comaroffs. Like consciousness that is simplistically conceived of as on or "un," hegemony and ideology are not polar oppositions, but a continuum of possibilities, their variety and relations to one another to be explained. What matters is describing the concrete historical and cultural conditions that transform tacit power into articulate, contestable power and vice versa.

However taken-for-granted the premises of power become, hegemony is never total. It remains vulnerable to that which it excludes. The "vitality of the forms of life it thwarts," and the contradictions between "the world as represented and the world as lived," offer a space for criticism (Comaroff and Comaroff 1991:25, 26). As the worldview constructed by BR engineers and their advocates became naturalized and institutionalized within the agency, people grew less capable of appreciating its distinctiveness and less aware of its effectiveness in editing the world for its members.

From a distance, our image of bureaucracy is of massive, impenetrable, unchanging organizations. They are labyrinths, defined and defended by arcane and elaborate rules, occupied by interchangeable, faceless people devoted to paperwork. This image resembles Weber's conceptual device, the ideal-typical bureaucracy, minus the history. But history is crucial for apprehending the distinctiveness of bureaucracies, for understanding where they come from, how they endure, and why, sometimes, they do change. And history is needed, too, to grant identities and agency to bureaucrats, to give them faces.

This chapter gives the history needed to appreciate the distinctiveness of this powerful bureaucracy. In it I explain the powerful worldview that emerged within the Bureau of Reclamation and how this became inscribed in the organization, appropriated and adapted by its constituents, and sustained for decades. This ethos presented an image of the BR and a lens for interpreting its place in the world. Understanding how this vision informed the commitments, actions, and conceptual frames of BR employees is crucial for understanding how its constituencies were defined and its projects were defended, why the agency built so many dams, why the American West developed as it has. It is crucial, too, for appreciating employees' often deep loyalty to the agency, their pride in its accomplishments, and the capacity of its projects to forge identities for those who became invested in them. This ethos, enacted organizationally and politically, provided the scripts, meanings, and passion that members of the Old Guard used to transform Orme Dam from a solution to a goal, from dam to symbol.

But exclusion can stimulate organizational identities just as incorporation can. Described by members of the New Guard as an "engineering culture," this worldview ensured their marginality by defining them as irrelevant or even opposed to the agency, and these atypical employees rallied in reaction against a vision that served to exclude them. Their presence, their efforts to redefine the agency's constituents as they struggled to define themselves and to devise technologies for inclusion were also responses to this worldview. And so understanding the impact of this ethos is also important for understanding the New Guard's commitments: to one another, to rationality, to public participation.

The environmental response that was galvanized by BR projects was also refined against the bureau's ethos. Written into laws and mobilized as social movements, environmental values penetrated this dam-building agency only gradually. They appeared in the form of EISs that, after the National Environmental Policy Act of 1969, had to be written, and they were adopted by the people who eventually came to write them. Their capacity to change the BR reflects yet another consequence of the bureau's ideology. The reclamation ethos that helped legitimate BR projects, once institutionalized and naturalized, shaped how the agency members responded to changes in the world, including changes it helped engender. As a frame of both reference and irrelevance, this ethos encouraged bureaucrats to ignore threats, dismiss opponents, and underestimate the New Guard's project. In engendering both loyalty and threat, identities of inclusion and exclusion, substantive and instrumental values, this ideology frames the Orme dispute for supporters and opponents alike.

The Old Bureau and the New

For the 5,000 residents of Boulder City, Nevada, a place one journalist described as "as parched and barren a patch of wind-swept rocky desert as could be found" (*Fortune* 1933), September 30, 1935, was a day for celebration. Boulder City's normally quiet streets were bustling, as cars jammed the roads and people in their Sunday clothes crowded the sidewalks (Stevens 1988:243–48). The occasion was the dedication of Boulder (now Hoover) Dam, the world's biggest and the reason that Boulder City first sprang to life in the middle of the Mohave Desert.

Franklin and Eleanor Roosevelt had taken the train from Washington, DC, along with FDR's Secretary of Interior, and crucial backer of the dam, Harold Ickes. Harry Hopkins, the head of the WPA (Works Progress Administration) had come, as had the governors of six of the Colorado River Basin states; the commissioner of reclamation, Elwood Mead, for whom the 118-mile reservoir would be named following his sudden death four months later; and dozens of other luminaries. Frank Crowe was there too. The former BR engineer who had supervised the whole project, the man called the "best construction man [they had ever] known" by his peers, "the greatest field engineer in the world" by historians, and "Mr. Hurry Up" by his laborers, was already beginning to wonder what challenges life could possibly hold after this dam (Stevens 1988:37, 252; Lear 1985:89).

Representatives of Six Companies, the hastily formed partnership of construction companies that built the dam, smiled broadly from the platform. They had much to smile about. Their contract to build Boulder Dam was the biggest ever granted by the federal government; thanks largely to Crowe's supervision, their company had finished the dam more than two years ahead of schedule and, for their efforts, stood to earn nearly $55 million, with net profits estimated between $10.4 and $18 million (Stevens 1988:252, 255–58; Lear 1985:91).[1] For the men who had worked on the dam, twice as big as any dam before it, and for the wives and children who followed them to this godforsaken place, it was a proud moment, one to savor a lifetime. The whole world was admiring their handiwork, and it was impossible not to be awed at the magnitude of their accomplishment or sobered by the sacrifices it embodied.

All told, some twelve thousand people that day would fill every inhabitable space near the dam, some even clinging to cliff sides to watch the ceremony and admire the stunning structure. Millions of Americans listened by radio as Harold Ickes, a champion of public power and public works, started the speeches. "Pridefully, man acclaims his

---

1. Boulder Dam was the first of many huge government contracts awarded to these initially relatively inexperienced partners, a consortium including Bechtel, Kaiser, Shea, MacDonald & Kahn, Morrison-Knudson, Pacific Bridge, and the Utah Construction Company. The fame and fortune attending the dam launched their industrial empires.

conquest over nature," he began, a conquest motivated by public good, not individual gain, one whose wealth would benefit generations of Americans (*Reclamation Era,* hereafter *RE,* 1935b:209–10). FDR, visibly awed by the dam, noted that "ten years ago the place where we are gathered was an unpeopled, forbidding desert," a "cactus-covered waste" in a "gloomy canyon," carved by a "dangerous, turbulent river." He proclaimed the "transformation wrought here a twentieth-century marvel," as he deftly linked the dam's triumph over nature with the government's triumph over unemployment: "Labor makes wealth. . . . To employ workers and materials when private employment has failed is to translate into great national possessions the energy that otherwise would be wasted. Boulder Dam is a splendid symbol. The mighty waters of the Colorado were running unused to the sea. Today we translate them into a great national possession" (*RE* 1935a: 193–94).

The speeches that day invoked the classic themes of reclamation, the basic tenets of the BR's engineering ethos: the conquest and possession of nature as a source of wealth and redemption; the transformation of what was dangerous, wasteful, and remote into something compliant, useful, and accessible; how taming nature revealed man at his best— heroic, dominant, intelligent. The speeches also show the political appeal of a big dam in providing a platform for, as well as a dramatic symbol and irrefutable evidence of, the state's efficacy. The world celebrated the stunning execution of these values. The dam marked a turning point for the Bureau of Reclamation, the agency that dreamed it, designed it, and oversaw its construction. Boulder Dam become its reigning symbol. It also marked a new era in reclamation, characterized by bold, expensive projects and a new logic for justifying its work. The bureau's stunning success with Boulder Dam launched a dozen other big dams, transforming it from a vulnerable, nearly bankrupt organization into a huge, powerful bureaucracy, one Donald Worster calls "the most famous and accomplished desert conqueror in world history" (1992:70).[2]

More than sixty years after FDR dedicated Boulder Dam, Bruce Babbitt, former governor of Arizona, failed presidential candidate, and Bill Clinton's secretary of interior, presided over a ceremony at a different dam site. After pushing a button, pulling a lever, and twisting a wheel,

2. BR dams proliferated quickly on the Colorado River. Hoover was followed by Parker, Davis, Morales (in Mexico), Laguna, Palo Verde, Headgate Rock, Navajo, Flaming George, Seedskadee, Savery-Pot, Hook, Meeks, Cabin, Vernal, Bonneville, Rifle Gap, Joes Valley, Paonia, Blue Mesa, Morrow Point, Crystal, Soap Park, Crawford, Silver Jack, Lemon, Frying Pan–Arkansas, and Glen Canyon in 1963, just a bit smaller than Hoover (Worster 1992:70–71).

Babbitt sent millions of gallons of Colorado River water cascading down from Glen Canyon Dam in a thunderous waterfall that reverberated throughout the walls of the Grand Canyon (*New York Times* 1996a). Babbitt created the first big flood in the canyon since the Glen Canyon Dam had been built thirty years earlier. The release lasted seven days, lowered Lake Powell by three and one-half feet, and represented about $2.5 million in power revenues forgone. This intentional flood was a modest effort to replicate the pre-dam natural floods, typically three to four times bigger than this release, that annually accompanied the melting snowpack. By creating new sandy beaches, widening rapids, introducing organic nutrients, and stirring up sediment in what had become a muddy, warm river, scientists hoped the flood would help restore the habitat of endangered fish species and generally improve the ecology of the river (*New York Times* 1996b; DIOS 1996).

The release was the culmination of thirteen years of study, dozens of reports, and a 1995 EIS that reanalyzed the operations of Glen Canyon Dam and generated over 33,000 letters from members of the public. It marked the first time the agency had, on such a grand scale, changed the way it operated its dams. This flood was for fish, birds, and trees. The reason why the reporters and camera crews came, why Babbitt was there wearing his hard hat and a big smile, why he declared this release "a new era in reclamation" was that this event was to mark the emergence of the "New Bureau." Dedicated to undoing past sins, the New Bureau was putting itself out of the construction business.

Babbitt later declared the experiment a "brilliant success," one that foretold "a sea-change in the way we operate large dams. We have shown that they can be operated for environmental purposes as well as water capture and power generation." He was careful to list all the agencies that had helped in the process, the inclusion of "stakeholders," like members of the Hualapai Tribe who lived along the river, and the elaborate public involvement process undergirding the decision. This experiment had worked, he stressed, because of the sound science that informed it and because the agency had listened to the people (DIOS 1996).

For an agency whose members refused for decades to acknowledge publicly the harmful effects of its big dams, who considered floodwater an enormous waste of money and natural resources, who viewed nature as an adversary to be fought rather than a model to emulate, this was a notable shift. Controversial, incomplete, too radical for some, too superficial for others, this change is central to the Orme Dam saga. These two well-publicized, carefully orchestrated, highly symbolic events—the dedication of Hoover Dam and the release of floodwaters in the Grand Canyon—separated by six decades, were understood by participants as pivotal moments in the history of this agency and in the way the nation managed its natural resources. The decision about Orme Dam was an important moment in this shift.

It is not too much of an exaggeration to say that the Bureau of Reclamation is a federal agency born of one social movement and reinvented by another. The federal irrigation movement of the late nineteenth century culminated in the 1902 Reclamation Act that created the agency. The environmental movement of the 1960s and 1970s, in challenging old notions of progress and development and old methods of valuing nature, in vigilantly applying environmental laws, and in introducing new kinds of employees to federal agencies provided the weapons that critics used to challenge its mission and recast its constituents, a process unfolding under the banner of the New Bureau. The New Bureau is still in process, and many agency critics are deeply skeptical of its efforts to transform itself, to wear the "green hat" after decades of dam building. What is clear, however, is that the sometimes indirect influence of the environmental movement is crucial for explaining why Orme Dam was not built, and why the agency is attempting to reinvent itself.

The Bureau of Reclamation originated in the vision and politics of Progressives, and matured and thrived under the New Deal. For both Theodore and Franklin Roosevelt, the agency played an essential role in their domestic programs. From its inception, the BR has confronted numerous threats: from private irrigators and others who opposed federal intervention in resource development; from fiscal conservatives, eastern legislators, midwestern farmers, budget cutters, and private utilities; and from those hostile to pork-barrel projects, whether out of principle or politics. The agency survived these threats to irrigate nearly ten million acres on more than 150,000 farms. The shape and politics of the West today are testament to the bureau's handiwork. It has built more than 350 diversion dams, 322 reservoirs, over 15,000 miles of canals, and more than 50 power plants (USBR 1977b:1–2).

But now the agency's future remains uncertain. Its original mandate to reclaim and settle the West has been accomplished. Its prolific dam building has left few empty dam sites. The uncertainty over what to do next has left the agency vulnerable to threats emanating from new and, for older engineers, improbable quarters: environmentalists who passed new laws and who attacked its projects and mission, and nontraditional employees who endorse their values and promote a broader accountability. The failure of BR engineers to counter or even, for a long time, to notice this threat indicts the insularity of their power and the hegemony of their worldview. But this insularity was punctured by a world that changed when these bureaucrats weren't looking. Despite these new challenges, the BR remains a tenacious bureaucracy. Because of these challenges, it is a transformed bureaucracy, one grappling for an identity.

The Beautiful and the Dammed: A Brief History of the Agency

Major John Wesley Powell, one-armed veteran of the Civil War, explorer of the Colorado River, founder of the U.S. Geological Service, and social visionary, is considered "the father of reclamation" in the United States. On the basis of his studies and explorations, Powell created an impressively comprehensive plan for the developing the West, most of which was ignored. Powell was the first to argue the then heretical idea that large-scale irrigation was necessary to settle the West and that government, not private industry, ought to help develop it by helping its citizens organize, by providing the scientific information they would need.

Powell recognized earlier than most that the resources, technology, and coordination required to develop irrigation on the scale needed to sustain agriculture in the West were far beyond the means of individuals or private industry, and that land and water speculation would destroy private irrigation. His *Report on the Lands of the Arid Region* in 1878 was the first important stimulus to the national irrigation movement. Ten years later, Congress finally approved an irrigation survey of the West which Powell launched, along with Frederick Newell and a host of young, eager engineers. Powell's enemies stopped the survey before it was finished, but he was able to convince some political leaders that reclamation was doomed without federal assistance (Worster 1985:135–37).

About one-third of the United States, including most of the West, requires irrigation to sustain tilled agriculture. The Homestead Act of 1862 had helped settle the Missouri Valley, but settlers further west were fighting a losing battle to develop agriculture. Water was the main factor limiting western migration, and the demands of large-scale irrigation overwhelmed farmers. As Marc Reisner (1986:112–13) describes their predicament: "It was one thing to throw a ten-foot-high earthen plug across a freshet in order to create a two-acre stock pond— though even that taxed the resources of most farmers in the West. . . . It was quite another thing to build a dam on a stream large enough to supply a year-round flow, and to dig a canal—by horse and by hand— that was long enough, and deep enough, and wide enough, to irrigate hundreds or thousands of acres of land. The work involved was simply stupefying."

Many Western rivers flow intermittently or fluctuate widely, requiring big, expensive dams to control them. The demand for irrigation created a flurry of private irrigation companies during the 1870s and early 1880s. Relying mostly on eastern capital, hundreds of private irrigation companies tried to make some fast money from western farmers' predicament. When most of the companies went bankrupt within ten years, the irrigation boom became a bust (Gressley 1966:viii). Several states, beginning with California, tried different plans for subsidizing irrigation, but these efforts all failed owing to poor planning, bad design, and underfunding. Ten years of drought, beginning in 1888, and an international depression dried up both the soil and the funding for irrigation. As a result, farms failed, people left, and some farmers began calling on the federal government to invest in irrigating the West (Worster 1985:131).

William Ellsworth Smythe, an early crusader for federal irrigation, helped to forge the movement's ideological base. For Smythe, a man of big ideas, "irrigation was the biggest thing in the world . . . not merely a matter of ditches and acres, but a philosophy, a religion, and a program of practical statesmanship rolled into one" (Smythe 1905: 267). Smythe believed that irrigation would solve many of the country's woes. It would decrease conflict, redress the "immigration problem" by creating jobs and redistributing the population, and, in creating irrigation districts, would forge new democratic institutions; irrigation would also spur scientific progress, enrich one's relationship to God, hasten progressive social evolution, and, because irrigation required small farms and cooperation among neighbors to tend ditches and regulate flows, it could ease the loneliness of rural life.

Smythe helped create in 1891 the National Irrigation Congress (NIC), funded mainly by the railroads, and from 1891 to 1896 edited its journal, *Irrigation Age*, which became the mouthpiece of the irrigation movement. Despite Smythe's best efforts, by century's end the irrigation movement still lacked the broad support it needed. The main problem facing supporters was their deep differences over what role the federal government would play. Most wanted federal subsidy without federal control, a hard position to sell to nonwestern legislators.

George Maxwell, a California lawyer interested in irrigation as a tool for lessening urban crowding, became the movement's next national leader (Hays 1980:9–10). Maxwell created the National Irrigation Association, a permanent, well-funded, and effective lobbying organization (McCool 1987:25). He helped unify the various factions among irrigation proponents and, with a sophisticated public relations campaign, broadened support for the movement, enough to prompt all three major political parties to endorse federal irrigation in their 1890 platforms.[3]

While Maxwell was mobilizing public opinion, Francis Griffith Newlands tried to mobilize Congress on behalf of federal irrigation. Newlands had lost half a million dollars in the Truckee Irrigation Project

3. Orme Dam was once named Maxwell Dam in his honor.

in Nevada. This unhappy experience convinced him that privately developed irrigation was impossible. After several failed attempts to get irrigation legislation passed, Newlands introduced legislation that he and Maxwell devised, but it was not until Theodore Roosevelt became president that Maxwell, Newlands, and reclamation had an ally powerful enough to sway Congress and overcome westerners' aversions to federal intervention (Hays 1980:14–15; Lear 1985).

Roosevelt was a strong backer of the federal development of irrigation, and reclamation became the centerpiece of his domestic policy (Roosevelt 1919:429). In his first address to Congress in 1901, he called for the creation of a federal reclamation service, declaring that its mission would be that of "homemaker to the nation." As Samuel P. Hays argues, the ideology and policies of the Progressive Era derived from these early attempts at western water development: "The modern American conservation movement grew out of the firsthand experience of federal administrators and political leaders with problems of Western economic growth, and more precisely with Western water development. . . . The movement to construct reservoirs to conserve spring flood waters for use later in the dry season gave rise both to the term 'conservation' and to the concept of planned and efficient progress which lay at the heart of the conservation idea" (Hays 1980:5). With some adroit political maneuvering by Roosevelt, the Reclamation Act was passed on June 17, 1902, creating the Reclamation Service as a new branch of the U.S. Geological Service.[4]

Newlands's bill gave the secretary of the interior, not Congress, the power to authorize, study, locate, and construct irrigation works. Supporters hoped bypassing Congress would minimize regional politics and avoid the logrolling that accompanied authorization of the Army Corps of Engineers' water projects. Legislators soon realized what they were missing, and when the depleted Reclamation Fund needed money, they used that opportunity to establish their right to authorize projects. Irrigation projects were supposed to be paid for from the federal Reclamation Fund, with revenues generated by the sale of public lands to settlers. The fund would be gradually replenished from the sale of water, interest free, to water users. While irrigators would have preferred a more direct subsidy, this repayment scheme made it politically palatable to congressional skeptics.[5]

4. In 1907 the Reclamation Service was moved from the USGS to the Department of the Interior and in 1923 was renamed the Bureau of Reclamation.

5. The subsidy on what amounts to a long-term interest-free loan is substantial. Rucker and Fishback (1983:53) have calculated that the interest exemption alone, at 10 percent over fifty years, amounts to a subsidy of ninety-one cents on the dollar. Repayment obligations were repeatedly relaxed and the proportion of "nonreimbursable" costs (e.g., for

The Reclamation Act was conceived and sold as a regional home-building program. Western families, not large landowners, were supposed to benefit from this law. This was partly a political strategy to appease legislators who worried that subsidized water for large farms would create unfair competition for eastern farmers. But this position also reflected the social agendas of men like Smythe, Maxwell, and Newlands, who believed that many of America's woes stemmed from overcrowded cities, and that what was needed was a means of encouraging immigrants to create productive, family farms in unsettled areas. This thinking led to two restrictions in the bill: irrigation projects were authorized only for land west of the hundredth meridian, which bisects states between North Dakota and Texas, and water from federal irrigation projects could only go to landowners with 160 acres or less.[6]

Once created, the Reclamation Service was quickly flooded with requests for projects. In just three years, it authorized twenty projects. Teddy Roosevelt wrote that "the impatience of the Western people to see immediate results from the Reclamation Act was so great that redtape was disregarded, and the work was pushed forward at a rate previously unknown in Government Affairs" (1919:431). In the selection of early projects, those that created farms on reclaimed public land, or ones that would sustain communities threatened by a lack of water, were supposed to be given priority. In practice, however, private land was often developed first. Donald Worster (1985:172) calculates that by 1910, of the thirty reclamation projects under way, incorporating over two and one half million acres of land, more than half were on private property. According to Worster, the main effect of these early projects was not to create family farms for urban migrants but to concentrate wealth and enrich speculators. The Warren Act, passed in 1911, permitted the agency to sell surplus water to nonfederal lands. So, less then ten years after its creation, the plan to use public land to foster homesteading and to replenish the Reclamation Fund was largely abandoned.

---

flood control, recreation, power, and dam safety) were expanded, which greatly reduced the amount paid by water users. In reviewing six BR projects, the General Accounting Office's found that irrigators repaid less than 10 percent of project costs (1981). Leveen (1978) estimates that irrigators would pay only 3.3 percent of the over $3.6 billion spent on irrigation. These studies are cited in McCool (1987:71); see also Devine (1995:68).

6. Both restrictions have long frustrated the BR. The regional limitation aided its rival, the older Army Corps of Engineers, in bitter turf battles. The acreage limitation, seen as even more restricting, was soon expanded to permit 320 acres for husband and wife. Violations are common in this laxly policed restriction. By 1980, 60 percent of the land irrigated by BR water was in holdings exceeding 320 acres, with 48 percent of reclamation land controlled by 9 percent of the landowners (USBR 1980; cited in Welsh 1985:75–76). In 1982 the acreage limitation expanded to 960 acres, a limit that is still routinely violated.

The Salt River Project in Arizona, one of the first projects authorized in 1903, illustrates what became prominent patterns in BR water development. First, as Worster notes (1985:172), while the agency had a formal homesteading mission, it contained no public domain land. Its primary feature, Roosevelt Dam, located at the confluence of the Salt River and Tonto Creek about seventy-six miles northeast of Phoenix, embodied state-of-the-art engineering. It was the bureau's first great structure and became the prototype for subsequent high, arched dams.

The Salt River Project also spawned the Salt River Valley Water Users Association, uniting the many smaller water-user groups that already existed in central Arizona.[7] John Orme, an ardent supporter of federal irrigation, was elected its first president. This organization was responsible for negotiating repayment schedules and for operating and maintaining the facilities of the project and exists today as the Salt River Project (SRP), one of the state's largest utilities and irrigators. SRP is still responsible for maintaining and operating Roosevelt Dam; it remains a powerful actor in regional water politics and was an influential participant in CAWCS. Groups like the Salt River Valley Water Users Association that were created to coordinate and maintain bureau projects often became skilled irrigation lobbyists, both locally and nationally. Irrigation districts and water-user groups became key constituents in the politics of federal water development (McCool 1987:84).

Claiming Reclamation: Engineers, Progressive Reform, and Professional Authority

From the beginning, the Reclamation Service attracted the nation's best civil engineers, and these early days were a heady time for the new profession. As Reisner (1986:118) notes, the chance to reclaim the desert was a far more enticing mission than designing steel mills, so idealistic young engineers headed west "to take on the most intractable foe of mankind: the desert. But the desert suffers improvement at a steep price, and the early Reclamation program was as much a disaster as its dams were engineering marvels." The thrill of designing big dams and the definition of reclamation as primarily an engineering problem diverted attention from pressing problems and were partly to blame for the failure of many early projects. Michael Robinson, in his sympa-

---

7. The Salt River Valley Water Users Association became the Salt River Project (SRP), one of two utilities serving the Phoenix area. SRP lobbied heavily during CAWCS for flood control and improved water-storage facilities. Much earlier, the association tried to remove the Yavapai from their reservation in order to confiscate their water rights and develop irrigation in the area.

thetic portrait of the agency, describes the "tendency for some engineers to view public works as ends in themselves. . . . As a result, the Service regarded itself primarily as an 'engineering outfit'" (1979:37). Donald Worster, in his critical evaluation of reclamation, provides a similar diagnosis: "Although there were many problems that plagued federalized irrigation, the central reason for the failure was a yawning gap between economic and technological ambitions on the one hand, and social vision and understanding on the other" (1985:170).

The agency's technological emphasis meant that people ignored such mundane concerns of irrigated agriculture as whether soils or climates were suitable for farming, or whether there was a market or a means of distribution for farm products. No one made sure that repayment schedules were realistic or taught inexperienced farmers how to maintain irrigation ditches. By 1922, only 10 percent of the money loaned by the Reclamation Fund had been repaid, and a staggering 60 percent of irrigators had defaulted on their interest-free repayment obligations (Reisner 1986:121). Speculation was a serious and persisting problem. A glimpse of agency surveyors was often enough to generate a flurry of "homesteaders," hoping to sell the land once its value escalated (Worster 1985:171). Despite widespread failure, the value of irrigated farms skyrocketed, sometimes selling for fifty times their original price once projects were completed (Reisner 1986:122). By 1927, a least one-third of all reclamation farmers had sold out, mostly to wealthy land speculators. Politics also jeopardized early projects by subverting careful planning studies; bad projects were built if they were supported by powerful people (Robinson 1979:38).

With early proponents' emphasis on irrigation as a medium for social reform, it may seem surprising that reclamation quickly became so identified with engineering solutions. But reformers' vision did not prevent the aspirations and values of engineers from overwhelming all other goals. This was an important coup for an emerging profession, and there are several reasons why engineers came to dominate. First, beginning with Powell's protégés, many engineers were among the original and most active proponents of federal irrigation. Progressive faith in the objectivity and authority of expertise contributed to engineers' privileged status. According to Edwin Layton (1971), the struggling, status-conscious profession created its own version of Progressivism. This "engineering progressivism" was espoused by an influential group of engineers both within and outside the agency who tried to unify their fractured, and somewhat insecure, profession around an idea of engineering as a vehicle for social reform. This view held that the technical elite should take the lead in making public policy, since their training and dispositions made them more rational and impartial. Having internalized the norms of science, engineers were best equipped to engineer not only technical but social reform.

Second, the engineers who first headed the agency were charismatic leaders who attracted the best in the profession. Both Frederick Newell, the Reclamation Service's first director, and his successor, Arthur Davis (Powell's nephew), were also committed public proponents of engineering Progressivism. Both were later elected president of the American Society of Civil Engineers, and their dual role as founders of the agency and leaders of their profession reinforced the links between reclamation and engineering. Davis, like Smythe and Maxwell before him, embraced the Jeffersonian ideal of a country of small, independent farmers; like them, he believed that land monopoly, overcrowded cities, and the poverty and crime that these bred threatened the moral fiber of country. Reclamation, in redistributing and helping cultivate western land, could avert the crisis (Hundley 1986:10–11).

As Davis would learn, however, it was easier and far more rewarding, politically and professionally, to build dams than to resolve complex social problems. By the time this was apparent, reclamation was securely identified as the domain of engineers. So successful and charismatic were these early engineers that they not only succeeded in capturing the new agency for their profession but also managed, with a few exceptions, to eliminate its potential competitor.[8] As the Reclamation Service grew, opportunities for irrigation experts outside government diminished, creating what Worster calls "technical hegemony in western water development" (1985:171).

Watering the West: The Frontier in Bureaucratic Mythmaking

Although engineers triumphed, the reformers' vision remained powerful. For Teddy Roosevelt, reclamation proved that government could exert "business-like control" over its resources. In addition to its "material accomplishment," however, reclamation also created the stable institutions on which the whole country depended and substituted "actual homemakers" for "huge, migratory bands of sheep" (Roosevelt 1919:434). Beliefs about frontier society and western expansion figure prominently in America's conception of itself and its history.

As John Walton has observed, books about the American West generally either sustain or debunk frontier myths. He argues that our preoccupation with the "real" West must be balanced with analysis of how

---

8. The BR's only rival was the Army Corps of Engineers. Flood control, ACE's primary mission, does not demand the mammoth structures that irrigation does, since water is not moved as far.

"legend is socially constructed and selectively used in collective action" (1991:6–7). He shows how, in different periods, Owens Valley residents invoked a reconstructed frontier heritage to legitimate their claims and publicize their struggle to control its development. BR employees created their own version of the mythic frontier, one featuring the agency's role in making the West habitable for (white) settlers. The government's centrality is nicely summarized in a cartoon the BR published in the newsletter it sent to its irrigators (see Fig. 1).

Where Walton's citizens emphasized the rugged individualism of early settlers and their lonely struggles to irrigate and farm the land, the bureau's version highlights the essential role of the federal government in reclaiming the West and the political and economic significance of the irrigation districts it created in extending democracy to western citizens. Like most versions of frontier myths, the agency's is silent on the contributions and sacrifices of many groups. Taming the West is a technological feat in an interpretation that ignores the women, workers, and subjugated native peoples whose labor and land were prerequisites to its projects. Those who bore the costs of these projects disappear in official accounts.

The agency's mythmaking takes varied forms. The family farm is a prominent feature of the bureau's settlement narrative. It is portrayed as the prime beneficiary of BR water in its frontier myth, a point underscored by its largely symbolic acreage limitations. Without federal irrigation, this essential American institution could not have survived western transplantation. A much-reproduced photograph features an Idaho couple during the terrible droughts of the 1930s holding a homemade sign amid the vast barren desert that proclaims: "Desert-Ranch. Have faith in God and US Reclamation."

Farming as a means for producing a distinctively American character is a prominent theme in agency publications. The "Irrigation Farmers' Creed," featured in its newsletter, conjoins sound irrigation techniques with the moral virtues of rural life. It begins:

> I believe in a permanent agriculture, a soil that shall grow richer rather than poorer from year to year.
> I believe in a rotation system of water delivery, with charge for service, based on the quality of water delivered.
> I believe in striving for maximum yields, and I shall not be satisfied with anything less.
> I believe in the farm boy and in the farm girl, the farmer's best crops and the future's best hope. (*RE* 1914)

Bureau reports romanticize frontier society. The first Central Arizona Project report relays, with no intended irony, that after the "subjuga-

THE STORY OF
AN IRRIGATED FARM

Fig. 1. The story of an irrigated farm, *Reclamation Record*, April 1915.

tion of the Indians by military force . . . the area was settled under the typical Western attitude, 'Open to all comers, everybody welcome'" (USBR 1947:r-1). Reclamation leaders were commemorated with the dams, lakes, and cities their efforts helped create: Davis Dam, Lake Powell, and Page, Arizona, are a few examples. As former employee William Warne notes, "The great names connected with the building of the West are linked with Bureau of Reclamation works, just as those of Darius and Valerian are associated with ancient irrigation projects. . . . In all likelihood, the modern works and names will prove to be equally enduring" (Warne 1973:47).

When Grand Coulee Dam was criticized in the press in 1941, agency leaders suspected that journalists had been bribed by private utilities to discredit the project. Commissioner Mike Strauss responded by hiring Woody Guthrie to write folksongs praising BR dams (Reisner 1986: 167). Guthrie complied with songs like "Talking Columbia" and "Roll on Columbia," which celebrate the dam's role in fighting fascism, creating jobs, and watering the land.[9]

The bureau's image as farm builder and settler of the West is one still celebrated nearly a century later. Written into law, this image was often contradicted in practice. In the rush to build projects, farmers' concerns were subordinated to engineers' desire to create important structures. During the New Deal, power, not irrigation, was the main motive for agency projects, and its revenues subsidized irrigation. While the BR publicizes the irrigation districts it creates as an extension of democratic practice with its national lobby, the National Water Resources Association, and dozens of regional and local lobbying organizations, it has methodically cultivated a powerful water elite to promote its projects.[10] Intended to foster family farms, the strict limitation on irrigated acreage was ignored as often as it was enforced, and agribusiness remains a prime beneficiary of the bureau's subsidized waters.

Despite these contradictions, the bureau's association with home-

9. Woody Guthrie's "bureau" songs continue to appear in BR publications and are sung on ritual occasions, including the fiftieth anniversary of Grand Coulee Dam (*RE* 1983:24).

10. Irrigation districts are official governing structures organized to construct and/ or collectively operate and maintain irrigation works. Usually the creation of state law, irrigation districts often have considerable power. For example, they can make and enforce contracts related to building and maintenance projects, tax property owners, or in some cases even take land by the power of eminent domain. Although many irrigation districts were created before bureau projects, if an area did not have one in place to negotiate and enforce water contracts or to maintain and cordinate water delivery, the bureau would help farmers create them. They might help draft the appropriate state laws, offering models to emulate and so on.

steading was ideologically potent, such that the settlement implications of BR projects are part of the standard repertoire for justifying them. In populated areas, this is an awkward task. The 1947 CAP report includes a section entitled "Settlement Opportunity," never mind that the project land is mostly settled. The section concludes hopefully that the conversion to irrigation might permit subdivisions of existing farms, thereby increasing the number of farm families. The report also warns that without the project, currently irrigated land would return "to idleness" (USBR 1947:r-46, 3).[11]

The agency's origins in the Progressive movement, with its linkage between reclamation and reform, left their mark. Water as social equalizer, as stimulus for family farms; nature as demanding taming, rationalizing; the BR as the settler of the West; dispassionate engineers as innovators, reformers, enlightened adjudicators of the collective good—these ideas shaped how members understood the organization and their place in it. They remained powerful justifications for the agency's projects for years, and, for an administration desperate to mitigate a depression, they offered the promise of prosperity, symbolic politics of a most tangible form, and jobs.

Dams as Symbols: Hoover Dam and the Romance of Reclamation

> It is the human answer to human need,
> Power in absolute control, freed as a gift,
> A pure creative act, God when the world was born!
> It proves that we have built for life and built for love
> And when we all are dead, this dam will stand and give.
>
> May Sarton, *The Lion and the Rose*

The Depression launched the "golden years" for the Bureau of Reclamation, which was a prime beneficiary of FDR's Public Works Program. Never before or since had the agency expanded so quickly or juggled so many huge projects. Hoover, Grand Coulee, and Shasta Dams were all built during this period. Already considered a large bureaucracy during the Hoover administration, with from 2,000 to 3,000 employees, by the time FDR died, the agency had nearly 20,0000 full-time employees (Reisner 1986:152–53). Before 1933, the average annual budget for the BR was $8.9 million dollars; from 1933 to 1940 it was $52 million. Under Secretary of the Interior Harold Ickes (who also

---

11. Projects are still justified this way. In 1985, the development of an additional 500,000 irrigated acres in eastern Washington, an extension of the Columbia Basin Project, was still promoted as a stimulus to family farms. Despite unprecedented bankruptcies and record subsidies for overproduced crops, proponents still described the new farms that result from converting dry land to irrigated farming as a boon to farming.

directed the Public Works Program), public power became an explicit end, and the rules for western water development were radically and permanently changed.

Hoover Dam marked a turning point for the bureau. After Hoover, the BR no longer needed to rely on irrigation to justify its projects; hydropower became the cash cow of irrigation, subsidizing boondoggles that instantly became "economically viable projects." Once hydropower was a legitimate goal, the unit of analysis in agency planning shifted from dam to river basin. This shift gave rise to its infamous "river basin accounting," where projects included multiple dams, some designated as "cash register" dams, whose sole purpose was to generate the power that subsidized irrigation and paid for the project. In the cost-benefit analysis conducted by the agency, hydropower was so lucrative it virtually demanded that dams be built. Hoover Dam was the first, extraordinary example of this logic. The Central Arizona Project was another.

Hoover Dam offers a useful vantage point from which to understand the content of the BR's engineering ethos, how this ethos transformed dams into symbols, and how these symbols gained such currency in American politics. Emile Durkheim argued long ago that the more abstract the social relationship, the more crucial that it be represented symbolically, so that people are easily able to conceptualize the relationship, to invest it with emotion, and to create ways to interact with it, collectively and individually.

Public works, because of their genesis in the state, have symbolized the role the state plays in American politics and culture and what government can accomplish for individuals. Public works are a means for individual citizens to see or to "visit" the state, to witness the resources it provides them, to celebrate its power and accomplishments or challenge its policies and authority. The scale of these works, their permanence, the publicity and politics that surround them from the beginning, and the sheer number of participants required to promote and build them enhance their symbolic appeal and shape their interpretation. Public works are simultaneously means of enacting and conveying state power.[12]

---

12. Public works as emblems of state power merit more scrutiny than they receive. They are culturally interesting not simply because they are, to borrow Ann Swidler's (1986) metaphor, useful ideological tools in the cultural tool kits of the parties and organizations that promoted and built the works; also interesting is how other, sometimes larger groups adopt them as significant cultural and political symbols, how their meanings change over time, becoming linked to new concerns. Chandra Mukerji's (1994) analysis of French state gardens as both a mechanism and marker of state power is an example to emulate.

Dams possess characteristics that make them especially useful symbols of government. First, they are tangible in distinctive ways. Their staggering and inspiring physical dimensions, and the work that they do, allow them to be experienced in ways unlike other public works or monuments. They are spatial, offering a place and a reason to go. Dams can be walked through and driven over, and their work observed; their transformations of rivers to lakes are obvious, requiring only that we turn from one side of the structure to the other. The buzz of electricity emanates from their power stations, and we can swim in, boat on, camp near, or drive around their lakes. They offer a form of immortality to those who build them, and their transformations are not transitory. And many dams are beautiful, meshing nicely with America's fascination with size, technology, and progress as we conceive it. The impressive "materiality" of dams reflects their symbolic weight.

Hoover Dam, the most publicized project in American history, was the bureau's fifty-first dam. It remains its preeminent symbol, and like all symbols, the dam condenses a rich variety of ambiguous and shifting meanings that have been appropriated and embellished over time. To BR engineers, the dam exemplifies their work, their organization, them. For FDR, the dam was a triumphant vindication of public works, of the potential of government.[13] For millions of Americans during the Depression, it was a welcome diversion, a source of inspiration (Reisner 1986:165–66). For Donald Worster (1992), Hoover Dam is the perfect symbol of modernity, exemplifying the hubris of our efforts to dominate nature, the folly of instrumental reason run amok.

Before construction on Hoover began, skeptics doubted that a governmental agency was capable of managing such a big, complicated project. A special board was appointed by the American Engineering Council and the Associated General Contractors of America to study the matter. The joint committee enthusiastically endorsed the project, concluding in 1931 that "every age has produced its builders. For centuries they devoted themselves to the business of immortalizing their own memory in temples, palaces, tombs. . . . Ours is a utilitarian age. . . . The harnessing of the Colorado River will be a lasting memorial to the Federal authorities who ordained it" (Warne 1973:36).

Considered its "masterwork" and featured prominently in agency

---

13. Joseph Stevens (1988:259) writes that both Roosevelt and Ickes saw Hoover Dam "as a compelling demonstration of the social and economic benefits they believed would flow from centralized resource planning, public-power development and federally funded public-works projects. The political popularity of the Hoover Dam undertaking was not lost on them, either."

publicity, Hoover Dam is a monument to many things: to engineering skill and vision, to the Depression and the drastic measures it prompted, and to the ability of the country to mobilize vast resources. Unlike other BR projects, the dam was paid for entirely by federal dollars: hydropower revenue meant no reimbursement costs to irrigators, so, for the first time, money was no object. Perhaps Hoover Dam's most remarkable features is that its construction was completed in 1936, just three years after it had commenced.[14] The dam was a massive undertaking, and building it required creating, from scratch, an entirely new city, where as many as 5,000 construction workers could live, a power line that crossed 200 miles of desert, a new railway 30 miles long, several new highways, a gravel screening plant, and two huge concrete-mixing facilities.[15] At 726 feet, Hoover was the highest dam in the world, creating the largest man-made lake, and included the largest power plant in the world.

Given the demands of its size and location, the construction of Hoover Dam required a long series of technical innovations. As Commissioner Elwood Mead said before construction began: "On the whole, this construction is a research school in engineering" (Warne 1973:39). Nearly every feature of the project set records. Huge new trucks had to be built to carry all the rock. The dam's design, the result of years of experimentation and testing, was an innovative hybrid of the gravity and the arch dams the agency had already built. The dam's 6.5 million tons of concrete (more than three city blocks wide at its base) required an imaginative cooling system composed of refrigerated water run through an elaborate system of pipes. Without it, the structure would have taken 150 years to cool. Even the concrete poured represented an engineering advance, the culmination of years of research that resulted in a stronger, more uniform mixture that used less water.

The agency is less eager to acknowledge the sometimes tragic costs of executing this technology. Building the dam was extraordinarily difficult and dangerous work, and safety was the first casualty of speed: 115 men died during its construction. The contract included a back-breaking schedule and exacted high penalties for failure to meet deadlines, so contractors and agency overseers were ruthless in their pursuit of production. Men who protested working conditions were fired on the spot. The attempted strike promoted by IWW (Industrial Workers of the World) representatives failed miserably. The agency sup-

14. The BR designs, inspects, and maintains its dams, but the actual construction work is contracted out to private companies.

15. Boulder City remains the bureau's regional office for the Lower Colorado Basin.

pressed reports of the terrible working conditions and the deaths these caused.[16]

For a country enduring a terrible depression, the construction of Hoover Dam was a valued source of good news. The most publicized public work in America, the dam captured the public's imagination. Each week, the BR released the best work of Ben Glaha, the official photographer, and for many newspapers, including the *New York Times,* his photos were nearly a weekly feature (Warne 1973:31). Magazines like *Fortune, Harper's,* and *Literary Digest* featured articles on the dam. Like FDR, the whole nation was eager to see the dam as embodying the best of America, its "resourcefulness, skill, and determination." Marc Reisner calls bureau dams "the reigning symbols of the era. . . . The dams announced that America could still do great things" (1986: 165–66; *RE* 1935a:194, 196). For another author, the complexity of Hoover Dam mirrored the complexity of America: "No other single piece of man's handiwork in this vast wilderness hinterland has epitomized so well during its construction all the strange and complex ramifications of our American Way—all its democratic faults and virtues . . . the political interlocking of local, state and federal governments, the meshed and rival economies of public and private enterprise, the conflicting needs of urban, agrarian and industrial groups" (Waters 1946: 337).

Hoover Dam remains a tangible manifestation of the skill and vision of bureau engineers, and of the values of their profession. To them, the dam is a powerful, permanent symbol that defines their aspirations and standards. Virtually every professional publication of the day lauded the sophisticated engineering that the dam required and the sheer nerve of those who undertook the project. BR engineers were praised for not being dissuaded by naysayers who lacked the vision and faith that the project required. They were commended for embodying what was best about America: their daring in the face of great adversity, their faith in their ability to shape and use nature in accordance with their wishes, and their technological skill, dedication, and public

16. With hundreds of men scaling canyons walls, miles of electrical wire crossing the canyon, thousands of tons of explosives being detonated day and night, tons of heavy machinery moving across rocky terrain and inside tunnels, the noise was deafening and accidents were common. Rock avalanches, collapsing tunnels, slips, falling debris, electrocution, and carbon monoxide poisoning were common causes of death. Heat prostration also killed dozens of men and even some of their family members. Twelve-hour shifts round the clock, seven-day work weeks, flash floods, poor sanitary conditions, the difficulty of getting water to workers, and exhaustion and isolation all increased accidents, nervous breakdowns, and the spread of disease among workers and their families. See Stevens (1988:60–65, 101–6, 197–202, 236–37).

mindedness. Contemporaries compared the dam to the seven wonders of the ancient world, convinced that centuries later, people would continue to marvel at it and the men who had built it. The thrill of participating in something of great public and historical importance was a heady experience for those associated with the project. As Frank Crowe, the engineer who supervised construction for Six Companies, said in 1943, "There's something peculiarly satisfying about building a great dam. You know it will stand for centuries" (*Fortune,* August 1943:214).

For bureau engineers, dams are both beautiful and useful. The glamour of Hoover Dam extends to more modest dams and exemplifies the aesthetic significance of good engineering, of controlling nature. Early on, the BR engineers who designed the structure were mindful of its aesthetic potential, and an English architect was hired to advise BR engineers on the style and details of its facade. His efforts to streamline the structure and to eliminate extraneous detail enhanced its verticality and emphasized its function (Stevens 1988:30), making it a thoroughly modern structure. As one former employee describes the dam, "The completed structure, with its clean, utilitarian lines, is unadorned beauty" (Warne 1973:45). Comparisons with other great works of art are common. For example, one writer saw it as "the Great Pyramid of the American Desert, the Ninth Symphony of our day" (Waters 1946: 337). Another described it as "a visual symphony written in steel and concrete—the terms of our mathematical and machine-age culture— it is inexpressibly beautiful of line, magnificently original, strong, simple, and as majestic as the greatest works of art of all time and all peoples, and as eloquently expressive of our own as anything ever achieved" (Stevens 1988:244).

The engineering aesthetic encompasses more than beautiful dams. It also embodies a particular view of nature, one first articulated by Progressive conservationists. Nature is understood both as a potential resource and as a respected adversary. Water that is left "unharnessed" or "untamed" is characterized in agency reports as "unproductive" and "wasted." River systems with empty dam sites have "gaps." "Uncontrolled" water is dangerous and threatening. BR projects enhance the appreciation of nature because they make it available for more people to experience and use. The rugged, beautiful, and inaccessible Black Canyon was transformed into an enormous desert lake that attracts boaters, campers, fisherman, water skiers, and swimmers; the dam is a major tourist attraction, and each year nearly a million visitors take reclamation tours. The highest expression of nature and one's "appreciation" for nature, according to this conception, is when man has exerted control over it, when he has imposed his will and his reason on it for socially useful purposes, rendering it safe, accessible, and available. This relationship improves man just as it improves nature.[17]

Efforts to "tame" nature with intelligence, skill, and physical prowess produce some of man's finest achievements, a testament to his existence. This view of nature is tied to the experience of and the beliefs about western expansion in the epic struggle to make land not just habitable but sustaining. The challenge for engineers, according to Donald Worster, was to make nature rational: "No competent earth designer . . . would have left over a million square miles of the American land without sufficient rainfall to raise a crop. . . . A rational nature, a healthy nature, would be a nature of uniform productivity, where there was no waste, no excess, no deficiency, nothing but a steady yield of the useful forever and ever. In that world, rivers would be transformed into models of reason. . . . Science demanded nature without flaws. The word used by engineers to refer to that work of rationalizing the rivers of the West, and nature in general, was 'conservation'" (Worster 1985:154).

Dams as Worship, Dams as Identities

For the religious, there was the special satisfaction of knowing that their dams pleased God. The biblical admonition that man exercise dominion over the earth sacralizes this view of nature. Early in the irrigation movement, William Smythe elaborated the theological and philosophical implications of irrigation. In a rousing conclusion to his book, written in 1899, he explains why irrigation is a form of worship, where man completes the world begun by God: "There are conditions in Arid America which make men peculiarly conscious of their partnership with God. . . . Irrigation, for example, is a religious rite. Such a prayer for rain is intelligent, scientific, and worthy of man's divinity. And it is answered. To put knowledge in place of superstition is the first step which men take in entering into partnership with God" (1905:327–29).

Smythe was not the first to make the connection between irrigation and religion, between developing nature and worshiping God. The Mormons were the first European settlers to create a regional economy based on irrigation, first in Utah and later in Arizona. As Robinson (1979:4) explains, their early success was partly due to the cohesiveness of their community, their unity in purpose. Reclaiming the desert was

---

17. Ickes expounded this view in his dedication speech: "No better example of understanding cooperation between man and nature can be found anywhere than this imagination-stirring project that, in grandeur of conception and in skill and speed of execution, ranks as one of the greatest engineering undertakings in the history of the world" (*RE* 25, no. 11 [Nov. 1935]: 209).

an act of devotion since it involved "building up the Kingdom of God on Earth." Worster attributes their success to the strict hierarchy of the church and its exacting control over its members. This view of nature as an unfinished product, as raw materials provided by God, is well captured in Walter Young's reflections. Young, the engineer who supervised construction of Hoover Dam for the bureau and who earlier helped select the dam site, wrote: "Observing the beautiful symmetry of Hoover Dam, one can hardly help thinking that, knowing future requirements, the Lord provided the dam site" (Warne 1973:107).

Hoover Dam represented an important moment in the political legitimation of the agency's mission, proof positive that it could design engineering masterpieces and effectively marshal and manage unprecedented sums of money. And the dam still inspires pride among agency employees who invoke it as evidence of their skill, the virtues of their engineering ethos, and the wisdom of spending huge sums on water projects. As engineers, as members of an organization, as individuals, they found that their identities became intertwined with structures, the one signifying the other. The standard reply to queries about the agency is still: it built Hoover Dam.

For many engineers, most now retired, contemplating Hoover evokes a wistfulness for a glorious era that has ended. Too young to have worked on Hoover, some were lured to the agency by its grandeur, their pride in the agency's accomplishments predating their arrival, their careers encompassing an era when their work was widely celebrated. As one man told me: "All my papers in high school were on Hoover Dam or the Colorado River. The bureau had a fabulous reputation at that time. The bureau built all the big dams in the West. Hoover, Coulee, Shasta, Glen Canyon, Roosevelt. Take Hoover Dam— you can't find a crack in that dam even today. It's surface still looks like marble. And that's because of the bureau's discovery of cooling the concrete using pipes. . . . The process was developed in the bureau."

The engineering values culminating in Hoover Dam were symbolically and spatially extended to the agency's other great structures, each bearing witness to a world where nature is an adversary and a resource that engineers tame, where their exploits are evidence of America's greatness, where well-designed structures are aesthetic as well as technological feats, and where those who create dams are deeply and singularly identified with them.

These values are now institutionalized. They are used to promote new projects, rebut critics, explain one's work, and construct one's identity, both professionally and personally. As one retired engineer confided: "I feel lucky to have worked on the projects I did. Glen Canyon is a beautiful dam, and I can go and see it whenever I want. Now

I don't get up there very often, but I know it'll always be standing right there where I left it. There's something really wonderful about being able to see your work working and to know that it will go on working long after you do."

Even now, critics are told that if the BR had listened to "common sense" or to any number of skeptics from an earlier time who doubted their abilities or their vision, Hoover or Grand Coulee or Shasta might never have been built, and life as we know it would not exist. Harold Ickes relished reminding the critics of Grand Coulee Dam (sometimes referred to as "Ickes' Folly"), who doubted a market existed for all its power, that "today we cannot supply enough power from Grand Coulee, or from all of our great hydroelectric plants combined, to satisfy the demand" (Warne 1973:91).

Echoes of Ickes reverberate in the agency. I have heard skeptics rebutted by BR engineers who spoke of the need for vision, for not limiting future opportunities with "small-minded" thinking today. In some cases, those who object are told what project critics had said in the past about Grand Coulee or Hoover or Shasta Dam. Before and after pictures are standard props in attempts to persuade the doubtful. The dramatic images of desert "wasteland" are compared with acres of irrigated agriculture and happy farmers to prove the worth of BR projects to doubters. Such pictures are standard props during public meetings and congressional hearings. These images, helpful in responding to critics, also supply a framework for understanding the agency's past and how work in the present relates to the organization's goals. As indisputable evidence of the value of reclamation, the pictures routinely appear in both agency publicity and internal documents. They decorate the lobbies of local project offices and sometimes hang in private offices. These images are literally and figuratively part of the agency's furniture. So taken-for-granted are these images that current employees joke about their work as another day spent "making the desert bloom."

Much has changed since Hoover Dam was built: the West is settled, few empty dam sites remain, and environmentalists have discredited dams in some people's view. Why has this ethos persisted for so long? Certainly, people's investment in ideas that make sense to them, and of them, may become a motive for retaining them. And it is clear that powerful material and political interests, booming economies, and the people these attract benefit from the agency's projects for developing water and energy in the West. From agribusiness to those who wished to develop flood plains, to those desert residents who take their swimming pools for granted, a broad range of interests became aligned with the Bureau of Reclamation. Effective ideology, the agency's ethos became their ethos. But this rendering gives a partial view. In what follows, I will suggest some of the mechanisms by which the engineering ethos of this agency was reinforced and reproduced.

An Institutionalized Ethos

Engineering and reclamation were inextricably linked for most of the agency's history. The history of the agency is often presented as a chronology of dams. Its organization reinforced this emphasis, facilitating the agency's emergence as the world's preeminent dam builder. Alfred Golze (1961:ix), a former assistant commissioner of the bureau, describes reclamation as evolving from a domain restricted to civil engineering to one that gradually incorporated other engineering specialties, and eventually even some economists and lawyers.

With its reputation for engineering excellence, the BR continued to attract the best engineers, and they enjoyed a special status within the agency; they were hired in greater numbers, trained more methodically, and promoted faster than those with other specialties. To develop their skills and facilitate their integration, the agency systematically rotated new engineers through different departments, positions, and projects. They were assigned career "mentors" who, as more powerful and experienced employees, carefully monitored their experience. The diversity of their experience allowed new employees to acquire a "big picture" of the bureaucracy quickly, including a sense of its division of labor, how its parts fit together, and an early appreciation of who was important and who controlled which resources.

Top agency positions went almost exclusively to engineers. All of the agency's commissioners were engineers, excepting Floyd E. Dominy, commissioner from 1959 through 1969. Dominy joined the agency as a land settlement specialist and rose quickly through the ranks by virtue of his extraordinary bureaucratic savvy, political skill, and the sponsorship of Senator Carl Hayden of Arizona. The prospect of the Bureau of Reclamation's being led by someone other than an engineer was so disconcerting to members of the profession, however, that the Association of Civil Engineers twice petitioned President Eisenhower to block his appointment.

The institutionalization of an engineering ethos was also facilitated by the role that projects play as fundamental categories, as organizational units of analysis, in defining the important boundaries of experience within the bureau. Agency history, more often than not, is expressed simply as a chronology of its structures. The role that projects play in the agency's budgets and administration is important, especially after some famous abuses prompted Congress to try to impose tighter control over the BR by appropriating money exclusively on a project-by-project basis. Money that is not designated for a specific project is unavailable. As a result, all incentives are geared toward designing and building large projects.

Big projects generate big budgets, which enhance the visibility, stature, and discretion of those who design and manage them. Employees are rewarded for finding reasons and places to build dams. Since careers and reputations are closely tied to specific projects, building dams and building careers went hand in hand. From the commissioner on down, a person's contributions to the agency were inevitably described in terms of the projects that he (rarely she) helped to build. This reinforced people's close identification with "their" projects and their collaborators. Big projects require large staffs, and managers' status is tied to the number of employees they supervise. As one informant told me: "Our budgets are built around projects. Projects pay our salaries. Projects keep the organization afloat. We get rewarded for building projects, not for maximizing preferences and certainly not for stopping bad ones."

The inflexibility of the bureau's budget also reinforces commitments to particular projects. Any budgetary change amounting to more than 10 percent of the allocation has to be reauthorized by Congress, a time-consuming and risky enterprise. This creates powerful disincentives for tinkering with budgets or modifying projects once they are authorized or funded, even when it makes sense to do so. This limits managers' ability to adapt to changes in the political environment or to new information quickly and efficiently. For example, if managers learn that a project will perform worse than expected, the money designated for that project cannot be diverted to a more promising project without reauthorization. Legislative control over budgets helps explain why projects persist as what some rational choice theorists have termed "lumpy goods," things which cannot easily be made divisible.

The need for congressional approval for each phase of a project politicizes the process. As John Ferejohn (1974), Helen Ingram (1990), and Daniel McCool (1987) have all noted, nothing attracts legislators like public policy with tangible, local benefits and dispersed, national costs. Members of Congress have long appreciated the political hay that can be made from having a large water project built in one's district. Not only does such a project pump millions of federal dollars into the local economy and generate hundreds of jobs, but the end result is also a tangible, photogenic public work, a monument to one's political clout. McCool (1987) shows how these qualities combine with other features of water development to create strong incentives for the formation of "iron triangles," where policy domains are controlled by a coalition of powerful congressional committees, governmental agencies, and interest groups.[18]

The duration of projects influences employees' and constituents' identification with projects. Long before any BR project is built, it goes through many planning stages. One manager described project development in the BR as a continuum, "ranging from very conceptual plans, to detailed planning, to discussion with Congress regarding final authorization, to construction design and management, and finally to maintenance and management of existing facilities." At each crucial step in the process, Congress must appropriate money. Congressional authorization, while requiring extensive planning and lobbying, is just the first and usually the easiest step in the process; securing the necessary funding to plan and complete the project is a long, arduous process. As a result, employees may invest a large chunk of their careers on a single large project. This long involvement encourages employees to identify with projects.[19]

Despite the pervasiveness of this engineering ethos, employees' identification with projects does vary depending on how long the employees have worked on them, the kind of work they do, their responsibilities for promoting them, and the nature of their political alliances. This explains why people affiliated with project offices are often the most ardent project supporters, since they are most minutely acquainted with it, are most responsible for mobilizing support for it, and work on it longest. Secretaries are generally less invested in projects than are engineers, but for some, their work is valorized by its ties to big, important structures. They, too, tell their children that they work for the people who built Hoover Dam.

Congressional authorization requires durable constituencies for water projects, so cultivating these is a priority. These relationships take time to develop and require trust between the parties and loyalty to the agency and to specific projects. Often constituencies are organized (with the bureau's encouragement) as powerful, political lobbies supporting the project. This inevitably creates a "water elite" made up of

18. See also Lowi (1979) and McConnell (1966).

19. For those working on smaller projects, or those whose specialty involves work that is completed early in a project (e.g., surveyors), the opposite effect can also produce loyalty. Some BR employees, like members of the military, lived itinerant lives, where wives were expected to pack fast and follow. One effect of this mobility was that it, too, fostered loyalty to the agency and to the projects that one worked on. Being new in town and knowing that your job was a temporary one meant that you needed your colleagues to be your friends and that your place in town was determined by your work on the project.

powerful, knowledgeable, and interested parties whose main task is to cultivate support for the project. This water elite receives special treatment by the agency; they are consulted often, are better informed than other public groups, and, like agency employees, become strongly invested in their projects. In Arizona, the Central Arizona Project Association, an organization composed of representatives of Phoenix's economic, political, and media elite, lobbied on behalf of this BR project for more than twenty years. Funded solely through the contributions of members (often representing large organizations or interests), the group employed full-time lobbyists to write speeches and press releases, attend hearings, and track the politics surrounding the project. Their investment in this project was as deep as that of members of the agency, and the boundaries between the BR and the lobby blurred over time.[20]

The powerful political and administrative incentives for building big projects and rewarding engineers helped reproduce a commitment to engineering excellence, building sophisticated structures, and using science to improve nature. This engineering ethos prevailed for decades within the BR, providing members with a framework for understanding their organization's place in the world. Institutionalized as career tracks, rituals, budgets, and the curricula of engineering, made tangible in dams, canals, reports, and photographs, this ethos incorporates and elaborates the ideas of Progressive reformers and visionaries like Powell and Smythe who helped invent conservation. The strong, enduring consensus about what the agency stood for elicited deep personal investments in its projects and fostered strong organizational loyalty. These qualities help explain why there are so many big dams in the West, and why some found it so hard to abandon Orme Dam.

In addition to these organizational mechanisms, the historic link between water and power also explains the durability of its ethos. Water, as well as what happens to it, is a visible and widely understood symbol of political power in arid lands. Ideology that is appropriated by some powerful group or actor often becomes more influential, acquiring the power of its proponents. That the bureau's fundamental task involves the delivery and distribution of water and energy to arid lands explains its economic and political significance. But in generating some of the more notable public works, it became a privileged producer of

---

20. Groundbreaking ceremonies, dedications, and celebrations marking first deliveries of bureau water are crucial institutional rituals that reinforce this identification. Speeches carefully acknowledge and allocate credit to supporters, allies, and employees. The agency plans these rituals almost as carefully as it designs its structures.

important political symbols, and this, too, explains the durability of its ethos.

Bureaucracies as Institutions

In Philip Selznick's (1957) language, the BR's engineering ethos, with its capacity to cultivate commitments and confer identities on organizational members, transformed the agency from an organization to an institution. Where the former is an expendable tool, a means for accomplishing more abstract goals, the latter becomes an end in itself, with the values that infuse it becoming substantive values. In the BR, this was expressed generally as dams for dams' sake and, specifically, as people's deep investments in particular projects. This substantive commitment favored dam building over farming. When combined with the politics of rewarding allies and bailing out failed irrigators, the result was the development of private, not public, land. Once Congress gained control over authorization, the process was further politicized, making it important for the agency to cultivate strong local constituencies to support its particular projects, as well as a federal constituency supporting reclamation. The social goals of the federal irrigation supporters were quickly undermined by the agency fixation on technology and the politics of authorization.

Another expression of the BR's commitment to dams as ends was the devotion of vast resources to engineering research and strong organizational incentives promoting engineering innovation and excellence. This precluded the agency from broadening its mission and its constituency, but the agency soon became the world's premier dam builder, possessing a virtual monopoly of dam-building expertise. As both the quality and number of undeveloped dam sites diminished, dams became technically more complex and too expensive to be paid for by irrigators. This gave rise to both new goals and new units of analysis. Hydropower became an official organizational goal, one that heavily subsidized irrigation.

This pattern of goal displacement is a familiar one. In his classic study of the Tennessee Valley Authority (TVA), another federal resource-development agency, Philip Selznick (1984) describes parallel processes. The TVA, like the BR, was a new government institution that represented a significant extension of government responsibility. Like the BR, this new institution was understood as an important symbol of good government that demonstrated how federal intervention can promote public welfare; the TVA, as an example of decentralized administration dedicated to unified, regional economic development and committed to participation at the grass-roots level, was also under-stood as an example of how the centralized power of bureaucracy could be constrained by more democratic planning.

As a new, innovative, and contested organization, what Selznick terms an "insecure" one, the promoters and members of the TVA, as in the BR, produced elaborate ideological accounts of the organization that became important lenses through which they understood the agency and their relation to it. These accounts helped recruit talented, dedicated employees, overcome local hostility to the TVA, and secure some autonomy from civil service control. To gain the needed support, local elites and local institutions were co-opted by the agency by incor-porating them into the agency decision making and making them con-duits for implementation.

This legitimacy came at a price. Many, though not all, of the TVA's original goals were subverted by local elites in ways that bolstered their wealth and influence. The TVA also abdicated control over some of its programs by diverting responsibility for implementing them to other institutions. Despite members' strong commitment to its official doc-trine, the TVA's efforts to extend democratic participation in adminis-tration failed because of mechanisms of co-optation and the institution-alization of commitments to the values, expectations, and goals of particular constituents.[21]

In the BR, co-optation was notably mutual. The BR's dependency on Congress for funds was muted by the political and economic value of the expertise the agency controlled. The strong constituencies they forged to back local projects created elites who were able to influence policy, often in the form of sustaining support and political pressure for "their" projects, and sometimes influencing locations and operations. There were occasions when the BR leaders were forced to promote or build projects that even they felt were unwarranted in order to appease powerful politicians. But the agency could threaten to impede or with-hold projects, and competition between regions over projects and their allocations also provided the agency with leverage over its local and national constituents. The mutual co-optation that did take place helped to foster an "iron triangle" in water development dominated by federal agencies like the BR, federal supporters, and regional water elites. The result was a powerful bureaucracy unresponsive to citizens outside its carefully cultivated constituency.

21. Other well-known analyses of how co-optation, conflict, and accommodation dis-place or subvert the goals of organizations or social movements include those by Michels (1949), Gusfield (1955), Messinger (1955), Clark (1956), Perrow (1961, 1963), Zald and Denton (1963), and Zald and Ash (1966).

Selznick's distinction between organizations and institutions is most helpful if it is appreciated less as a dichotomous characteristic and more as a continuous variable to be explained. Like Weber and Michels, Selznick analyzes the pressures that transform bureaucracies from means into ends, from administrative apparatus into a distinctive form of domination that concentrates power into fewer hands. Each has emphasized different intervening mechanisms in this transformation: Weber highlights the possession of distinctive knowledge—as technical expertise, knowledge of rules and official secrets, and the possession of files; elsewhere he also suggests the power of habit to confer normative meanings. In his words, "It is by way of conventional rules that merely factual regularities of action, i.e. usages, are frequently transformed into binding norms, guaranteed primarily by psychological coercion. Convention thus makes tradition. The mere fact of the regular recurrence of certain events somehow confers on them the dignity of oughtness" (1976:326). Michels argues that the leaders of organizations develop interests in the survival of the organization and in reproducing their power within it. These distinctive interests can lead to a subversion of organizational goals and a lessening of their public accountability. Selznick's analysis of the TVA shows how efforts to adapt organizations to institutionalized environments can produce this shift.[22] All three portray this transformation as mostly one-directional and, if not inevitable, as exceedingly hard to inhibit. Although I believe Alvin Gouldner (1950) exaggerates in positing a generalized "iron law of resistance to bureaucracy," my analysis suggests that under some conditions, "institutions" can be pressured into becoming more like "organizations." That is what happened within the Bureau of Reclamation.

Confrontation

The engineering ethos constructed by the BR provided its members with powerful strategies for interpreting the world. But it also conferred an insularity that allowed its leaders not to notice or acknowledge that the world had become less enamored of its big dams and that the consensus within the organization was no longer so easily translated into assent outside it. With the confidence that comes from power and the certitude that comes from attending only to your supporters, it was just too easy to dismiss dissenters as radical, irrelevant and unrealistic. This hubris, shared by many Department of the Interior

22. Selznick (1957) also suggests that leaders can play a crucial role in shaping and reinforcing the institutionalization of values and that this may not always be bad, since the commitments characteristic of institutions are ways of making organizational memberships more meaningful.

bureaucrats, was often first expressed as "tolerant contempt" for the scorned "sentimentalists" and "bird-watchers" (McConnell 1971:433). With their zeal for new projects dampened by the diminished capacity of well-dammed rivers and the declining number and quality of empty dam sites, bigger, more expensive "cash register" dams were needed to work the financial magic that made new projects "economically viable." And so the BR inadvertently helped to mobilize and politicize modern environmentalists. By antagonizing conservationists with the promise of big dams in spectacular settings and by overestimating their own ability and the appeal of the projects, the BR helped to launch the modern environmental movement.

For environmentalists, bureau dams are good targets. The same qualities that make dams such evocative symbols of the state and monuments to political clout also make them potent symbols for insurgents: the duration of their genesis, their scale and permanence, the publicity that swirls around them, and their violent transformation of landscapes all make dams useful symbols for challenging the premises of Reclamation's engineering ethos. That the best dam sites are inevitably found amid breathtaking scenery enriches their symbolic appeal for opponents. But bureau leaders could not appreciate the polysemic potential of their dams. It took time to understand that their own awe was a contingent response, that their version of nature could be denaturalized. Their response to environmentalists who attacked their projects shows how dominant the agency's ethos had become. Their response also reveals how contradictions can fuel dissent.

Bureau versus Brower

The BR deserves much of the credit for radicalizing David Brower, the world's most charismatic "archdruid."[23] Brower's twin gifts for inspiring supporters and splintering organizations made him a pivotal figure in contemporary environmental politics.[24] A passionate nature lover, Brower would become the Sierra Club's most controversial and, some might argue, most effective director, the founder of Friends of the Earth (1969), the League of Conservation Voters (1970), and the Earth Island Institute (1984). But Brower's first foray into national politics was catalyzed by the bureau.

23. John McPhee's (1970) rendition of David Brower and Floyd Dominy's raft trip on the Colorado offers astute and entertaining portraits of both men. Reisner (1986:293–99) and Gottlieb (1993:40–46, 143–57) also provide helpful accounts of Brower's influence on the environmental movement.

24. Two helpful accounts of U.S. environmental movements are Gottlieb (1993) and Schnaiberg and Gould (1994:143–64).

Since the mid-1940s, the BR had proposed a dam and power plant at the confluence of the Green and Yampa Rivers near the Utah-Colorado border. Located in Echo Park, a part of Dinosaur National Monument, the dam would flood one of the West's most beautiful canyons and one of David Brower's favorite places. A ten-year battle over the park ensued, led by the Sierra Club and the Wilderness Society, two mainstream protectionist groups composed mainly of formerly unconfrontational outdoor enthusiasts. To save Echo Park and to avoid charges of obstructionism, both groups reluctantly agreed in the mid-1950s to a compromise plan that included a huge dam in a more remote, less familiar desert canyon, one not formally designated a park. That dam was Glen Canyon in Arizona.

The legacy of Echo Park is mixed. This was the first time that the bureau had been forced to swap its preferred dam site for another, the first time conservationists had defeated the powerful water lobbies. The Sierra Club and Wilderness Society experienced a surge of confidence and also gained new members. The struggle made both groups more visible and provided their leaders with valuable political experience. Leaders in both organizations concluded that a new law to protect wilderness areas was desperately needed. For nine years, protectionist groups were absorbed in the frustrating process of trying to get a wilderness bill through Congress. They were forced to settle for a much diminished bill that initiated a long, draining period of bureaucratic wrangling with the Park and Forest Services.

Some see the Echo Park conflict as a pivotal moment for environmentalism. Grant McConnell (1971:432) emphasizes the battle's semantic significance. It prompted John Muir's "spiritual heirs" to begin reclaiming the term "conservation," to rid it of Progressive associations with economic development and rational efficiency and reassert its older, more literal meaning of protecting nature. By doing so, participants simultaneously challenged and appropriated a powerful legacy. This process of re-vision and self-definition, crucial to many social movements, was empowering. Yet divisions remained. The tensions generated between those who saw compromise as necessary to accommodate growth and those who began to question the logic that drove development would polarize participants and distinguish environmental organizations for decades.[25]

The compromise to save Echo Park would haunt David Brower. In a journey of despair, he rode the Colorado through Glen Canyon, which had remained virtually unknown since Powell's excursion a

---

25. Allan Schnaiberg's (1986) analysis of the "treadmill of production" is one of the most trenchant critiques of the forces of development.

hundred years before. The dam under way, Brower was heartbroken by the canyon's beauty. He blamed himself for understanding, too late, what he had conceded. He vowed never again to sacrifice a canyon for a dam.

Brower's resolve was soon tested. Instead of being sobered by this defeat, in a stunning display of hubris, the bureau publicly launched plans in 1964 for two huge dams in the Grand Canyon as part of its Central Arizona Project. Brower swung into action, assembling experts to debunk the agency's strained economic justification for the dams and to create ads for a national publicity campaign. Their jobs were made easier by the bureau's arguments.[26] After the bureau claimed that the dams would boost tourism by making the canyon more accessible, one legendary ad asked whether the Sistine Chapel should also be flooded to give tourists a better view of the ceiling. The Sierra Club's ads in newspapers across the country generated an outpouring of outraged letters that were literally delivered to the bureau in dump trucks. CAP supporters knew the canyon dams were lost when first *Reader's Digest,* then *Life Magazine,* and finally the *Weekly Reader* attacked them. As Daniel Dreyfus, Dominy's top aide and one of the bureau's most effective lobbyists, remembers, "Then we got plastered from *Weekly Reader.* You're in deep shit when you catch it from them" (Reisner 1986: 299).

But Commissioner Floyd Dominy did not want to hear that the dams were doomed, not from the thousands of schoolchildren who sent letters, Daniel Dreyfus, Secretary of Interior Stewart Udall, or anyone else. CAP supporters waited until Dominy was out of the country to work out a compromise in 1967 that exchanged the dams for shares in a newly coal-generated power plant on the Navajo Reservation. Today, the smoggy haze that fills the canyon and obscures tourists' views is a legacy of the deal to save what became the bureau's last giant water project.

The tactics deployed during this fight were more confrontational than those used during the Echo Park controversy. In addition to the ads, the skillful lobbying, and the letter-writing campaigns, supporters protested during congressional hearings and picketed public meetings. The IRS revoked the Sierra Club's tax-exempt status in retaliation for its ads. Although this generated publicity, sympathy, and another surge of new members for the organization, some board members be-

---

26. My account relies on Reisner (1986:295–300). Jeffrey Ingram, a young mathematician, discovered that the bureau's financing of these very expensive dams amounted to a shell game. The bureau planned to pay for them with power revenue from Hoover, Parker, and Davis Dams once their costs were paid, a scheme that was both ludicrous and illegal.

gan to question Brower's aggressive leadership, and he was soon forced to resign.

Dominy, and many others in the agency, wished to reduce environmentalism to the grandstanding of a handful of hyperactive protesters. At first dismissive of Brower, Dominy became obsessed with him. Bureau employees were charged with tracking his movements, attending his speeches, and reporting back to Dominy on what they learned. Fearing for their jobs, they told Dominy what he wished to hear: that Brower's talks were emotional tirades, unsubstantiated by facts, that he was less formidable than feared, and that any unbiased audience would see through Brower (Reisner 1986:298). Dominy, like many other reclamation devotees, could not admit that public opinion was changing, that the trouble went deeper than David Brower.

The stakes of conservation had seldom been higher or clearer than in the battle for the Grand Canyon. For Marc Reisner (1986:295), the fight was "the conservation movement's coming of age." It is hard to imagine a more dramatic expression of agency arrogance than its plan to flood the Grand Canyon. For many Americans, it was inconceivable that a federal agency would propose such a thing. For the first time, some began to see how ruthless the commodification of water had become, how uncontainable were the pressures for development, how irrational were the terms of instrumental reason in which truly nothing is sacred. The bureau's justifications were finally beginning to sound hollow.

CAP supporters had convinced themselves that since Bridge Canyon Dam was located just outside the official park boundaries (but within Grand Canyon National Monument), this would appease critics. They did not seem to grasp that it was not the park boundaries that most concerned critics, but the 120 miles of inundated canyon that mattered. In a speech in Denver, David Brower explained that he would accept Grand Canyon dams so long as the bureau would build a comparable canyon somewhere else. He received a rousing ovation from a crowd easily convinced of the Grand Canyon's incommensurability.

Savvy environmental leaders like David Brower, media eager to publicize this battle over this national treasure, and the hubris of agency leaders all helped defeat these dams and begin to soften public support for reclamation. Some contemporary BR engineers will now concede, reluctantly, that arrogance and insularity may have produced an "engineering bias" within the agency, that maybe the organization should have paid more attention to the public and used other sorts of criteria when designing its projects. Some, but not all, will acknowledge that the Grand Canyon dams were a bad idea. The product of conflict and of collective action, this awareness was prompted and shaped by law.

And it is superbly ironic that NEPA, the law most responsible for the emergence of the New Bureau, was shaped by someone with intimate knowledge of the Bureau of Reclamation.

Daniel Dreyfus, one of the agency's most effective lobbyists, the man who had helped sell CAP, who had written speeches extolling the virtues of dams in the Grand Canyon, was undergoing a crisis of confidence in the late 1960s. Dreyfus found that he was no longer persuaded by his own reclamation rhetoric, that he was sick of Dominy's arrogance and unwillingness to admit the obvious. As Dreyfus put it, "The mood of the country was changing, but Dominy refused to let the Bureau change. You got the feeling that you belonged to the Light Brigade" (Reisner 1986:261). Disenchanted, he left the bureau to become an aide to Henry Jackson, the senator from Washington and one of Dominy's few western foes. One of Dreyfus's new jobs was to help Jackson devise legislation that would encourage federal agencies to protect the environment. Better than most, Dreyfus understood the unseemliness of water politics. When he went to work on NEPA, he knew just how hard this would be.

Legislating Rationality: The National Environmental Policy Act of 1969

NEPA changed everything; well, maybe not everything—we still build dams more or less the same way—but it sure seemed like everything else changed after NEPA.

                                                                    BR Director

Like the engineering ethos it was designed to subvert, NEPA defined the contours of the Orme Dam dispute. NEPA, sometimes explicitly and sometimes quite subtly, structured the relations between the Old Guard, the New Guard, and the Yavapai community. NEPA is crucial for appreciating the insularity of the BR's engineering ethos; their response to NEPA in the Orme decision turned a controversy into a crisis, demonstrating how their assumptions informed their politics. NEPA explains the emergence of the New Guard, not just as aberrant individuals in a strange agency, but as a group that, in amplifying NEPA's mandate, made rationality a mission. NEPA as implemented by the New Guard may have displeased some Yavapai people, but it ensured their participation in the process and provided both a forum and an avenue of recourse if need be. Understanding NEPA is a prerequisite to understanding these relations.

For a law that "changed everything," one many regard as pathbreaking legislation, NEPA's origins are notably inauspicious. With its many close friends in Congress, the Bureau of Reclamation was normally adept at monitoring legislation that affected its business; but NEPA, as it progressed, never registered on the radar screens of this or any other development agency.[27] As laws go, NEPA is short. Less than four pages long, it has just two titles and was uncontroversial when it was passed. Nixon signed it just ten months after it was introduced, an extraordinarily speedy passage. Hearings in the House and Senate only took a few days, and the media barely noted them. The bill did not even merit a roll-call vote. Compared with earlier, narrower, and far less significant environmental legislation, NEPA sailed through Congress (Liroff 1976:10).[28]

NEPA's origins were surprising in other ways. In creating and passing NEPA when it did, Congress was more proactive than reactive, according to Lynton Caldwell, one of NEPA's framers (1982:52). A "political anomaly," NEPA was not drafted by lobbyists or the subject of much lobbying by either developers or environmental groups. Mainstream conservation groups supported NEPA, but they were marginal players throughout the legislative process. It was only after NEPA was passed and some tried to weaken it that the law developed what could be termed a "constituency." Caldwell (1982) argues that this was an important step in defining an environmental constituency. In this respect NEPA was both a product and a catalyst of the environmental movement.

The Act

NEPA has three main provisions: it declares environmental quality a national priority by outlining a national policy for the environment; it requires all federal agencies to help protect the environment by establishing procedures for including environmental issues in agency decision making; and it creates the Council on Environmental Quality (CEQ) to coordinate and manage federal environmental efforts.[29] The CEQ established the guidelines for how federal agencies were to comply with NEPA.

27. The interior department's official position on the House bill, when formally solicited, was "no objection" (U.S. Congress 1969:11–12). Accounts of NEPA's legislative history are found in Finn (1973), Liroff (1976:10–35), Anderson (1973:1–14), and Espeland (1992:63–71).

28. In retrospect, Wayne Aspinall, Colorado's prodevelopment representative, known as "Mr. Reclamation," most accurately anticipated NEPA's influence. Aspinall objected to NEPA's scope and feared it would change the mission of every agency (Liroff 1976: 27). The most notable accomplishment of the League of Conservation Voters, one of David Brower's organizations, was its role in 1972 in defeating Aspinall, then the seemingly invincible chair of the House's Interior and Insular Affairs Committee.

29. National Environmental Policy Act of 1969, 102 U.S.C. 4332 (1970).

Section 101 of Title I, the substantive part of NEPA, sets out its goals (Gray 1979:361). It calls for the federal government to use all practical means to ensure a safe, pleasing, and healthful environment; to attain the "widest range of beneficial uses" of the environment without degrading it; to preserve important historic, cultural, and natural resources; to maintain a diverse environment and a "balance" between population and our use of resources; and to improve renewable resources. This section concludes by recognizing that each person should enjoy a healthful environment and is responsible for helping to preserve and enhance the environment.

Section 102, drafted by William Van Ness and Daniel Dreyfus, the former bureau lobbyist, became the most controversial part of NEPA. Often described as the "procedural" section, it requires federal agencies to prepare what are now called Environmental Impact Statements in advance of federal action that affects the environment. In what became known as its "action forcing" component, NEPA stipulates that federal agencies incorporate natural and social science into their decisions, devise procedures for including "presently unquantified environmental amenities and values," describe the environmental impact of proposed action, and identify unavoidable adverse impacts, any irreversible and irretrievable commitments of resources, and alternatives to proposed action. This section effectively changed the procedures used by federal agencies to make decisions, something no other law had done before.

Dreyfus knew that for agencies to consider seriously the environmental consequences of their actions, these consequences would need to be incorporated into the "decision documents" accompanying their proposals (Liroff 1976:17–18). Doing so would make environmental impacts part of the routine review processes of both Congress and the Bureau of the Budget. Since most agencies never developed alternatives to their recommended proposals, requiring them to assess environmental impacts for a range of alternatives would broaden their planning and, they hoped, generate policy that was less environmentally damaging (Liroff 1976:18).

Title II of NEPA calls for the formation of a Council on Environmental Quality, which was responsible for advising the president, preparing annual reports on the state of the environment, and advising federal agencies in revising their guidelines.

NEPA as an Example of Rationalization

The novelty of NEPA, according to Serge Taylor (1984:7), is that it substituted "analysis for reorganization." Instead of changing the legal mandate of each agency or creating an all-powerful regulatory agency, the traditional strategies of bureaucratic reform, NEPA tried to change the premises of decisions by changing the information that agencies routinely collect and process. While the extent of reform varied across agencies and took years to become institutionalized, NEPA generally rationalized decision making. That is what its supporters wanted, and that is why the EIS requirements approximate a rational decision model. NEPA also rationalized in a Weberian sense by expanding the role of technical experts, further depersonalizing authority, and by standardizing and incorporating more calculation into administrative decision making.

NEPA's supporters clearly intended it to promote a more rational environmental policy. That environmental policy was being made by literally hundreds of different agencies with widely divergent missions meant that coordination and control were crucial problems. NEPA was supposed to be a device for coordinating policy, for addressing cumulative, integrated environmental effects, and for rectifying the "ad hoc incrementalism" that characterized federal environmental policy. Jackson, one of NEPA's sponsors wrote: "Over the years, in small but steady and growing increments we in America have been making very important decisions concerning the management of our environment. Unfortunately, these haven't always been very wise decisions. . . . The present problem is not simply the lack of a policy. It also involves the need to rationalize and coordinate existing policies" (*Congressional Record,* hereafter *CR,* 1969). NEPA's framers also believed that science could help resolve conflict. In establishing an explicit environmental policy to inform agency decision making, in creating a structure to coordinate and integrate the environmental action of different agencies, and in promoting the use of scientific information about the environment, NEPA supporters clearly thought they were legislating rationality.

NEPA legislation, as implemented according to the CEQ guidelines, roughly conforms to classical models of rational choice. NEPA establishes the protection of the environment as a broad federal goal and then requires agencies to consider this goal when making policy decisions. It also requires that agencies develop a set of alternatives (including a "no-action alternative") to predict their expected outcomes or consequences and to specify the causal connections implicit in these predictions. These predictions must include environmental consequences (both the costs and benefits) of each alternative.

NEPA does not require agencies to select the alternative that maximizes environmental values, but it forces them to document and compare environmental impacts across alternatives, so they have been prompted to provide more elaborate defenses of their choices. Neither

NEPA nor its guidelines require that the categories for evaluating alternatives be made commensurate; nevertheless the explicit comparisons made in EISs have prompted many strategies for making evaluative categories commensurate.[30]

The act also promotes rationalization as Weber uses the term. Although he refused to collapse all the forms of rationalization in his analyses, Weber recognized that these distinct processes cumulatively produced a distinctive Western rationalism. Three "unifying themes" characterize Weber's analysis of rationalization: the expanding significance of knowledge and technical expertise in everyday life; the increasing "objectification" of structures of power and authority; and increased control, grounded in standardization and calculability, over material objects, relationships with others, and oneself (Brubaker 1984: 29–35). NEPA promoted rationalization along each of these dimensions.

NEPA requires that new forms of environmental knowledge be generated and incorporated into agency decision making, thereby creating a demand for specialized, technical knowledge that has changed the composition of agency personnel and sustained a consulting industry. The structure of the EIS emphasizes causal relations between actions and future consequences. This fosters the "intellectualization" of life, where "there are no mysterious incalculable forces that come into play" (Weber 1946:139). NEPA institutionalizes the belief that it is possible to "master" the environment through causal knowledge of the impacts of our actions.

The act also promotes rationalization by objectifying power and depersonalizing authority. Costs, benefits, and impacts are to be calculated objectively by credentialed experts who subscribe to an ethic of impartiality. Decisions must be couched in terms of their utility for society as a whole, as objectively determined according to explicit criteria and not in terms of the whims or preferences of the decision makers. In practice, value is often determined by estimating market prices for various resources or activities, and as Weber notes, market transactions are the most impersonal of all social relationships (Weber 1978:636–37). In estimating value according to market principles, the "impersonality" of the market and its system of valuing are incorporated into the decision making of the agencies.

30. CEQ guidelines do require that environmental impacts of the proposal and the alternatives be presented in comparative form in order to sharpen the issues and clarify the choices. EISs are public documents prepared in several stages, preparers must solicit comments from other relevant agencies and from affected groups, and the reasons for rejecting alternatives must be provided. These factors have also produced more elaborate justifications and greater commensuration.

Finally, NEPA expands calculation and further standardizes decision procedures. EISs must predict a greater range of the environmental and social impacts than were considered before NEPA. When prepared according to the detailed CEQ guidelines, the resulting EIS is a public and highly standardized document. Paradoxically, NEPA's requirement (Title I, Sec. 102, B) that "presently unquantifiable environmental amenities and values" be incorporated into decision making prompted a surge of research on how to quantify previously unquantifiable entities. Already in 1973, the lack of good quantitative environmental indices was cited as a serious impediment to implementing NEPA. After NEPA, manuals with explicit directions for measuring and quantifying such elusive concepts as "quality of life" and "social well-being" were prepared by agency personal and hired consultants (Curlin 1973: vi, 3).[31]

The act's proponents clearly wanted to change federal environmental policy, and they relied on procedural mechanisms to do so. NEPA does not, and perhaps could not, dictate which federal projects be implemented. NEPA only requires that environmental impacts be documented for a range of alternatives. Agencies remained free to select any alternative, providing they complied with NEPA. As Andrews describes it: "The law does not establish environmental policy. It declares what the policy ought to be and then requires agencies to prove that they paid attention to these policy goals" (1976:xii). The publicity surrounding the NEPA process provided important constraints on decisions and would often require stronger justification of the choices an agency might make. Yet there was nothing explicitly in NEPA which would force agencies to make different kinds of decisions. Underlying this was an implicit belief that information changes values.

In NEPA, legislators were trying to accomplish substantive rationality by enhancing instrumental rationality. As in some versions of rational choice theory, the gap between facts and values, goals and procedures, is built into NEPA.[32] Legislators wanted to change the values of decision makers concerning the importance of environmental impacts. Most believed that this would be accomplished simply by providing them with better information about the environmental consequences

31. See, e.g., the "Social Assessment Manual" prepared for the BR by Apt Associates, a social science consulting firm.

32. NEPA guidelines make an explicit distinction between impacts and effects. Environmental impacts are scientific, "factual" judgments or projections about expected environmental consequences associated with a specific plan. An impact is a causal relationship. An effect is a value judgment about whether an impact is good or bad. Scientists assess impacts; it is less clear who is supposed to assess effects, since these are subjective value judgments.

of their projects. But as I shall show in later chapters, the relations and tensions between goals and method, substantive and instrumental rationality, facts and values, science and politics are far less straightforward than they had hoped.

NEPA in Court

NEPA, more than any other piece of legislation, defined the field of environmental law. It has been called "the most famous statute of its kind on the planet" (Rodgers 1994:801). NEPA first introduced comprehensive environmental issues to the federal courts and expanded the scope of judicial review over administrative actions for a wide range of policy (Anderson 1973:16). NEPA was also widely copied, both by states and internationally.

Although courts have become the main enforcer of the act, NEPA supporters did not anticipate this, and judicial review was virtually ignored during the legislative process. Anderson gives several reasons why the courts have proven so willing to review NEPA cases so vigorously (1973:15–23). First, courts tend to enforce statutory procedural requirements strictly when they have no recourse to the substantive decisions that agencies make (Jaffe 1968:566). Also, environmental policy enacted by agencies often has implications for life, health, and safety, areas most subject to judicial intervention. Most intriguing, Anderson suggests that the parallels between the goals of NEPA and those of judicial review may explain the court's close scrutiny of agency compliance. NEPA's procedures are similar to those contained in the Administrative Procedure Act, which helped define review procedures. Both NEPA and the standards of judicial review ask agencies to establish procedures for "principled" decision making, to assess the risks associated with proposed action, to evaluate alternatives, to explain the selected action, to interpret public interest broadly, and to increase public participation. Anderson concludes that Section 102 of NEPA offers courts a "surrogate review mechanism" (1973:17–18).

"Good Faith" and Its Defenders

NEPA litigation is massive and varied, and patterns of judicial review have changed over time. For the crucial, early decisions, how the courts defined and defended agency rationality, the relationship between procedural and substantive compliance, and the problem of commensurability are most important for my purposes. Courts have ruled repeatedly and emphatically that the EIS must be a "reasoned document,"

one "sufficient to permit a reasoned choice."[33] The EIS should demonstrate the rationality of an agency's decision-making procedures and
of the decision itself. What constitutes rationality has been interpreted
both positively and negatively. Judges have characterized a "reasoned
document" as a thorough presentation of alternatives that is detailed
and exhibits good faith. It cannot be arbitrary or perfunctory, nor can
it be a promotional document or a post-hoc rationalization (see Rodgers 1977:730–35). The "good faith" test, cited in many cases as a reason
for reviewing NEPA compliance, was introduced in the landmark *Calvert Cliffs Coordinating Committee v Atomic Energy Commission*.[34]

Calvert Cliffs was among the first NEPA cases to reach the appellate
court and is still widely cited. Plaintiffs charged that the Atomic Energy
Commission's rules for compliance with NEPA were inadequate. The
court ruled that the commission could not wait until the Calvert Cliffs
Nuclear Power Plant was constructed before considering environmental factors at the licensing stage. Evidence of "bad faith" included how
long the commission took to devise rules for complying and its rule
that environmental data merely "accompany" an application through
review, one that Judge Wright argued "made a mockery" of NEPA:
"What possible purpose could there be in the [EIS] . . . if 'accompany'
means no more than physical proximity—mandating no more than the
physical act of passing certain folders and papers, unopened, to reviewing officials along with other folders and papers? . . . NEPA was
meant to do more than regulate the flow of papers in the federal bureaucracy" (p. 1117).

Other courts elaborated the "good faith" doctrine. The timing of reports signals how seriously the EIS was taken. Courts have ruled that
the EIS must be prepared early enough in the process so that its findings may actually influence the outcome.[35] Thorough documentation
is another sign of good faith. By explaining its reasoning, an EIS makes
it possible for courts to determine if compliance is genuine or perfunctory, whether the EIS treats the decision as "an impending choice" or
"a foregone conclusion to be rationalized."[36] A detailed administrative
record is "both a spur to reasoned decision making and a protection
against criticism. . . . But the agency must go beyond mere assertions

33. *Natural Resources Defense Council, Inc. v Morton*, 458 F. 2d 827 (D. D.C 1974).

34. 449 F. 2d 1114 (D. D.C. Cir. 1971). Before NEPA, "good faith" was a standard
applied to contractual parties.

35. *Citizens for Clean Air v Corps of Engineers*, 349 Supp, 708, 2 ELR, 20665 (D. Kansas,
1973); *Saunders v Washington Metropolitan Area Transit Authority*, 159 U.S. App. D.C. 55,
486 F2d 1315 (1973). See also Anderson (1973:180n. 8)

36. *Ely v Velde*, 451 F.2d 1130, 1139, 1 ELR 20698 (1st Cir. 1973); *I-291 Ass'n v Burns*,
517 F2d 1077 (1975).

and indicate its basis for them."[37] Disclosure protects against noncompliance.

Embedded in these opinions is a conception of rationality that is closely linked to procedure. To be rational, a decision must neither be nor look capricious, alternatives must be carefully weighed, and the logic underlying the choice must be retrievable. But proceduralism alone does not confer rationality. Rationality also depends on actors' intentions, on their believing and using the requisite information. Rationality demands more than faithful application of technique; it requires "faith" in procedure.

The courts' linking of good faith and rationality suggests several things. First, the courts implicitly understood the potential for official compliance "decoupled" from decision making. Their strategies for discerning good faith were their means for trying to distinguish and discourage the symbolic rationality conferred by procedural compliance from the "real" thing. What they hoped to find in their procedural mechanisms was a way to identify a commitment to reason, the normative component of rationality they were unwilling to relinquish. Good faith, the court's strategy for mediating NEPA's substance with its procedures, was also an effort to reconcile administrative procedure, substantive law, and procedural review. There is something poignant in relying on "faith" to resolve the bedeviling tensions between formal and substantive rationality. But as believers have long understood, the realm of faith is hard to reconcile with the lived world, and the distance between the two is no more easily or logically bridged than is the distance between substance and procedure. In interpreting NEPA, faith and substance were subordinated to procedure.

Procedure over Substance

The distinction between procedure and substance and the courts' role in reviewing each have been vigorously debated by judges and legal scholars. Their compartmentalization is built into NEPA. Section 101 of Title 1 of NEPA sets forth its substantive goals; Section 102 outlines the procedures that agencies should follow to accomplish these goals. Not surprisingly, courts have labored over their relation and how to ensure that the latter accomplishes the former. While opinions have varied, courts have generally emphasized strict compliance with NEPA's procedural requirements while ignoring or downplaying its substantive goals. As one scholar puts it: "Virtually all judicial opinions reviewing the [EIS] process so far have dealt exclusively with proce-

37. *Silva v Lynn*, 482 F. 2d 12822 (1st Cir. 1973).

dural questions" (Gray 1979:362).[38] Judicial response to NEPA's substantive goals has been either to assume that these will follow automatically from its procedures, which they rigorously enforced, or to rule
that it was inappropriate or too difficult for courts to supersede agencies' discretion and expertise.[39] Most courts concluded that if an agency
followed NEPA procedure, they could not overrule its decision on the
basis of NEPA's substantive goals. Judge Skelly, in the Calvert Cliffs
opinion, helped establish this position: "Section 102 of NEPA mandates
a particular sort of careful and informed decision making process and
creates judicially enforceable duties. The reviewing courts probably
cannot reverse a substantive decision on its merits . . . unless it be
shown that the actual balance of costs and benefits that was struck was
arbitrary or clearly gave insufficient weight to environmental values.
But if the decision was reached procedurally without the . . . balancing
of environmental factors . . . it is the responsibility of the courts to
reverse." This opinion is widely cited. A few judges have used it to
claim authority to review the substance of agency decisions, but more
often the case is cited to support limiting such review.[40]

Environmentalists were disappointed with judicial refusal to over-
turn administrative decisions based on NEPA's substantive goals.
Since NEPA's procedural mandate is no guarantee that its substantive
mandate will be met, some saw NEPA as fatally flawed. And some
bureaucrats, including those who prepared the first EISs on the Central
Arizona Project, saw a strict procedural interpretation of NEPA as offering legal protection; once they scrupulously documented a project's
environmental impacts, they could ignore these and build what they
wanted, since NEPA legitimized their discretion. During the early
stages of implementation, EISs were so biased that compliance with
NEPA became another forum for lobbying for an agency's pet plan.

NEPA's effects, however, extended beyond the courtroom, as subsequent chapters will show. The courts may not enforce substantive

38. See Rodgers (1977:741n. 23) for a list of decisions where NEPA is recognized as
having created substantive rights.

39. In *Stryker's Bay Neighborhood Council Inc v Karlen et al.*, 444 U.S. 223, 100 S Ct. 497,
62 L.Ed. 2d 433 (1980), the Supreme Court argued that the court's role was simply to
ensure that agencies had considered environmental consequences. In *Vermont Yankee
Nuclear Power Corp v NRDC* (435 U.S. 519 [1978]), it held that the duties NEPA imposes on
federal agencies are "essentially procedural." Justice Marshall's dissent rejects reducing
review to the "mindless task" of documenting the inclusion of environmental factors,
regardless of their effect.

40. See, e.g., Gillham Dam, *Environmental Defense Fund v Corps*, 325 F. Supp. 759 (E.D.
Ark. 1970), and *Environmental Defense Fund, Inc. v Corps (Tennessee-Tombigbee)*, 348 F.
Supp. 933 (D. D.C. 1971). *Natural Resources Defense Council, Inc. v Morton*, 458 F. 2d. 827
(D. D.C. 1974). See also *Citizens to Preserve Overton Park, Inc. v Volpe*, 401 U.S. 402 (1971).

goals, but the public could endorse them. CEQ guidelines requiring public participation and more elaborate justifications for selected policy offered new forums and new tools for project opponents. At the same time, the gradual introduction of new kinds of employees into agencies challenged taken-for-granted values. These new decision procedures took time to become institutionalized but, once they did, disrupted routines and redirected employees' attention. In ways that neither legislators nor judges nor bureaucrats had expected, these consequences of NEPA shaped both the political and the organizational context of environmental decision making.

Commensuration

Courts have treated the issue of how, under NEPA, agencies are to commensurate competing values and objectives as a question of "balance." In nuisance cases, courts have long balanced the gravity of harm against the utility of conduct. But in nuisance cases, judges perform the initial balancing instead of merely reviewing it, and the issues involve conduct between private parties. NEPA is silent on the proper role of the courts in reviewing how agencies balance conflicting goals. Again the Calvert Cliffs opinion offers the framework for doing so: "NEPA mandates a case-by-case balancing judgment on the part of federal agencies. In each individual case, the particular economic and technical benefits of planned action must be assessed and then weighed against the environmental costs; alternatives must be considered which would affect the balance of values. . . . The point of the individualized balancing analysis is to ensure . . . that the optimally beneficial action is finally taken."[41]

Anderson (1973:256) suggests that this endorsement of balancing was probably intended to suggest the loose, common-sense notion of trade-offs. But the courts' language often implies a precise calculation and certainty that agencies could never attain. Judges may not have meant to proliferate cost-benefit techniques, but that is what happened in many agencies, including the Bureau of Reclamation.

Neither Congress nor the courts prescribed methods agencies should use to perform this balancing act; nor does NEPA specify the relative weights that should be assigned to environmental values; nor have courts developed a consensus about how to review this balancing. The only consensus to emerge was that it was the court's duty to ensure that a careful balancing did occur. As a result, agencies were scrambling to find ways to balance environmental, economic, and technical goals

41. 449 F. 2d 1114 (D. D.C. Cir. 1971).

without guidance from those who would be reviewing them. Their so-lutions were mainly variations on cost-benefit (CB) analyses (Barem 1980:477).

The courts were sympathetic to agencies' problem with how to bal-ance competing values, and some judges criticized Congress for failing to provide them with more guidance. Judge Bazelon criticized legisla-tors for abdicating their responsibility to make the "hard value choices" for administrative agencies that cannot "resolve value conflicts through the relatively simple expedient of a show of hands" (Barem 1980). But their sympathy for agencies did not keep them from scrutinizing how this balancing was accomplished. In the Calvert Cliffs decision, the court ruled that agency discretion was questionable when the bal-ance of costs and benefits, however derived, was "arbitrary" or "capri-cious." After Calvert Cliffs, the appropriateness of an agency's balanc-ing became the criterion for reversing its substantive decision. For the first time, under NEPA, an agency's CB analyses came under judicial review. Before NEPA, agency CB analyses were not reviewed.[42]

Judicial scrutiny revealed some remarkably biased analyses. In the Gillham Dam case, the Army Corps of Engineers' CB ratio for the pro-posed dam included as "benefits" estimates of the value of enhanced water quality.[43] That dams enhance water quality was a dubious claim in light of what was already known of their effects on silt and salt. The EIS argued that since the proposed dam would increase development and population density (not considered an environmental impact) around the newly formed lake, this would increase pollution (again, not included as a project liability). Since the dam would permit greater regulation of water flow, this could be used to dilute this new pollution and would therefore enhance water quality. In the EIS, the recreational benefits associated with the new lake were calculated, but not the costs associated with losing river recreation.[44] Although the project was two-thirds completed, a temporary injunction was granted until the EIS could be revised. In *Sierra Club v Froehlke*, the court asserted its jurisdic-tion to review agency CB analysis, formerly the exclusive domain of

42. Taylor (1984:190); see *U.S. v West Virginia Power Co,* 122 F. 2d (4th Cir. 1941).
43. *Environmental Defense Fund v Corps of Engineers,* 325 F. Supp., 59 (E.D. Ark. 1970).
44. ACE ignored testimony on the sensitivity of their CB ratio to interest rates and on the operationalization of the "life" of the project. Lower interest rates, those used when the project was first authorized, were used to calculate the cost of the project, rather than current higher rates. The life of the project was defined as 100 years, the old unit, rather than the now standard 50-year life. CB ratios are vastly improved when low discount rates are used for projects with large initial costs and a long stream of benefits, typical of large water-resource projects. The ACE refused to update its assumptions, which greatly inflated project benefits. The early CAP EISs show a similar pattern.

Congress.[45] The court found that the balance struck in the CB analysis was "arbitrary" and gave "insufficient weight to environmental values." The agency was directed to redo the EIS, including its CB analysis (Anderson 1973:263–65).

Despite these seemingly promising rulings, environmentalists' efforts to change the rules for CB analyses mostly failed. Their court challenges to the low discount rates used in old projects prompted Congress to pass a law "grandfathering" the lower rates to when the projects were first authorized (Taylor 1984:191). Attempts by environmental groups to change the CEQ guidelines for calculating costs and benefits also failed. Judicial review of CB analysis did not lead to the wholesale incorporation of environmental values into the techniques. It did, however, generate a surge of interest in devising new methods for doing so.

This new intrusion of the courts into the administrative decision making of government agencies created a new arena for contesting and claiming legitimacy, one characterized by evolving rules provided by courts and regulatory agencies and new, public audiences. The courts' emphasis on procedural over substantive compliance with NEPA, their reluctance to intrude too far into the discretion of executive agencies, combined with the need to document the balancing of environmental and nonenvironmental interests, and the general lack of guidance about how to do this prompted many agencies to experiment with new ways to quantify and commensurate disparate values. The response of many agencies to the NEPA litigation was to become procedurally scrupulous (Taylor 1984).

Procedural scrupulousness does not eliminate bias. In some cases, bias simply took a new form after NEPA, as bureaucrats manipulated alternatives, decision factors, and measures in ways that supported their policies. It was clear to the courts and to those who filed legal challenges that many early EISs were symbolic documents "decoupled" from agency decision making (Meyer and Rowan 1977). In the most egregious examples of decoupling, the courts intervened, trying to spell out the terms of good-faith decisions.

NEPA's effects were not limited to the symbolic gestures of compliance that characterized early EISs, however, and judges' influence was broader than case law might suggest. Knowing that judges, lawyers, and other economists would be scrutinizing one's work promoted more scrupulous analyses. BR employees would sometimes regale me with stories (perhaps apocryphal) of the malleability and partisanship of CB analyses in the "old days," of how a call from a senator could

45. Trinity River-Wallisville Dam, *Sierra Club v Froehlke,* 395 F. Supp. 1349 (S.D. Texas 1973).

miraculously boost the benefits of some pet project overnight. But the moral of these stories was always the same: we couldn't get away with that now. As a bureau planner told me, "Knowing you are going to have to publicly defend your analysis does tend to make you more careful, less partisan." Serge Taylor (1984) found the same pattern in his analysis of two other federal agencies.

The act did prompt some fundamental changes in how agencies carried out their work. For many agencies, being forced to create and evaluate alternative policies represented an abrupt departure in their decision-making routines. Many in the past had simply proposed and evaluated one plan, considering only minor modifications. Others, like the BR, might consider several dam sites, selecting the one that best met their engineering criteria. But gradually the practice of comparing alternative plans became institutionalized, and the characteristics of these plans have shifted over time.

NEPA forced agencies to perform explicit comparisons of alternatives that must include a "no-action" plan, although I never heard of an agency that decided that status quo was preferable to their proposed policies. Some alternatives evaluated in EISs, especially early ones, seemed designed for rejection: either too utopian or expensive to implement, or more ecologically destructive than the agency's pet plan. Others EISs created alternatives that represented minor variations on a theme, formalizing in EISs past practices of deciding among nearly identical plans. But NEPA, judicial review, and politics all exerted pressure on agencies to broaden the range of alternatives they considered. It took several decades, but some agencies are now writing EISs to evaluate policy designed to improve the environment. EISs are providing the means by which traditional operations are being reevaluated. The Grand Canyon flood that Bruce Babbit presided over dramatically illustrates this shift. While many might question the effectiveness of such remedial measures, there is no doubt that this represents a radical departure for an agency that had been dedicated to damming the West.

Decoupling and Recoupling: Myths That Matter

Those who study organizations have long been concerned with how their legitimacy is maintained. Neoinstitutional theory has taught us that the extent to which organizational arenas are institutionalized and rationalized may explain more about an organization's structure and activity than the sort of technology it employs or the resources it requires. There were many incentives for agencies to try to finesse NEPA with symbolic compliance decoupled from "real" decision making. Early EISs provide ample evidence of how egregious decoupling could be, and the task of defining the acceptable limits of decoupling fell to courts. As Weber pointed out, there are no rationally valid means adopting or choosing one substantive value over another, and there will always exist irreconcilable tensions between substantive values and instrumental ones. When the necessary gap between substantive and instrumental values becomes especially obvious or problematic, this is perhaps a situation that most requires the construction of "myths" that make this chasm less troubling. One such myth is that procedural scrupulousness can somehow substitute for, or signal, substantive compliance and that the documentation of procedural compliance ensures that behavior somehow measured up. As Feldman and March (1981) have suggested, the symbolic properties of information become paramount when concern centers on the representation of a vague, uncertain value.

For courts, signaling concern for the environment ultimately came down to marshaling new kinds of information in a new form; the form, which emphasized the balancing of information and which led to a proliferation of commensuration in agency reporting, cultivated the appearance that the new information was being treated the same as the old information. Besides documenting that the new information was collected and attended to, commensuration—while spelling out differences in the weighting of information in precise ways—also suggests that the new information was accorded the same logical status as the information that had traditionally been collected by the agency in making its decisions. The commensurate form itself suggests a sort of evenhandedness in attention.

The symbolic potential of procedures, nevertheless, is sometimes hard to contain. Myths and methods can be potent, sometimes resulting in a recoupling rather than a decoupling of practice. When groups within an organization become invested in the authority of procedures, or when these can be publicly scrutinized and contested, when myths become politicized, then these can become autonomous in ways that threaten the status quo. The chapters that follow explain in more detail how, in reacting against or mobilizing around NEPA, the law shaped the way members of all three groups interpreted both their and one another's interests and identities in the Orme dispute. I will describe how the Old Guard's response to NEPA shifted over time, eventually culminating in their appreciation of the tenuousness of the worldview that had once been hegemonic. I will investigate the conditions that allowed members of the New Guard to exploit and elaborate NEPA in ways that made it more than the paper tiger that many bureaucrats first imagined it to be. And I will describe how NEPA, as interpreted by the New Guard, influenced how members of the Yavapai community understood themselves, their adversaries, and their strategies of resistance.

~~~~~ **Three** ~~~~~

The Old Guard: Stand by Your Dam

Water is life in the desert. . . . The Central Arizona Project is a very old dream. I first heard about it from my grandfather.

Morris Udall

Orme is at the confluence two rivers. There is no more strategic place than that to build a dam. It is a good dam site. There is no way you could improve on it. You could only take something less, which is what they did.

Retired BR engineer

[W]e must say to Central Arizona's water needy posterity that we wound up being so cowed by our adversaries that we were willing to settle for an improvised answer to our most critical problem when in our hearts we know it was more of a political escape for decision makers than a trustworthy answer.

Howard Pyle, former governor of Arizona,
Orme Dam supporter

One of Chuck's earliest memories was about water. It had been a dry summer in Oklahoma, and all the grown-ups ever seemed to talk about was how much they needed rain. Under all that casual talk he knew, as children often do, that this was serious for his parents and for other farmers like them. He recalls standing by the side of the farmhouse one hot summer day when he spotted a big, dark cloud headed his way. Well, here comes something, he thought; it was finally going to rain and things would be alright. But the cloud turned out to be dust, not rain, and his five-year-old's excitement gave way to a disappointment so powerful he can still retrieve it some seventy years later.

When Chuck graduated from college with a degree in engineering, he had several good jobs to chose from. He decided to work for the Bureau of Reclamation, because, as he put it, "I was more interested in water. . . . I got my interest in water from my father." As a boy, Chuck would tag along to help his father dig wells, and he came to appreciate just how much water meant to dry-land farmers and arid communities. He believed in water development. He understood how water could change lives.

Like many BR engineers, Chuck loved his work. He was deeply loyal to the agency that employed him, proud of its accomplishments, and relished building projects. In his words, "You want to find a viable project, build it, and leave something behind that people will benefit from." Chuck's loyalty to the organization and his identification with its mission were characteristic of many bureau engineers. In the previous chapter, I described the history of the agency and the emergence of an engineering ethos that shaped its members' understanding of their work and their response to broad political and cultural changes. This chapter examines these processes closer to the ground, as they affected one relatively small, but important, group within the organization, a group of bureau employees I call the Old Guard. In it, I explain how the engineering ethos that evolved in the bureau informed the Orme dispute: how these men invested in Orme Dam, how they forged a remarkably powerful and enduring constituency that included politicians, business and media leaders, farmers, and an Arizona populace wary of Californians out to "steal" their water, how they fought their political battles, with water rivals, environmentalists, and Yavapai leaders, and why they lost control of the decision framework.

Members of the Old Guard did not think of themselves as a group, at least not until they began to feel threatened by changes in the world and in the agency. The qualities they shared were ones shared by many BR employees, and for much of their careers they did not need to understand or defend themselves as distinctive. They were men, most were engineers or people, like surveyors, who worked closely with engineers. Most have retired or are nearly ready to, and most have spent much of their careers with the Bureau of Reclamation. As regional directors, assistant directors, managers or assistant managers of local project offices, or the chiefs of divisions within the various branches of the agency, they were powerful men who had risen through the ranks. What most united them was their passionate support of the Central Arizona Project and Orme Dam. Several members of the Old Guard worked in the Arizona Project Office for most of their careers; many worked there for a decade or longer, coming to Arizona after having worked on other projects, in regional offices or in Washington. Because CAP was such a large project that took so long to build, people who worked on it spent longer on the same project and were less mobile than were many other BR employees.[1]

The Old Guard's loyalty to the agency was not a new phenomenon.

1. While I emphasize bureau employees in this group, it is appropriate to include the long-term CAP and Orme supporters, the carefully cultivated "water elite" of Arizona who worked closely with BR people to promote the project: local and federal politicians, lobbyists, members of state water agencies, civic leaders, farmers, and developers. While their attachments to Orme are different, some were deeply invested in the dam and felt the same sense of loss and betrayal when an alternative was selected.

According to Samuel Hays, when the policies of Frederick H. Newell, the first director of the Reclamation Service, were attacked by the secretary of the interior, *Engineering News* (Jan. 13, 1910; cited in Hays 1980: 154) was among the many newspapers and journals to defend him vigorously. Many engineers were so committed to the agency that they turned down higher-paying jobs in the private sector so that they might continue to support the federal program. William Warne, a former assistant commissioner, sees this strong loyalty as one of the agency's most distinctive features. He characterizes the bureau as a "high morale" outfit, where time spent in the agency would "mark a reclamation man for life." He argues that the bureau's legacy fosters employees' attachments: "The men of reclamation participated in one of the most exciting phases of the winning of the West. Whole communities of pioneers followed them into the land of sagebrush and stayed as settlers when the reclamation men went on to their next job. Their names became known worldwide as the reputations of their projects spread. The men of reclamation look back with satisfaction at having built something that people find worthwhile. . . . Meet one of them in any desert of the world where . . . if you happen to have been one of them, together you will toast the bureau with a beer" (Warne 1973:v–vi).

Members of the Old Guard, like Chuck, remain extremely loyal to the agency and, as Warne might have predicted, closely identify with its work and with its legacy. When asked what he liked about his job, another man told me: "I like what I'm doing. Where else could you be involved in the type and scale of projects that the bureau does? The bureau has a long history of setting the standard in civil engineering, in building something everyone said was impossible to build. What other governmental agency can you think of that has created projects like Hoover or Coulee, projects that are recognized worldwide as state-of-the-art? . . . When I'm driving home from work, sometimes I look at all the development, all the new homes, the families that have moved [to Arizona] and I think about how bureau water and bureau power made it all possible. Starting with Roosevelt Dam. You know, most people never remember that."

The Old Guard's commitment to Orme Dam, like their loyalty to their employer, is a political and organizational accomplishment. Orme Dam was part of an old dream that eventually became known as the Central Arizona Project. Invented in the BR and embraced by water users in Arizona, CAP was a dream that the BR, local politicians, farmers, businessmen, the local media, and community leaders had spend decades and millions of dollars promoting. And old dreams die hard. Orme Dam became emblematic of many of the conflicts the agency faced. It represented the old way of doing business, before environmental interests, NEPA, multiobjective planning, and rational choice models had intruded, back when the politics of water development meant learning how many projects you had to dole out to get yours. Part of the Old Guard's investment in Orme was an investment in the politics of the past and fear of losing control over the future. For those whose power had become naturalized, uncertainty and the threat of losing that power were a frightening prospect.

The Central Arizona Project

The Colorado River is the most politicized, litigated, regulated, diverted, and just plain used rivers in the world (Fradkin 1981:15–16). That point is about the only one agreed upon by environmental groups, the BR, and the dozen or so other federal agencies that manage natural resources and national parks tied to the river, and the dozens of Indian reservations, seven states, and two countries that make up the Colorado River Basin. As Marc Reisner (1986:126) put it, "To some conservationists, the Colorado River is the preeminent symbol of everything mankind has done wrong—a harbinger of squalid and deserved fate. To its preeminent impounder, the U.S. Bureau of Reclamation, it is the perfection of an ideal."

Not surprisingly, the Colorado River is terribly polluted, carrying the most silt and salt of any American river through some of the world's most spectacular scenery. The use made of the river is such that unless rains are heavy enough to generate local flooding, no river water has reached the Pacific Ocean, the natural outlet of the Colorado River, in the last twenty years (Fradkin 1981:16). Back in 1968, the National Academy of Science already cautiously reported that "the Colorado Basin is closer than most basins in the United States to utilizing the last drop of available water for man's needs" (Fradkin 1981:15); 1968 was the same year that CAP was finally authorized by Congress. For Carl Hayden, Arizona's congressman since statehood in 1912, the authorization had been his mission for over twenty-five years. The Central Arizona Project, his lifelong dream, was now his political triumph.[2]

CAP was the bureau's grand plan to divert water from the Colorado River to central and southern Arizona through an elaborate system of

2. Carl Hayden was first elected to the House in 1912 and to the Senate in 1926. An ardent reclamation supporter, Hayden, after serving on the powerful appropriations committee for twenty-five years, became chair in 1953. McCool says of Hayden: "If one individual were to be plucked from the panorama of American politics and credited with the success of the reclamation program, it would be Hayden" (1987:730). Hayden retired from the Senate in 1969, fifty-seven years after first being elected to Congress and one year after CAP was authorized.

dams, canals, and aqueducts. It was the largest, most expensive, and most politically volatile water-development project in U.S. history; it was also the most ambitious basin project that the bureau had ever attempted. (A basin project is one with interconnected features at different sites in the same river basin, where, typically, the power generated by one dam is used to pay for the other features.) The original plan for CAP called for pumping 1,200,000 acre-feet of water annually from Lake Havasu, the reservoir created by Parker Dam, via a giant aqueduct, to central Arizona. The power needed to lift the water 900 feet from the reservoir to the aqueduct would be generated by two new dams near the Grand Canyon: Bridge Canyon Dam and Marble Canyon Dam. Bridge and Marble Canyon Dams would be the project "cash registers." The excess power would be sold commercially to subsidize the rest of the project. Without this revenue, the cost of building the rest of the project would have overwhelmed its benefits.

In addition to these dams and the nearly 400 miles of aqueduct, the project would build five other new dams and enlarge one existing dam. These dams were designed to help store and regulate water and provide flood protection. To make all this work, four new pumping stations, a series of smaller canals for distributing the water to irrigators, and transmission lines would also be built. Orme Dam, located at the confluence of the Salt and Verde Rivers, was one of the new dams proposed (USBR 1947:R16–R27).

The Bureau of Reclamation first became involved with the plan to divert Colorado River water to central Arizona in 1940, when it made an agreement with Arizona to jointly fund preliminary investigations of a Central Arizona project. A 1945 report explored various diversion routes, and another in 1947 compared the two top contenders (USBR 1947:5). Long before that, men like George Maxwell, the national leader in the federal irrigation movement, and Fred Colter, a flamboyant state legislator, were already dreaming of finding ways to get Colorado River to the deserts of central Arizona. As far back as 1918, something called the Arizona Engineering Commission proposed diverting water from the Colorado to one of its tributaries, the Gila River, in order to irrigate land in southern Arizona. By 1922, the energetic George Maxwell was already lobbying for his plan. Maxwell was persuasive enough to get Phoenix businessmen to pay for a survey of an aqueduct to carry the Colorado water. Arthur Davis, then BR chief engineer, called Maxwell's plan "a mad man's dream" (Johnson 1977:13–14). This "mad dream" would obsess Arizonans for another seventy-five years.

How to develop the Colorado River was the hottest political issue in the state, and, for years, where you stood on that question sealed your political fate. According to Dean Mann, the issue was capable of "making or breaking politicians from county sheriffs to governors" (1963:81). For twenty-two years, due largely to Fred Colter's influence, Arizona had refused to sign the Colorado River Basin Compact that Herbert Hoover had negotiated. This compact divided up the Colorado River for the seven states that comprised the Colorado River Basin: Arizona, California, Colorado, Nevada, New Mexico, Utah, and Wyoming. Locals were convinced that since nearly half of the river either flowed inside the state or marked its boundary, Arizona ought to enjoy unrestricted use of the water.[3]

Fred T. Colter, a wealthy businessman who spent six terms in the state senate, was the originator and most prominent proponent of this view. His political battle cry, "Save the Colorado for Arizona," was one voters endorsed for years. Although Colter created elaborate plans for how Arizona ought to develop the river for its exclusive and "sovereign" use, supporters found themselves continually on the defensive as they tried, unsuccessfully, to block California's aggressive attempts to develop the Colorado River for its own ends.

Unfortunately, positions that are wildly successful with local audiences often seem absurd to a national one. Besides using political means to try to stop the ratification of the compact, Arizona filed three unsuccessful lawsuits trying to stop California water projects, a costly political blunder. When repeated attempts to negotiate a compromise with California also failed, even more extreme tactics were deployed to prevent California's appropriation of "Arizona's" water. In 1934, Arizona's Governor Benjamine Maour called on the state militia to stop the construction of Parker Dam, which was to designed to divert Colorado River water to Los Angeles. Besides earning the state a well-deserved reputation for obstructionism and the enmity of most of Southern California, Arizona succeeded mainly in delaying getting any water from the Colorado River, prolonging the fight with California over water rights, and ensuring that California's congressional delegation would reject any legislation designed to send water to Arizona.

Despite Arizona's best efforts, California kept developing elaborate systems to supply itself with water, including sending Colorado River water to burgeoning Los Angeles. Some local Arizona politicians worried privately that the state's obstructionism was playing into California's hands, recognizing that California was much better organized, politically and financially, to push through the projects its backers wanted. At that time, Arizona had no organized, well-funded means

3. Norris Hundley Jr.'s (1975) analysis of the Colorado River Compact is the definitive treatment of this landmark event in western water politics.

for lobbying on behalf of its water interests. To try to redress that problem, the Central Arizona Project Association (CAPA) was formed in 1946 to lobby for the Central Arizona Project. A private, nonprofit organization, CAPA was originally composed of about 100 "prominent" citizens, virtually all with a direct economic interest in water and energy development. Founding members included farmers, bankers, merchants, water lawyers, managers of local utilities, and local political leaders.[4]

In 1947, the bureau completed its planning report on CAP and submitted it the secretary of the interior for approval. Wasting no time, Senator Earnest McFarland of Arizona introduced S. 1175, the first legislation calling for the authorization of Central Arizona Project legislation. One of the first tasks of the CAPA was to organize and coordinate the testimony on this bill during the hearings before the Senate Subcommittee on Irrigation and Reclamation (Johnson 1977:30, 31).[5]

Orme Dam, circa 1947

The strategy of CAP supporters early on was to paint CAP as a "rescue" operation, one that was necessary to replace the "exhausted" ground-water supply in order to save the local economy. As Senator Carl Hayden testified, "This legislation is just based on sheer necessity. We have in central Arizona a desert . . . we have to irrigate our land. We have done it by impounding all the water in the streams in Arizona. We have done it by digging wells until we have exhausted the underground water supply. It is absolutely essential that a supplementary water supply be obtained, and the only source is from the Colorado River" (U.S. Senate 1947:3–4). Bureau officials reported that "without Colorado River water about one-third of the productive capacity of the agriculture development will be lost, which will result in large scale abandonment and migration" (U.S. Congress 1951). Local supporters adapted the themes of the agency ethos in defending CAP. During the hearings, Arizonans testified that without the project, re-

4. California's lobby—the Colorado River Association—was formed to stop CAP. Funded by six local power and water agencies, including the powerful Metropolitan Water District of Southern California, this organization lobbied against any further effort to develop the Colorado River, which members believed would threaten their investments (Terrell 1965:28–29). All of the seven basin states had comparable organizations that monitored Colorado River policy.

5. A year later, the Arizona Interstate Stream Commission was created to act as the official state representative on issues pertaining to Colorado River development. CAPA wrote the state law creating the agency, and most of those appointed to the commission were members of CAPA as well. Young Barry Goldwater was also appointed, in his first foray into politics.

claimed, productive land would be ceded back to the desert. Wayne Aktin, the president of a farm management company and of CAPA, declared: "I have tried to convey to you the vital nature of the problem facing the whole irrigated farming community of central Arizona. This empire, which we have created from the desert, is in grave danger. The situation is desperate" (U.S. Congress 1951:114–15). As Jesse Udall explained to senators, "[Land] is on the verge of reverting back to the desert. The sight of burning crops, dying trees, parched lands that once were fruitful makes a close observer wonder if this generation is keeping faith with the generations of pioneers that carved an empire out of the deserts. It also raises questions as to what this generation's responsibility is to the next. . . . It is imperative that additional sources of water be brought into central Arizona. . . . In Arizona it isn't acres, but acre feet that spell prosperity and success" (U.S. Congress 1951:171).

Arizonans' efforts to cast the CAP as essential for keeping the desert at bay, protecting community in Arizona, and preserving the legacy of pioneers carried no weight with California's representatives. The strategy of portraying CAP as essential to stave off imminent disaster ultimately proved embarrassing; as the fight for CAP dragged on for years, opponents would note that the predicted water crisis, economic decline, and population exodus had not occurred (Johnson 1977:33; Terrell 1965:261–62). The Senate passed McFarland's bill in 1950 and again in 1951, but both times California's delegation blocked the bill in the House, arguing that there was too little water left in the Colorado River to sustain the project. California was already using nearly a million more acre-feet of water annually than was allocated to it under the Colorado River Compact. California wanted Bridge and Marble Canyon Dams as a source of inexpensive power for Southern California and not for CAP revenue. To delay further, the California-controlled House Subcommittee on Irrigation and Reclamation passed a motion requiring that water rights on the Colorado be adjudicated before any CAP legislation could be sent to the floor. Angry and frustrated, project backers filed suit against California. The Supreme Court finally agreed to hear Arizona's case.

Arizona v California

Arizona v California was a monumental case.[6] Judge Rifkind, the court-appointed special master of the case, described the trial as "the greatest struggle over water rights in the latter day history of the West" (Mann

6. A detailed description of the case is found in Johnson (1977:73–146); see also Mann (1963:89–96).

1963:94). The case was filed in 1952, and the Supreme Court finally issued its decree on March 9, 1964. Two special masters presided over 340 witnesses and the 50-plus lawyers that worked on the case and reviewed 25,000 pages of testimony. The pretrial conference alone lasted more than two years. At twenty-two hours, it was the longest oral argument ever heard by the Supreme Court (Moss 1967:11). The court finally sided with Arizona, allocating the state 2.8 million acre-feet of Colorado River water annually.

Retired members of the Old Guard remember the dramatic changes attending the decision. During the court battle, as representatives of a federal agency, they could not look too partisan for fear of jeopardizing their relations with California's water elites. Behind the scenes, local bureaucrats strongly supported Arizona's case. The long legal battle kept local engineers in limbo, their funds and their patience dwindling. Their thirty-person Arizona Project Office dwindled to six as engineers transferred out. Once the court ruled in Arizona's favor, however, it was recruiting season in Arizona, and within a year one hundred people were hired. They were eager to start construction on CAP, but once again their patience was tried as the struggle for authorization ensued.

Arizona's celebrated judicial victory over California was neither the final word nor the thorough vindication that supporters had hoped for, as politics incrementally retracted what the court had awarded. In order for Arizona to receive the allocated Colorado River water, Congress first had to authorize and then fund the projects needed to deliver the water. Though not quite as protracted, obtaining congressional authorization of CAP proved to be as exasperating and as time consuming as the Supreme Court case had been, requiring an additional five years of haggling, arm twisting, and, above all, logrolling. The end result was that much of what Arizona was granted by the courts was negotiated away in order to secure the support of the other Colorado Basin states.

Beginning the day after the Supreme Court issued its opinion in 1963, the introduction of CAP legislation in countless varieties was a regular feature of each congressional session. Hayden would repeatedly introduce the authorization legislation in the Senate, hearings would be held, and the bill would be approved in the Senate only to be buried in some House committee. As one member of the Old Guard recalled: "Arizona wasn't exactly politically naked: we were exposed, but not buck naked." The arithmetic was simple: In the Senate, where Hayden reigned over the mighty appropriations committee, CAP fared well. In the House, where California had thirty-five representatives to Arizona's one, and where Colorado's Wayne Aspinall controlled the Interior and Insular Affairs Committee, CAP died multiple, inventive deaths.

From 1963 until 1968, over twenty-five CAP related bills were introduced in Congress, some to advance the project, some reflecting compromises, others to derail it.[7]

CAP authorization was complicated in 1965 when David Brower's
coalition of conservation groups launched their campaign to stop the
construction of Bridge and Marble Canyon Dams in the Grand Canyon.
For CAP supporters, the loss of these dams threatened the feasibility
of the entire project, since their power was what made the project "economically viable." These dams were especially significant to bureau
engineers. According to Helen Ingram: "The bureau's hopes for a
bright future for itself were particularly pinned to the Bridge and Marble Canyon Dams. These two great structures were to be built on the
two remaining best dam sites on the Colorado River . . . the bureau
had been experiencing difficulty in finding flood projects which met
economic feasibility criteria. These two [dams] were moneymakers on
paper, and they held particular glamour for dam-building engineers"
(1990:49). CAP supporters finally conceded that as long as CAP included those dams, it was doomed in Congress. Brower and his allies
had generated enough publicity and pressure so that even legislators
that usually supported western water projects felt they could not risk
damming the Grand Canyon (Ingram 1990:55–56).[8] Supporters reluctantly agreed to replace the dams with a coal-generated power plant
on the nearby Navajo Reservation.

The environmentalists' success was an unpleasant shock to CAP supporters, and especially to members of the Old Guard. For one man,
now in his eighties, mentioning David Brower can still raise his blood
pressure. He relishes telling stories highlighting Brower's arrogance,
his "misunderstanding" of water issues. He relishes the irony that the
air pollution of the Grand Canyon, currently a hot environmental issue,
is a by-product of the compromise plan the environmentalists negotiated. For BR engineers, the power plant represented a radical and unsavory departure for the agency; it was the first time that a project abandoned hydropower as a source of energy to pump water and make
money.

BR engineers were contemptuous of the environmentalists responsi-

7. For a careful, but partisan, account of all the legislative maneuvering, see Johnson
(1977:6–12). Johnson, as director of the CAPA, a member of the Arizona Task Force for
CAP in Washington, and executive director of the Arizona Interstate Stream Commission, was a central participant. Terrell (1965) provides the California prospective on the
basis of his experience as a publicist for their anti-CAP lobby, the Colorado River Association.

8. In 1966, opponents of CAP helped create new legislation to enlarge the boundaries
of Grand Canyon National Park as a way to stop the two dams.

ble for forcing this unappealing compromise. They were vilified as ignorant, irrational, wild-eyed radicals opposed to progress; they were
"dam haters." Only once, in the Echo Park dispute, had public pressure
forced the agency not to build a dam where it had been authorized to
build one. Having to abandon the Grand Canyon sites in order to have
CAP authorized may seem like a small compromise in such a big project, but to BR engineers it represented a stinging defeat and the unwarranted intrusion of "emotional amateurs" into what had been exclusively their turf. Their bitterness over this compromise colored their
reactions to subsequent challenges to their plans.

The stature of Carl Hayden and the goodwill he had amassed over
his long tenure prompted many legislators to want finally to deliver
to him, now a sick, old man, the project he had supported for so long.
The sentiment was gratifying to him, but Hayden had recourse to more
than goodwill. As chairman of the appropriations committee, he could
stymie every other proposed water project. While Hayden rarely re-
sorted to heavy-handed tactics, he had become so frustrated with all
the stalling that he finally used his clout to force Aspinall to air the
bill. Hayden threatened to stall money for the Frying-Pan Arkansas
water project in Colorado, Wayne Aspinall's pet project, and to attach
CAP legislation as rider to the Public Works Appropriation Bill, where
he could by-pass Aspinall's committee and block appropriations for
every other public works project that session (Ingram 1990:61; Reisner
1986:282; Johnson 1977:206–7).

The threat worked. Aspinall convened hearings on the legislation
beginning in late 1967. A similar bill had already passed the Senate,
and before the hearings began, the seven Colorado Basin states had
finally hammered out an accord acceptable to all. The bill was redrafted
to accommodate Aspinall and the agreement reached by the basin
states. Lyndon Johnson demanded quick action on the legislation, and
in May of 1968, after just four hours of debate, it passed with a big
majority in an unrecorded vote. On September 30, in a White House
ceremony, LBJ signed the bill, awarding to a somewhat dazed Carl
Hayden the ritual "first" pen as onlookers applauded wildly.

CAP was authorized as Public Law 90-537, the extraordinary legislation known as the Colorado River Basin Project Act. Described as "a
water development spectacular" (Ingram 1990:43), this act was the political conclusion to over forty-five years of regional water wars. For
critics, it was the ultimate pork-barrel legislation, buying regional support with projects. California came off best by renegotiating the forty-
five-year-old agreement that allocated water during shortages. The
"California Guarantee" gives priority to the state's allotment of 4.4 million acre-feet, so that Arizona receives no water until California's full

allotment has been delivered. Since apportionments were based on exaggerated estimates of annual flow, this was an important concession. California also obtained federal funding for an extensive study to look for new sources of water to augment the overextended Colorado River and to make the water allocated to Mexico in the Mexican Water Treaty a "national obligation." This meant that the depleted river required "augmentation" water added from some other source; the cost of providing for Mexico's share would not be charged to the other water users. As part of the bargain, California also insisted on a long-range study of the region's water supply.[9] Wayne Aspinall extracted five water projects for Colorado (costing nearly $400,000,000 in 1968 dollars) as his price. Projects in Utah and New Mexico were also authorized. In all, the act authorized nine projects in four states. Nevada was promised support for the Southern Nevada Supply project.[10]

Although CAP was controversial among regional water interests, and nationally among conservationists, eastern and midwestern legislators, and fiscal conservatives, within Arizona there was tremendous support for the project. So great was the official consensus regarding its virtues that even to question the project was treated locally as treasonous behavior. William Martin and Robert Young, two University of Arizona economists, published an article in 1967 which suggested that rather than build CAP, it would be wiser to rely on groundwater and to redistribute water from agriculture to municipal uses. They were publicly attacked, and their careers suffered for such "treason." Editorials in Tucson's newspaper about their work concluded that the best thing for Tucson and for the state was "a new source of water, and great deal less noise" (Ingram 1990:97, 47; Reisner 1986:309). The only other dissenting voices to the euphoric support of CAP were those of a few conservation groups. Morris Udall, who told these dissenters, "I think you people have done our state a great disservice," entered into the records of the congressional hearings of 1965 an endorsement of CAP made by the Arizona Conservation Council, a coalition of conservation groups that supported the project (Ingram 1990:45). Of course, this strong consensus was a manufactured one, since dissenters

9. This created the interagency Westwide study, the forum that stimulated interest in commensuration among early members of the New Guard.

10. In addition to CAP, the act authorized the Dixie Project and (provisionally) the Uintah unit in Utah; the Dolores Project, Dallas Creek Dam, West Divide, San Miguel, and the Animas-La Plata Project (shared with New Mexico) in Colorado; Hooker Dam in New Mexico. In addition, Arizona threw in some Gila River water for New Mexico. In exchange for his support, Henry Jackson of Washington demanded a moratorium on BR plans for "transbasin diversion": bringing water from the Northwest to the Southwest.

were often excluded or censored. When a small delegation of Yavapai residents paid their own way to Washington to the authorization in hearings in 1968, they were not permitted to testify.[11] It wasn't until 1973, five years after the project was authorized, that the bureau held its first meeting to discuss the project on the Yavapai reservation.

Arizona's longing for CAP overwhelmed the interests of the other states in reaching some accord over regional water development; as a result, Arizona was the only party wholly committed to building the requisite consensus, to creating a bill that would give all involved something that they wanted. The concessions required of Arizona in forging this consensus were controversial and hotly contested within the state. Figure 2, a cartoon that appeared in the local newspaper in 1965, nicely illustrates supporters' frustrations. Prominent CAP supporters worried that, for all their efforts, Arizona was left with less than its due. Some advocated an unrealistic state-built CAP. It was especially bitter to concede priority in water allocations to California, the state's nemesis. New Mexico's rights to Gila River water were also hotly debated. However painful those were, the loss of the Grand Canyon dams to the conservationists hurt worse since, for the first time, outsiders forced the compromise. As vehement as the regional water fights had been, they were between parties that ferociously supported federal water development. These were battles between familiar and legitimate foes, where conflict was over who got the water. The environmentalists had forced CAP supporters to grapple with the demands of the uncommitted, to relinquish two dams. For some of the more astute parties, it was a signal that times were changing. Helen Ingram concludes her analysis of the Colorado River Basin Act: "The Colorado River Basin Act is not a very logical or consistent piece of legislation. It does not establish any overall plan of development; [its] provisions are not complementary, and some of the bargains arrived at, such as the Mexican Water Treaty burden, appear as rather fantastic dodges from confronting basic problems of supply. . . . The really spectacular aspect [of the bill is] the political accomplishment of fitting together so many divergent interests" (1990:65).

The long political and judicial battle to obtain authorization for CAP left an indelible mark on its supporters and on the project. What had

11. Although kept from testifying, they lobbied individual legislators and officials, some of whom did not know that Indians still lived on the reservation; others were shocked to learn that residents were opposed to the project. During the long struggle for CAP authorization, Fort McDowell residents were not informed of the many hearings and never testified at one. Residents did not know that much of the reservation would be destroyed and that most of their homes and the tribal cemetery would be flooded (Khera and Mariella 1982:170–72; Butler 1978:17–19).

Fig. 2. Good to the last drop, *Arizona Republic*, August 29, 1965.

started out as the largest, most extensive water project ever proposed turned into a colossal regional water-development act and the renegotiation of decades-old water rights and water policy. As one engineer told me: "In order to buy the farm, we had to buy the whole goddamn surrounding city." CAP had been the preeminent political issue in the state for decades. Long-time supporters and many residents felt they were entitled to CAP. After years of bitterly watching other states develop and appropriate the Colorado River, they believed their efforts, the repeated failures, their patience, and all their compromising had to be rewarded. Like Carl Hayden, a number had spent whole careers supporting the project, and its authorization was personal and professional vindication. To them, CAP was more than just a water project: It was political affirmation and payback for all the yes votes on all the other projects. And through it all, members of the Old Guard had helped write the speeches, inform the editorials, generate the numbers, and prepare the charts and graphs.

There was great celebrating in Arizona when CAP was authorized. A grand dinner was held for all the long-term supporters, replete with toasts, speeches, and backslapping. Local papers entertained readers with tales of the behind-the-scenes political struggles that authorization required, and credit was lavishly heaped upon supporters. Authorization proved to be less a conclusion than a beginning of new political and legal battles. It took a while, but the exhilaration of authorization gradually subsided as attention shifted to more mundane concerns. Ever since the 1947 report, the official status of CAP within the bureau was that of a "Preliminary Planning Study." Following its authorization, CAP was now reclassified as an "Advanced Planning and Engineering Study." During this phase, the incomplete analysis of earlier investigations would be fine-tuned, and serious design studies would commence. Since this level of investigation would require more funding than provided in the Colorado River Basin Act, the Arizona congressional delegation, headed by John Rhodes after Hayden retired, was immediately charged with securing the funding.

New Decisions and Old Alternatives: The Changing Role of Orme Dam

During the next eight years, two events profoundly affected the future of CAP. The first was NEPA's passage in 1969. The project was authorized before NEPA, so CAP supporters thought it should be exempted from EIS requirements, but courts were ruling elsewhere that exemptions required legislation. The last thing supporters wanted was to provide Congress with a new chance to debate CAP, so members of the Arizona Project Office, CAP headquarters, reluctantly commenced writing an EIS. The inclusion of CAP on President Carter's water project "hit list" in 1977 was the second fateful event.

One of bureaucracies' most effective, least appreciated weapons is its tedious technical reports. Like frigid February elections in Chicago, these fat volumes dissuade all but the most faithful. Yet for partisans and scholars alike, careful scrutiny of bureaucratic documents is a necessary, and often rewarding, exercise. Since securing CAP was such a prolonged process, the supporting documents shows how BR policymaking evolved over time, and how the agency responded to broader political and economic shifts. The documents generated by Orme Dam provide a useful vantage point from which to compare the effects of NEPA and the influence of the New Guard.[12] BR documents figured prominently in the politics surrounding Orme. Along with testimony at congressional hearings, five BR documents are crucial for understanding the evolution of Orme Dam: the 1947 report on the Central Arizona Project (USBR 1947), the revised "Pacific Southwest Water Plan: Supplemental Information on Central Arizona Project" (USBR 1963), the "Central Arizona Project Final Environmental Statement" (USBR 1972a), the "Draft Environmental Impact Statement, Orme Dam Reservoir, Central Arizona Project, Arizona–New Mexico" (USBR 1976), and the 1981 EIS (USBR 1981b), written during CAWCS.[13]

Spanning nearly thirty-five years, these reports reveal important changes in how the agency made decisions and justified its proposed projects; they also show changing patterns in the information the agency collected, and how this did or did not influence its decisions. The effects of NEPA are especially apparent when comparing older and more recent planning efforts and the three EISs addressing Orme Dam. These comparisons reveal two striking conclusions: the role played by Orme Dam, technically and symbolically, changed dramatically; and however haltingly and half-heartedly the agency's endorsement of it, NEPA changed how the BR made and represented decisions.

Before CAP was authorized, Orme Dam was an uncontroversial and insignificant component. With the controversy over the cost of the Colorado River Basin Act, the Grand Canyon Dams, and regional battles over water flows, Orme was largely ignored in early reports and hearings.[14] Authorization changed all that. Despite Orme's insignificance

12. A detailed analysis of these documents appears in Espeland (1992:160–87). See Dorothy Smith (1982) for a perceptive analysis of documents as constituents of social relations.

13. The social and economic analysis of the Fort McDowell community in the 1976 EIS was based on a study entitled "Socioeconomic Study of the Fort McDowell Indian Reservation and Community with and without the Development of Orme Dam and Reservoir," which was prepared by consultants with the Natelson Corporation (USBR 1976a).

14. Orme was mentioned once during congressional hearings, when James Haley of Florida questioned Secretary of the Interior Stewart Udall about its effects on the Fort McDowell community. Udall explained that "the small but fine little reservoir we are

before authorization, the intensity and duration of the battle for CAP are crucial for explaining for why Orme eventually became so important to so many people.

In the early BR planning studies of CAP, Orme Dam, then named McDowell Dam, played a small and ambiguous role. It had nothing to do with Colorado River water, the main impetus for CAP. Instead, it was tacked on to the project to help store and regulate the flow of water on the Salt and Verde Rivers, the "local" water that would supplement the water brought from the Colorado River. The dam would also provide some incidental flood control. Mainly, Orme was there to fill an empty dam site; its role—how it functioned in relation to all the other features of CAP—was undeveloped.[15] As one engineer described Orme's role at this phase: "The first planning report [1947] on CAP was a 'reconnaissance report' in today's terms. In it they figured out a plan and a rough cost estimate. . . . At that stage, Orme does nothing in relation to the rest of the project; it just augmented water supply. It was just an add-on to the other project. One of the concepts we worked on in the forties was the idea of the continuing damming of the West. This was still a goal, a way of thinking. There were still increments that were undeveloped. We were still filling in the gaps. It wasn't a question of whether or not this was the best element. It was a good dam site that was empty, so you put a dam there."

The 1947 report provided the main documentation for the authorization, and no alternatives to Orme, or any other dam, were considered. Other than its cost, no negative consequences of CAP are mentioned. Anything that may have been construed as negative impacts is described as project benefits, with the logic that had characterized BR planning for years. CAP is justified as essential to "rescuing" an economy on the verge of collapse owing to water depletion. CAP benefits include its boon to agriculture, the economy, and progress generally, the development of new farm land (already privately owned), and its preventing the desert from reclaiming cultivated farmland. As well as the additional power (and revenue) generated, other benefits include flood control, salinity control, silt retention, recreation, fish and wildlife

---

creating . . . would be a tremendous economic benefit to the Indians" (Johnson 1977: 217). John Rhodes later inserted an amendment that gave the tribe priority in developing and operating the recreational facilities.

15. The original Orme was a modest dam with a concrete center and earthen embankment, 126 feet high, with a crest of 4,100 feet, a reservoir holding about one-half million acre-feet of water, and costing about $16 million to build. In contrast, Bridge Canyon Dam would be a concrete arch-gravity dam, 673 feet high, with a crest 1,950 feet, a reservoir containing nearly 2 million acre-feet of water, and costing about $192 million (USBR 1947:R17–R18).

conservation.[16] These benefits, estimated at $80 million, are important since they are deducted from the amount that irrigators have to repay the government. The financial feasibility of irrigation depends heavily on the proportion of cost that can be classified as "nonreimbursable." The loss of river recreation that would occur at eight sites, including two portions of the Colorado River running through the Grand Canyon, is not mentioned. Nor is the loss of riparian habitat or the impending relocation of the Yavapai. Construction cost estimates do not even include the cost of acquiring the reservation land. The only reference made to Indians is that reservations constitute a small portion of land that could receive irrigation.

Such skewed coverage may have reflected a political strategy for a public document or, more benignly, the current information-gathering routines of the agency. Investigators may have been ignorant of some of CPA's adverse effects, but the limited state of environmental or sociological knowledge cannot explain all omissions. People knew that forced relocations would occur and that the recreational benefits of the reservoirs came at the expense of free-flowing streams. Although the report was a preliminary study, the gaps in information are not evenly distributed. Most surprising is that this document remained the primary analysis of CAP throughout its authorization. Its only official revision before authorization is contained in the 1963 "Pacific Southwest Water Plan: Supplemental Information on Central Arizona Project."

Orme Dam, circa 1963

In the 1963 report, CAP is still justified as a "rescue" project, only this time, the doubling of population in the previous ten years makes the need more urgent. Economic development is assumed to be driven by agricultural development: without more irrigated farmland, urban growth (which also reduces irrigated acreage) will be stymied. Not explained is how the population grew so fast despite dire predictions about how water supply would limit economic development. No alternatives to a confluence dam, now named Maxwell Dam, are examined, although the structure has been slightly modified. The dam is still storing unused Colorado River water, regulating flows in the Salt and Verde Rivers, and offering Phoenix some flood control. In the latest bureaucratic jargon, Maxwell Dam now serves a "multipurpose role."

16. Silt retention, usually considered a hazard of dams, is a "benefit" here because the silt accumulated at these dams would lessen the build-up behind Hoover Dam. Similarly, new water would dilute the salt content of existing surface water; although over time the concentration of salts would increase owing to the effects of evaporation.

As in the 1947 report, the only "environmental" consequences acknowledged are either neutral or positive, although a bit more detail is provided. This report states that the habitat of the "agricultural service area" won't be changed but does not address how creating lakes and eliminating rivers affect the habitat. We are also told that the project will enhance lake fisheries and improve recreational opportunities, and that the flood control provided by the project will decrease the destruction of the white-wing dove nesting area. Not addressed is how flooding affects the dove's habitat or the significance of the loss of riparian habitat for other species of birds and animals.[17] On the last page of the report, the Fort McDowell community is mentioned for the first time in conjunction with CAP. Conclusion 12 states that the recreational opportunities from the dam will provide an economic stimulus to Fort McDowell Indians and to the neighboring Salt River Indian Reservation (USBR 1963:67). Again, no mention is made of whose land will be acquired at what cost for any of the proposed dams.

After CAP was authorized, design teams began working on integrating Orme Dam with the aqueducts. Where once the dam's role had been completely marginal to the logic of the project, the elimination of the other dams and the new design had recast Orme as what one hydrologist described as "the regulatory heartbeat" of the project. In his words, "Initially, [Orme's] physical location was its primary attraction. Local interest in Orme centered on the fact that it sat at the confluence of two rivers that flowed through Phoenix, and those rivers had a history of flooding. We thought, if we could interface with CAP, Orme could also conserve and store water while it controlled the local flooding. It would be a multipurpose dam. One of the catchwords of the sixties was 'multipurpose.'"

Orme Dam, circa 1972

The first EIS written on the entire Central Arizona Project was released in draft form in 1971 and in final form in 1972. Bureau officials had vainly hoped that NEPA would not change much. As one manager put it: "So many laws and regulations had been passed and ignored it was hard to figure out why this one should be any different. How were we supposed to know that this law would matter? That it would be any different from all the other laws they keep passing?" The 1972 EIS was one of the first major environmental statements ever written by the BR,

17. This "benefit" is suspect, since the dam would destroy the trees where the birds nest. The logic of the report seems to be that the occasional flooding of rivers harms birds, but the permanent inundation of their breeding site would not.

and certainly the first EIS the bureau (or any other agency for that matter) had written for such a large, complicated project. This EIS was intended to be a general investigation of the entire project, with more detailed studies to be conducted later for the specific project components.[18]

The draft EIS still justifies CAP as essential to sustaining Arizona's growth and development.[19] Fewer than four pages of the draft EIS are devoted to considering alternatives to this billion-plus dollar project, and the already eliminated Grand Canyon dams receive the most attention. The 1972 draft EIS was roundly criticized for failing to consider alternatives to CAP, so the Final EIS includes, in addition to these rejected alternatives, several dramatic new ones: manipulating the weather through cloud seeding (e.g., "Project Skywater"—see USBR 1972b), desalting ocean water, managing the watershed, which involves eliminating forests and replacing existing vegetation to enhance runoff, diverting water from the Northwest (which could not be pursued until 1978), and conserving irrigation water. Not surprisingly, these are all rejected as reasonable alternatives to CAP.

The requisite "no-action" alternative that assumes that CAP is not built is mainly a restatement of project benefits forgone. The most damning phrase was that without CAP, California would continue to use Arizona's water (USBR 1972a:198). The adverse impacts that would be avoided, including the forced relocation of the Yavapai community, are not discussed. The loss of important archaeological sites and river recreation are framed as beneficial in the BR's partisan logic: the impending inundation of archaeological sites will prompt excavation that might otherwise not occur. Hence, without CAP, "archaeological knowledge would suffer (197–98)." The EIS also fails to note that the river presents unique recreational opportunities in the area, whereas there are numerous man-made lakes in the area; also ignored is that

18. The difference between the draft and final versions suggests how comments and criticisms were addressed. NEPA required the bureau to solicit written feedback from people concerned with the proposed policy, to make that feedback public, and to provide a written response to it. The final EIS describes how the BR dealt with comments and includes a subset of comments and the BR's response. About 270 copies of the draft EIS were sent to other agencies, interest groups, and anyone who wanted one. The decision not to hold public meetings on the draft was defended by the number of copies sent out.

19. The "rescue" language is toned down in the final version, perhaps at the urgings of Rich Johnson, president of the Central Arizona Project Association, the private CAP lobby since 1946. Johnson writes that while he believes Arizona's economic growth would be "severely hampered" without CAP, as the EIS states: "I doubt the wisdom of making the flat, unqualified statement. We have been saying it for the last 30 years while our total economy continued to grow phenomenally" (USBR 1976:App. C, p. 72).

the normal fluctuation of the reservoir would create a lake surrounded by some fifty yards of mud flats during hot summer months. The Arizona Outdoor Recreation Commission reports that "this fluctuation . . . will have a tremendous influence on the design of recreation facilities and the use of such facilities" (App. C, p. 65).[20]

Both the draft and the final versions give a more detailed analysis of the design and the operation of the confluence dam, now called Orme Dam. This bigger, modified dam now plays a fundamentally different role than it did in earlier studies: Orme Dam and Reservoir are now integrated with both the existing Salt River Project water system and the Granite Reef Aqueduct, which moves water from the Colorado River to Phoenix. The reservoir acts as a sort of switching station/holding tank for water being diverted from and to different systems. It would also store Colorado River water during periods of low demand.

In the draft statement, no mention is made of Fort McDowell Reservation and the impending relocation. Almost as astonishing is the tepid response of the Bureau of Indian Affairs: "The effect of Orme Dam and Reservoir on the Fort McDowell Indian Reservation is one that should be mentioned. . . . Although the authority is granted in the legislation to obtain additional lands to replace those taken for the project and relocate those Indians living within the taking [*sic*] area, nevertheless the dislocation of these people from their ancestral homes and lands, as well as the destruction of this beautiful area, is in [*sic*] adverse result of the project" (App. C, p. 23). The Native American Defense Fund (NADF) and the Sierra Club are more forceful on the forced relocation on the Yavapai.[21]

Responding to these criticisms, and those from some of the recently hired New Guard, the final EIS briefly mentions that relocations would occur on the "mostly undeveloped" reservation. This is the first time the BR acknowledges that Orme Dam will harm the Fort McDowell Indian community by acquiring 14,000 acres and relocating fifty-three

---

20. Other examples of losses-as-benefits abound. The EIS claims that damming the river will improve the remaining riparian habitat. The Fish and Wildlife Service replied (p. 39) that "the replacement and preservation of fish and wildlife resources destroyed by the project cannot be claimed as a benefit" and replacing the species made extinct or threatened by the project with other species cannot be construed as beneficial. The EIS language is also noteworthy. Changes in habitat that are likely to obliterate species are environmental "alterations" or "displacements of species." "Benefits," an extremely malleable category, are highlighted and "costs" are often labeled "changes."

21. The NADF calls the EIS "totally inadequate" (App. C, p. 146), and the Sierra Club describes it as "replete with statements which are obviously subjective and not justified by data" (App. C, p. 121).

families. The report still claims that Orme will benefit the reservation economically and will bolster the "general welfare" of both the Fort McDowell and the adjacent Salt River Indian communities. The EIS report hedges on the cultural consequences of the dam, saying they are "not fully known." While acknowledging that "intangible cultural disruptions may never be mitigated," it portrays Orme's effect as adding to the influences of the expanding non-Indian development (136–37).[22]

The final 1972 EIS is a revealing document, though clearly not one that genuinely informs a decision. Critics' depiction of it as an elaborate justification for CAP seems warranted.[23] As I was emphatically told by members of the Old Guard, the whole task of preparing an EIS was a new, uncertain venture for bureaucrats given virtually no guidance from Congress, the CEQ, or courts. Writing an EIS required information that the BR did not have or could not obtain from their current staff. Nonetheless, internal memos and participants' reports show that most participants considered the EIS a legal hoop to jump through, a document that must withstand the attacks of the agency's new nemesis, environmentalists.[24] While the revisions made in the final report do include information about social and environmental impacts not mentioned in the draft, these are either stated so vaguely, or given such cursory treatment, or framed as beneficial, so that the final EIS remains

22. Another section concludes vaguely that constructing the dam will modify the "culture of the Fort McDowell Indian community. . . . The Indians' mode and standard of living will be changed and their burial ground will be inundated by the reservoir. These changes will have a long-term effect on the Indian community, especially as related to the cultural significance of the burial grounds. Memorialization or relocation of the burial ground may offset some of this long-term loss" (p. 180). The idea of relocating the cemetery or "memorializing" it, which elsewhere meant building an island in the reservoir where the cemetery once stood and putting a fence around it, was repugnant to residents, confirming that they were not consulted about this conclusion.

23. The Environmental Protection Agency concludes: "The final statement should overcome the draft's reticence to discuss the unavoidable adverse environmental effects of the project. . . . This draft is phrased as a justification for a project into which much money and planning have been devoted" (App. C, p. 13). The Bureau of Land Management reviewers conclude that "the prospective adverse impacts will be much greater than those described in the draft statement" (App. C, p. 24).

24. The comments of sympathizers who wish to make the EIS hard to challenge support this. For example, F. J. MacDonald, long-time CAP supporter and chairman of the Central Arizona Project Environmental Advisory Group, which the BR appointed to advise the agency on the EIS: "It has been my painful experience that each environmental impact hearing is a 'whole new ballgame.' As the statements are improved, the critics get more active in finding imagined or real problems (especially since there is no point at which they would say, 'O.K., go ahead . . . we approve.') . . . There should be no gambling with the environmental impact statement, since this is one sure way it can be delayed . . . interminably" (App. C, p. 51).

more a robust defense than an objective analysis of CAP.[25] In the language of the courts, "good faith" was lacking.

Orme, circa 1976

The 1976 EIS (USBR 1976b) was an important document, both for the changes it embodied and for its consequences. Devoted solely to Orme Dam, it was intended as the beginning of a series of EISs on the major features of CAP. It was the agency's first attempt to integrate EIS preparation with agency planning procedures, and the first investigation of the effects of Orme on the Fort McDowell reservation. The Orme EIS was what one manager called "two documents in one: it was an advanced planning document and an EIS. Normally an advanced planning document would be a report on where to begin the EIS process. It would look at engineering, cost estimates, and set forth the best plan. Then the EIS would come in and evaluate the environmental aspects from an environmental perspective. The EIS brings in a whole bunch of things normally planning documents don't. The social and economic and bugs and bunnies aspects; now its expanded to bring in cultural and historical types of impacts; This stuff was not included in advanced planning at that time." This EIS also became the forum for organizing and expressing opposition to the dam.

During the 1970s, Arizona's population was growing quickly and its economy was thriving, so mitigating declining ground-water supply, assuring long-range supply, and additional flood control were again featured project objectives. In this EIS, Orme's role is largely unchanged. The same alternatives are discussed, with little new information about them. The objectives of CAP have not changed, although Phoenix's expanding population makes the project benefits more valuable. The document's tone is still partisan, especially its general conclusions, but there is less reticence in identifying adverse impacts. These are now framed as being offset by Orme's greater benefits.

A small consulting firm was hired to assess Orme's consequences for the Yavapai community. On the basis of a survey of residents, this investigation concludes that although reservation residents strongly

25. One striking difference between the draft and final versions is the inclusion of useful biological inventories of the project areas. This is clearly a response to critics who complained that the draft contained no detailed information about the environment in the project area. Compiled by consultants, most inventories were relegated to appendices, with no attempt to integrate this information with the rest of the report. Project impacts on the inventoried wildlife and vegetation are not specified. This is the first time this kind of information is included in the bureau's planning documents even if it is not yet meaningfully incorporated. Public input was limited, but it did force the BR to include new information that would later prove useful to those opposing the project.

value their land, having survived several forced relocations in the past, they are likely to survive another. The report highlights the economic gains associated with the developing recreation on the reservoir as a much-needed source of jobs and revenue. These conclusions angered Yavapai residents and their supporters, reinforcing their doubts that the government could conduct a credible study.

The "PR" Problem in Phoenix: On Underestimating Opponents

The occasion sounds innocuous, even boring: the release of the draft 1976 Environmental Impact Statement on Orme Dam. The meeting in Phoenix was supposed to be a forum for presenting the BR's findings and soliciting the public's views on the project and its consequences. The BR had learned from experience that failing to hold them spurred critics and angered judges, who were beginning to scrutinize NEPA's public participation requirements. Public involvement was still a novel idea within the agency, and the guidelines for how to do it were minimal and evolving. This was the first time that the agency had actually constructed a "plan" for how to coordinate public input. Before this, as one manager told me, "We were just bootstrapping." And the BR's first public meeting proved to be a memorable one.

The BR had expected four or five hundred people, more than usual for a typical public meeting. When thousands showed up (one man estimated 5,000), there was no place to put them. There were more people outside than in, as busloads kept arriving at the Phoenix Civic Center. The seasoned and savvy supporters of CAP, used to the usual CAP celebrations for which Arizonans were noted, were completely unprepared for strong, local opposition. And their opponents, residents of Fort McDowell and their supporters, various environmental groups, and those who thought CAP was a waste of tax money, were clearly well-organized. Instead of the routine public meeting they had prepared for, it had become a political rally, a media event, or, in their words, "a bad dream," "a riot," a "PR nightmare." They had lost control.

According to one senior engineer, about 500 people spoke during the two-day hearings, with comparable numbers of supporters and opponents. The supporters—local politicians, Chamber of Commerce people, representatives of water-users associations, lobbyists, bankers, and farmers—spoke passionately of the impending water crisis, the virtues of development, the devastation of floods. Only this time, they were booed. Members of the Yavapai community and their supporters came, as did representatives of the Audubon Society and other environmental groups. Some wore swimming trunks and inner tubes to protest the destruction of Arizona's favorite site for tubing. As opponents explained why Orme Dam was destructive, unnecessary, and unfair, they were cheered.

Some twenty years later, the details are still vivid for members of the Old Guard, as decades-old arguments are rebutted with the fluency that comes from years of private rehearsals after the performance is over. Their explanations go a long way toward explaining why they had underestimated their opponents so badly. "It was great television," one high-ranking BR engineer remembers: "In terms of sheer numbers it was 50/50, pro and con . . . several million people were represented by mayors and the governor. . . . No one cared about that . . . on TV, nobody cared about the tribal representation who agreed with the plan. What the cameras cared about was the seventy-year-old toothless Indian who cried on cue . . . the grandmother who didn't want her ancestral land flooded. Cameras always focused on the emotional. Those who saw TV and weren't at the hearing, would come away with the sense of the emotional nature of it, not of the issues." Like a lot of Old Guard members, this man believed that the Yavapai community had mostly supported Orme Dam, enticed by the money and the economic benefits that would attend the dam. Orme may not be a "total answer to all their problems on the reservation" but would solve "at least 90 percent of them." This was the account of the Yavapai's position that project managers had given to superiors and politicians for years. Clearly the politically expedient view, it was perhaps easier to sustain this account in light of the agency's lack of interest in either providing the tribe with information about their plans or learning the residents' views on the proposed dam. Nevertheless, it meant ignoring a lot of contradictory evidence, including a telegram sent to the secretary of the interior by tribal members and the results of a poll taken among adult residents that showed 144 people opposed to the dam, 8 undecided, and 1 in favor.[26]

In providing incontrovertible evidence that many reservation residents opposed the dam, evidence that was impossible to ignore, this meeting forced members of the Old Guard to generate new accounts of the Yavapai's position. In explaining what became defined as sudden change of view, the senior engineer just mentioned blames the environmentalists: "Environmental interests infiltrated the Fort McDowells" and had "orchestrated and used the Indians very effectively . . . [to forge] a cohesive opposition group to Orme." In this man's view,

26. The bias of the state's two largest newspapers made it hard for residents to publicize their views. Both papers, owned by the same family, were ardent Orme supporters, and both failed to report the results of the tribe's poll, refused to print letters to the editor sent by residents, ran editorials that misrepresented the tribe's position and history, and minimized opposition to the dam.

"There were two serious and significant camps with the tribe: pro- and anti-Orme. The ones who came to public meetings, that cried on cue, were anti-Orme." (He did not explain why Orme supporters all stayed home that day.) Before this "infiltration," he described the tribe as working cooperatively with the agency through "legal representation"; once "infiltrated," reservation politics changed dramatically, and a new tribal chairman who vehemently opposed Orme was elected. That's when, according to this man, "the whole attitude of the Fort McDowells was starting to swing dramatically to anti-Orme instead of cautiously pro-Orme." He also dates this election as the beginning of what he describes as the political maturation of the community. In his words: "This was their political puberty. Suddenly they were less like children wholly dependent on us and on the secretary to make all the decisions for them. They were striving to make their own decisions for their own future for the first time. Prior to the mid-seventies, they were very childlike in the political process. They were incapable of making decision. All they would say was 'What's the right thing for us to do, Mr. Secretary?' Orme Dam became a rallying point for their political education." The Orme controversy clearly mobilized residents and honed such political skills as public speaking, lobbying, and managing media. This man's portrayal of residents as childlike dependents demonstrates both his ignorance of the reservation community and the potency of race as a political frame.[27]

This unanticipatedly disastrous public meeting (and the 20,000 separate comments that groups and individuals sent in response to the draft EIS) unsettled members of the Old Guard, such that they called in people from the Engineering and Research Center in Denver, the commissioner's office in Washington, the regional director's office in Boulder, and the local project office to assess the damage and decide how to proceed. The Old Guard's faith in the superiority and inviolability of Orme was not shaken, but new strategies seemed warranted. Mark, a senior engineer, recalls:

> After the Orme hearing, we regathered the troops . . . and said:
> 'We now have significant local opposition. How do we proceed?'
> We had to design a process from draft through final EIS that leaves

27. Racism was not unusual among some CAP supporters who wished to minimize Yavapai claims, but it was rarely this explicit. More often, it was expressed as bewilderment at the Yavapai's position [which may be, but isn't necessarily, racist]. Many supporters were unwilling to accept that Indians could know and articulate their own interests. Indians as pawns of environmentalists, as misguided innocents led astray by radicals, is perhaps, in their view, a charitable interpretation, since their shortsightedness can be blamed on the unsavory influence of outsiders. Peter, another BR manager, reported that after the EIS meeting, he told the tribal chairman, "Well, Chief, I hope you enjoy your poverty."

us in the position of being legally sufficient. After those public hearings we still all believed . . . that we were socially and environmentally correct on Orme from an agency perspective. We thought all we've got to do is tighten up the legal perspective. The agency-preferred alternative is still going to be Orme Dam. This was the consensus within Reclamation. We had to be legally tight . . . which means doing things by the book, no shortcuts. We had to comply with NEPA and with the agency rules and regs available at that time which controlled planning. The key was, no suits from the opposition on procedural matters. That was the modus operandi of environmental groups at that time.

The public hearing on the EIS was a turning point in the Orme controversy. The Old Guard's inexperience with public involvement was partly to blame for the fiasco that ensued, but the result also implicates their organizational ethos. Members of the Old Guard could not imagine that their comfortable assumptions about the world would generate such dissent. The Old Guard's insularity, a function of their power, their organizational ideology, and the prodevelopment water elite they had helped to cultivate, an elite who dominated local politics and shared their views, had been punctured by the public participation requirements of NEPA. Members now realized that there was no longer a consensus over Orme Dam. They now knew, for the first time, that they faced serious, organized opposition. Although their faith in Orme was not swayed, this meeting convinced them they had a "big PR problem," and they concluded that what was needed was a procedurally impeccable EIS, one capable of withstanding the attacks of their now mobilized opponents.

Carter's Hit List: The Death and Resurrection of Orme Dam

The PR problem became a political crisis a few months later, when the newly elected Jimmy Carter placed the CAP on his "hit list" of nineteen water projects to be deleted from the federal budget. Carter's announcement precipitated a mad scramble to save CAP. An interagency task force was created to reanalyze the feasibility of CAP in light of the tougher criteria Carter now advocated. A deal was made, based on the recommendation of this task force and compromises negotiated by the congressional delegation, to preserve CAP but to eliminate three of its dams, including Orme Dam.[28] Congress approved the compromise provided no funds would be spent on the deleted dams. The

28. In eliminating Orme, the White House cited the money saved, its effects on the Yavapai, and its harmful environmental effects (Office of the White House Press Secretary. "The White House Statement on Water Projects," April 16, 1977). One of the first "casualties" of Carter's list was the "Orme Division" of the Arizona Projects Office, which

regional director issued a controversial memo stating that no further efforts would be expended on Orme Dam or any confluence dam.[29]

For several months, Orme was a "dead issue," officially at least. Since Orme now played an important role in regulating CAP water, Orme's untimely demise was unacceptable to members of the Old Guard and to the Arizona congressional delegation.[30] Suddenly, the deleted confluence dam was referred to as the "high" Orme Dam in an effort to leave open the possibility for a redesigned, "lower" Orme Dam, and suddenly NEPA seemed a useful law. The regulatory storage and flood control that "High Orme" would provide were still needed, and could be provided by alternatives to High Orme, including different versions of a confluence dam. NEPA required that alternatives be assessed. Surely, Congress had not intended in deleting funding for Orme that the agency fail to comply with NEPA? Andrus, Bevil, and Stennis sent back word that neither Congress nor Interior would block the studies of alternatives to Orme. The regional director rescinded his order suspending all work on Orme Dam, and Orme Dam, or at least a close cousin, was resuscitated.

NEPA and the invention of High Orme allowed the agency to launch a new investigation and a write new EIS to replace the now-rescinded 1976 EIS. Worried that its reputation had been damaged as a result of the 1976 EIS, the agency believed that restoring Orme's legitimacy depended on its capacity to conduct a more credible investigation. Now that organized opposition to Orme had become an organizational "fact," the commissioner conceded that, however expensive, scrupulous evaluations were worth the investment. It was time to bring in new people, launch a new study, and be meticulous in compliance. And so in 1978 CAWCS began to take shape.

Retrenchment through CAWCS

"Do you want to know why I came West?" Chuck asks me politely, not sure what I want from him but eager to tell me the story. "It was

---

was quickly renamed the "Regulatory Storage Division" (Memorandum from the Lower Colorado Regional Director to the Chief of Planning Coordination, June 9, 1977).

29. Senate Report 95-301:85; House Report 95-379:92; Memorandum from Manuel Lopez, Jr., Regional Director, Lower Colorado Division, to Projects Manager, Arizona Projects Office, September 30, 1977.

30. Letter from Sen. Dennis DeConcini to John C. Stennis, Chairman, Subcommittee on Public Works, U.S. Senate, October 31, 1977; reply dated December 15, 1977; letter from Morris Udall, Chairman, House Committee on Interior and Insular Affairs, to Cecil D. Andrus, Secretary, Department of the Interior, November 14, 1977; February 7, 1978; see also letter to Keith Higginson, Commissioner, Bureau of Reclamation, from Sen. John C. Stennis, December 15, 1977.

Jimmy Carter. Jimmy Carter was elected president, and he had no appreciation for the West and its water needs and the ongoing work of reclamation. He's the reason I came West." Carter's hit list confirmed for Chuck his ignorance of water matters and his antagonism to the BR. It became personal for Chuck when Carter's staff occupied his office. These "so-called conservationists who believed every dam was bad, that no good comes from a dam" spent eight or nine months poring over projects, scrutinizing budgets, recalculating the numbers, all at close quarters. It was too much for Chuck to bear, and he began looking for a BR job that would get him out of Washington and away from those people, back in the construction business, his first love. He knew about CAP, knew it was a huge, important project, and he figured it would actually get completed. So Chuck moved to Arizona. One of his main responsibilities was to oversee the Central Arizona Water Control Study. It was his last job with the bureau, the job he retired from.

Members of the Old Guard were not involved in designing CAWCS. Several prominent members retired before it was completed. Others, like Chuck, had formal responsible for CAWCS, but the day-to-day management was left to others. For members of the Old Guard, CAWCS was an expensive vindication of Orme Dam, made necessary by environmentalists and Jimmy Carter. At this point, members of the Old Guard lost control of the EIS process and of the underlying decision framework to members of the New Guard. This proved to be a turning point in the balance of power within the agency, but the Old Guard did not understand this for some time.

The Old Guard's complacency attests to the power of agency ideology. Members were confident of their ability to get what they wanted, regardless of the framework used. Partly, this was a function of their power; they were so used to accomplishing their goals, it never occurred to them that marginal employees could jeopardize their interests. The imposition of a new framework and the use of new decision technologies seemed more inconvenient than threatening. They neither understood nor believed in the decision procedures that were being proposed, and consequently had no faith in their legitimacy or autonomy. Nor did they have much faith in the autonomy of the law which prompted these innovations. NEPA, at first ignored, became more bothersome than they first imagined. But it had also proven useful too, in resurrecting Orme, and these engineers started to think that the law could render them even more impervious to environmentalists. If they complied with the law, if they paid attention to the concerns of environmentalists, what recourse would opponents have when Orme Dam was vindicated?

Their experience told them that even when laws changed or planning procedures were revised, the dams they wanted would be built. In the past, their procedures always supported the results they wanted. As the early Orme documents attest, there were times when the agency came close to cooking the numbers, but often bias was subtler and less strategic than that. Within the worldview of participants, they were not systematically excluding damning information, or inflating benefits, or minimizing costs; they were making sound decisions on the basis of the kinds of information they possessed or routinely collected. And making sound decisions hinged on deciding where and what kind of dam to build. The engineering ethos informing their planning was so taken-for-granted, so deeply implicated in how they understood their jobs, it prevented them from even noticing what others would see as blatant bias. Their well-honed engineering sensibilities made nonstructural solutions, or nontechnical (design) issues irrelevant. And they could not imagine that nonengineering criteria might ever supersede good engineering.

Most important, however, in explaining the Old Guard's lack of concern about the impending changes was their faith in Orme's superiority. Orme Dam was a beautiful engineering solution to an engineering problem. Confluence dams are always more efficient than dams at other sites, since one dam, in controlling and regulating water from multiple rivers, could do the job of several. It was a technically superior structure located in an ideal dam site. In all this, it turns out, the Old Guard had badly miscalculated. Three different participants, all engineers, described the prevailing view during this period:

> We knew we'd get sued [by environmentalists], and we knew that EIS would be picked over, poked at, and scrutinized like nobody's business. We were still hearing about the last one. No one wanted to jeopardize CAP, but nobody was betting on anything but Orme. The idea was that we just had to provide irrefutable documentation on Orme and why it was the only thing that made sense. Nobody thought they'd come up with something else altogether. Nobody. We thought if you looked carefully at the only feasible alternatives, you'd have to build Orme. Guess we were wrong! [laughing]

> I never would have bet a plugged nickel that we would back away from Orme Dam. Even a few months before [the decision], I was sure it would be Orme.

> I guess I didn't think the bureau would ever cave in to public pressure [on Orme Dam], but then they hadn't seen pressure like that before.

Contrary to the predictions and expectations of the Old Guard, CAWCS turned out to be more than an affirmation of Orme. The design and evaluation of new alternatives, including nonstructural ones (read, no dams), were taken seriously. The negative consequences of the proposed dams were treated extensively, including the effects of the project on the Yavapai reservation. The information excluded from the analysis was less the result of partisan politics than of how hard or easy it was for it to be incorporated into their new procedures. An extensive, expensive, and effective public involvement program was an integral part of the investigation. The role of Orme was modified in the final stage of the investigation. Now referred to as a confluence structure, there were three versions included among the eight alternatives which varied by size, cost, and the amount of "space" dedicated to flood control and water regulation.[31] The investigation, despite occasional pressure to cast impacts in the best possible light, was a fair and honest attempt to understand, devise, and evaluate a set of alternatives. Compared with the earlier analysis, the CAWCS investigation was far less biased and much more accessible to the public. What was nonnegotiable for participants about the study was its framework and the goals that the alternatives were designed to accomplish.

The Symbolic Significance of Orme Dam

Just as the technical significance of Orme Dam changed over time, so did its symbolic significance. As the confluence structure evolved from an extra dam at a good site to the dam regulating water on three systems and providing flood control for the entire metropolitan area, Orme became a more potent symbol. For some engineers, Orme became an integral part of CAP and the two became synonymous. Partly, the increasing significance of Orme was simply a function of the engineers' and their supporters' closer identification and greater familiarity with the project. But this added intensity also reflected the long, hard-fought battle over CAP and the accumulated bitterness at having felt taken advantage of by California for so long, at having had to compromise on so many aspects of CAP, and above all, anger at what one engineer described as "losing the dams to the environmentalists." Hav-

31. The name Orme Dam was dropped during CAWCS to emphasize differences (mainly variations in size and cost) between the new confluence structures and earlier iterations. These differences had little effect on environmental and social impacts. Some naively believed that a smaller dam might be more acceptable to opponents, who viewed the name change in conspiratorial terms. One man dubbed the three confluence dams, formally known as "Plan 3, 4, and 5," as Orme, Son-of-Orme, and Orme-in-Drag. I refer to all the confluence structures as Orme Dam, as did most participants.

ing "lost" on Bridge and Marble Canyon Dams, Orme was now even more emblematic of the agency's mission and its legacy, its power, and was, for some, a harbinger of its future. Further losses would signal a dangerous decline in the Old Guard's power and the power of their organization. All this contributed to Orme supporters' strong sense of entitlement.

For Old Guard engineers, the investment in Orme was both professional and deeply personal. Orme Dam was a technologically superior and aesthetically pleasing structure. Part of its aesthetic appeal was its parsimony; one structure that can prevent floods, and store and regulate water from three rivers, is better than three structures for the same thing, even if the cost is comparable. In this regard, their tastes are like those of a mathematician who prefers a simple, elegant equation to a big, cumbersome one. Engineers are not prone to long lectures on the aesthetics of dams, or on any other aspect of their attachment to dams that does not fit easily into a debate on efficiency or performance. They are, however, aware of the plurality of tastes and defend theirs as legitimate as other people's. As one man told me: "Some people think rivers are pretty. So do I. Other people think there's nothing as pretty as a well-tended farm. Well I happen to think that a big, well-designed dam is beautiful. Who's to say who's right? Just because something is useful doesn't mean its not pretty; and just because God didn't make it and we did, doesn't mean it doesn't belong somewhere."

Orme became the new forum for debating (again!) the merits of CAP. But for members of the Old Guard, it also stood for ten, twenty, or even thirty years of people's professional lives. Dams embody not just the values of the profession, one's pride in one's affiliation with the profession but also one's ties to the agency, one's sense of belonging to an organization that knows how to build massive projects and tame rivers. Although they are reluctant to talk about it, there is, I believe, an ambivalence, perhaps even some anxiety, about their status as bureaucrats working for a big federal agency. These engineers know they could make more money in private industry and are sensitive to stereotypes of bureaucrats as pencil pushers with lifetime employment, people whose skills or work ethic was somehow lacking compared with those of people working in the private sector. This ambivalence, coupled with training that emphasizes building something, reinforces the importance of leaving tangible evidence of one's work. For the engineer who still takes his grandchildren to see Glen Canyon, or is willing to spend hours telling a stranger behind-the-scenes stories of dam building and dam politics, the significance of dams does not end with retirement.

While Orme Dam was not the masterpiece that Hoover or Coulee was, it was an "interesting dam," a "good, efficient structure on a terrific site," and one that would have been "fun to build." Unlike Hoover Dam, Orme Dam never became a national symbol of the potential of government or of Yankee ingenuity; it did become, however, an important regional symbol. For the Yavapai, it embodied the callous disregard of their life, home, and culture that has characterized their relations with the federal government and with non-Indians for decades. For environmental groups, Orme Dam symbolized the arrogance and power of a federal agency concerned only with perpetuating itself while dismissing the concerns of people who stand in its way. For the Old Guard, it symbolized their careers, their clout, and their commitment to the values of their profession and their employer. Orme was no longer, in their minds, simply a solution to a problem; the dam had become an end in itself, transformed from an instrumental to substantive value.

One memorable meeting brought many of these contradictions to the surface. Members of the New Guard were eager to conduct a pretest of the procedures they had devised for assessing the public's values about the proposed plans. Among those invited to help test the procedures were some members of the Old Guard. Their perspectives were especially useful since they were generally knowledgeable about the objectives of the project and some of the alternatives but had not played any role in designing the procedures being used. Also, since they included several high-ranking bureau employees, it was also important that they be informed of the proposed procedures. After being walked through the decision format, which included acceding to the stated goals and the factors being used to reflect preferences, this group performed the ranking and weighting task that was designed to determine which alternative maximized their preferences. The results enraged members of the Old Guard, who were, in effect, told that they "preferred" Plan 6, an alternative not including a confluence dam. For bureaucrats who had always derided the "emotionalism" of the Indians and the environmentalists, it was an impressive display of passion. Members of the New Guard were shocked at the response.

Part of the Old Guard's reaction can be explained by a deep ambivalence that some felt about cultivating and involving the public in the details of decisions that had formerly been made exclusively by the agency. The Progressive and professional legacy of the agency was to understand "conservation" as the rational management of natural resources, a task charged to trained experts, to the scientists and engineers who were most capable of designing, building, and managing the requisite technology. Ordinary citizens are not trained to make or understand the technology required to promote the rational use of resources. When the laws changed, requiring public participation in agency decision making, the agency's muffled contempt for public opinion, as well as an unwillingness to relinquish control, accounts for their begrudging response.

Many members of the Old Guard were deeply suspicious of the whole enterprise of formally incorporating public opinion into their planning process: In their view, the public was incapable of under-standing the details of the decision, and they would introduce values that really had no place in the decision. While public opinion had al-ways been crucial for generating the necessary political support, taking the public's values seriously in designing a project was another matter. The result was, according to a senior engineer, too often "paying more to get less." For this man, the real legacy of NEPA is the greater role of the public in agency decision making: "One thing should be clear in all this. The bureau isn't making the decision. The state of Arizona is making the decision. The decisions are really being made by Arizona and its elected officials. We could not, as an agency, commit to these additional costs. Public involvement validates public choice among the alternatives and permits us to spend more money for plans that meet their values. It allows the agency to step back from the decision process and allow others to make the hard choices. That is the real change that emerged from NEPA."

The Old Guard was also suspicious of the new techniques being promulgated. They were being asked to embrace a decision technology they did not understand, one they felt was capable of "hoodwinking us all," one they worried could be manipulated by those who created it. They felt as if they were losing control, that their experience in making decisions would be devalued. As Mark said: "I'm not going to support something just because some damn computer program tells me I should. Why should I trust some program to tell me what I want? Who the hell knows what kind of mumbo-jumbo is programmed into it. I already know what I want. After all, I've been working on this project for eleven years. I hardly think that some computer program that some-body dreamed up can match all my experience." When the rational procedures designed by the New Guard did not vindicate Orme Dam, the Old Guard rejected the validity of the procedure, not the rationality of their alternative. Rather than change their minds about which alter-native to support, they rejected the legitimacy of the procedure.[32]

32. Where members of the Old Guard had formerly been uninterested or agnostic about the new procedures for assessing public values, they became suspicious and even hostile after this experience. Some participants clearly would have liked to abandon the these procedures, although they had little choice but to use them, since they had no alternative procedures to offer.

Members of the Old Guard wanted the dam. They didn't want just better flood control, an improved water supply, or more lakes. Orme Dam had become, for many members of the Old Guard, an incommensurable value and as such could not be accommodated within the New Guard's rational choice frameworks. As one engineer told me:

> Asking me to back off [Orme] was asking me to say that I no longer believed in what I had been working on for the past twelve years. It's not easy to all of a sudden convince yourself that you've been wrong for so goddamn long. I know I was supposed to be a good soldier and sound real happy that a compromise had worked out. I guess I am happy that the project was still going to go forward and that something will get built; so if my choice is nothing or this [new] plan, I'd pick the plan. But you have to understand that I have been making speeches about that dam for years now, both in public and private. I'm still convinced it was the best solution, and it's hard to sound real excited about something you ultimately think is a mistake. I still believe that those Indians would have been better off with the money and the lake, and that Phoenix and the taxpayers would have been better off with Orme Dam.

Bob is more ambivalent in his interpretation of events. An engineer who had worked on aspects of CAP for nearly fifteen years by the time the study was concluded, he is happy that a workable alternative emerged and that the Central Arizona Project remains intact. He is even proud that the agency could, by means of CAWCS, forge a political consensus. But he still believes that Orme was the best solution. It was only because opponents were able to generate enough political controversy that Orme had to be abandoned. He was not ultimately swayed by any of their "emotional" arguments:

> The reasons why Orme got defeated were emotional, not factual. I hold that very dear. Orme Dam was still the best answer when *all* the factors were weighted . . . from an economic, social, and efficiency point of view, Orme's the best. The social evaluation said the Indians would be devastated by Orme. I don't believe it. It's hard to assess these things, with people coming on the reservation and creating the issue. The Fort McDowells would have been very happy to have that lakefront property with all the recreation as its future economic base . . . they're still struggling today with how to provide work for its members. . . . I wouldn't say that it's sad Orme didn't get built. From a CAP perspective, we got a workable alternative. The cost was horrendous to the taxpayers. . . . We have to do things at four or five places we could have done more effectively at one. That's the political reality. Any time you get into po-

litical controversy that means dollars. You can buy your way out
of politics.

One engineer, whose career spanned over forty years with the agency,
spent about thirty of those years working on some aspect of the Central
Arizona Project. In his words, "I lived CAP. I knew every nut and bolt
of that project. . . . I attended every hearing on that project. I always
had a great faith in the project." As he assessed the outcome, he was
alternately ambivalent and bitter. He is happy that Arizona is finally
assured of the delivery of Colorado River water, but is critical of the
process and the outcome: "All five [of the original] dams are out of the
project. . . . If the 1947 report had been authorized then, the cost of
CAP water would have been $4.30 an acre; now it's $100 an acre. With
all the delay and fooling around, and the environmental act [NEPA],
it cost us all the dams that were generating the power and the money.
Now the Sierra Club is fighting the steam plants it once supported. . . .
Nothing earns more money than a hydro dam. Water comes in and
falls down and runs through a generator, generating no smoke, no
nothing. But [laughing] I guess that's progress, to spend more to get
less."

It was not just engineers who became invested in Orme Dam. Supporters outside the agency became deeply invested in the structure,
both personally and politically, and this prevented some from backing
an alternative that they were assured would provide them with all the
benefits and fewer of the costs of Orme Dam. For those who understood local water politics, the day that Wesley Steiner, head of the State
Department of Water Resources and Governor Bruce Babbitt's closest
advisor on water policy, who was known locally as Arizona's "water
czar" and a long-time, ardent CAP supporter, publicly endorsed Plan
6 over Orme Dam as a way to solve the area's water problems was a
turning point in the controversy. Steiner's endorsement signaled that
the state water establishment had publicly backed away from Orme
Dam. Many insiders read this as the beginning of the end of Orme
Dam; members of the Old Guard and their allies read this as betrayal.
For example, Howard Pyle, a former governor of Arizona who was
himself a long-time and ardent supporter of CAP, wrote in a local
newspaper column entitled "Orme Dam: Surrender Is Sorry Chapter
in Long Fight":

> [Steiner's] shocking capitulation and explanation did little to build
> confidence among those of us who just don't believe in the surren-
> der involved. . . . Although I have tried to be, I am not persuaded
> by those who are trying to comfort us . . . under the banner of Plan
> 6. . . . [It] will be well to remember that we can no longer rely

on the Congressional clout of our venerable former Senator, the Honorable Carl Hayden. To this man more than to any other single person we owe the fact that the Central Arizona Project was authorized along with Orme Dam. It will be a sorry tribute to this great man in the history of Arizona's long and embattled fight for every drop of water to which the state is entitled if we allow ourselves to be "dickered" out of any part of what he worked so hard to gain for us. In his memory I suggest we remember the millions of acre feet of priceless water we lost forever in the last floods that paralyzed our river crossings. What a difference Orme Dam could have made. (*Tempe Daily News,* Oct. 7, 1981)

The passion surrounding Orme Dam is also stirred by the symbolic significance of water. Water, like the dams that hold it, have a special symbolic significance for members of the Old Guard. It is not something they talk about much, but those who know them well attest to their deep feelings about water. Wasting water, which includes letting rivers run unregulated and having to release floodwater, is reprehensible. A young economist working for the BR says that "water has a mystic quality to [the Old Guard]. It's life. It's not a commodity. Now, they can't express this, but if you work around them long enough, you pick it up. Water is the basis of life. It's unconscious, [but] its a rock-bottom value."

Incommensurable Dams: Emblems of Identity

The Old Guard's discomfort with the Orme alternative, which appeared to meet all the objectives of the project, objectives which they helped to define and articulate, was irrational if rationality is defined as consistency. But a conception of the self which overemphasizes cognitive consistency misses much about how people become invested in their actions and how they make them meaningful. Bernard Williams's criticism of utilitarianism is helpful in explaining why some members of the Old Guard reacted as they did. He asks, What type of actor is required in the utilitarian model of action? Williams describes a situation where someone, after taking into account his and others' interests, reaches a conclusion about which outcome will maximize the desired outcomes. But then, Williams asks, What if that action conflicts with (or in the case of the Old Guard, repudiates) a person's own projects that are central to his or her life? As Williams writes:

> The point is not, as utilitarians may hasten to add, that if the project or attitude is that central to his life, then to abandon it would be very disagreeable to him and a great loss of utility will be involved. . . . Once he is prepared to look at it like that, the serious argument

is over anyway. The point is that he is identified with his actions as flowing from projects and attitudes which in some cases he takes seriously at the deepest level, as what his life is about. . . . It is absurd to demand of such a man, when the sums come in from the utility network . . . that he should just step aside from his own project and decision and acknowledge the decision which utilitarian calculation requires. It is to alienate him in a real sense from his actions and his own convictions. It is to make him into a channel between the input of everyone's projects, including his own, and an output of optimific decision; but this is to neglect the extent to which his actions and his decision have to be seen as the actions and decisions which flow from the projects and attitudes with which he is most closely identified. It is thus in the most literal sense an attack on his integrity. (Smart and Williams 1973:116–17)

People are not simply invested in abstract goals or "states of the world," Williams argues; they are invested in projects and action, and in outcomes, sometimes ones they create themselves. For the Old Guard, who had invested years of their lives and a good chunk of their "selves" in Orme Dam, asking them to abandon the project in favor of an alternative that better captured their preferences was like asking them, in effect, to abandon their integrity.

Engineers perhaps feel this more keenly than most people. A common complaint among BR engineers today is that they never get anything built anymore. Many engineers told me that the reason that they chose their profession was their desire to see the tangible results of their work, to be able to point to some structure and say, "I helped build that." There is an underlying sentiment in such expressions that if nothing you have worked on gets built, you have missed an essential part of your professional experience: you have worked in vain. Deciding not to build something (however sound the reasoning) is deciding not to use your talents and not to leave your mark. As Williams notes: "We do not merely want the world to contain certain states of affairs (it is a deep error of consequentialism to believe that this all we want). Among the things we basically want is to act in certain ways. But even when we basically want some state of affairs, and would be happy if it materialized, we know that we do not live in a magical world, where wanting an outcome can make it so. . . . We do not want it merely to *turn out* that we produced it; we want these thoughts of ours to produce it" (1985:56). That we value not merely outcomes but outcomes we help create, and ones in which we are personally invested, helps explain the "irrationality" of the Old Guard.[33]

33. Williams's analysis complements Karl Marx's analysis of alienation. Marx criticizes capitalism for how it distorts a whole series of interdependent relationships by

What we care about it not simply abstract states of affairs, as the consequential logic of rational choice theory would imply. As Williams points out, we also care deeply about how we arrive at these states of affairs. As a result, preferences are not independent of outcomes but come to be deeply fused with our actions and with the projects in which we engage. As the Old Guard intuitively understood, and as some organizational theorists have argued, choice is not always about simply making a decision (Feldman and March 1981). A choice is also a statement about power, and a signal of one's stature and status, about whose values prevail, whose judgment is respected, and whose judgment is ignored. Choice can also be understood as an affirmation of one's career and one's identity.

For members of the Old Guard, the values and standards of their profession, the ethos that informed their bureaucratic practice, the structure of their agency, the time they devoted to CAP and to Orme, the bitter political battles that had ensued, and their reluctant but growing awareness that their agency's mission had largely been accomplished, that what they had stood for was out of sync with their time, all these conspired to create their deep, singular investment in Orme Dam. The boundaries we construct around our "selves" do not permit us to easily make our individual identities the subject of trade-offs, of calculations. The tight conjoining of dam and identity produces incommensurabilities, since we cannot practically understand ourselves as commensurate beings.

The rational procedures used to evaluate Orme Dam and the other CAWCS alternatives could not represent the preferences of the Old Guard. For them and their supporters, their preferences were the Orme alternative. So Orme, an incommensurate value, could not be the object of easy, abstract trade-offs. The dam was symbolic of their work, their power, and their profession, and they balked at the New Guard's calculus. At a time when the agency faced an uncertain future characterized by new laws and new audiences with new interests, Orme had become symbolic of a nostalgic past which had celebrated their work. The Old Guard saw in the eroding support for Orme Dam an end of era that they did not want to acknowledge. Plan 6 is not "their" alternative, just as Bruce Babbitt's New Bureau is not "their bureau," the agency

---

transforming ends into means, and vice versa, by transforming work into active alienation. The value of our work is not just in its product but also in the fact that *we* are doing it, which allows us to develop as rich, productive social selves and to understand our shared humanity. Marx's fundamental disagreements with classical political economic theory rest on its focus on the products of labor and its refusal to acknowledge what takes place in the process of labor, in the social relationships that this process embodies.

they love. As one retired engineer, a man who speaks proudly of his more than forty years of service to the agency, sadly conceded, "When I went to work for the agency, it was considered the finest engineering organization in the entire world. Now it is in shambles. Its glory days are over."

The Old Guard Now

Some members of the Old Guard have died. Of those remaining, most are retired. Retirement hasn't always been easy for men who were so committed to their careers. Some have found it hard to watch, from the sidelines, what they view as the dismantling of their agency. The Old Guard still understand themselves as "bureau men," but it has been hard for some to reconcile their loyalties with the agency's abandonment of Orme. "Their" bureau, the one they celebrate and cling to, is a historical organization. The symbolic boundary dividing the "old" bureau and the "new" is as salient for them as it is for members of the New Guard. They are saddened at the demise of what they finally understand was a distinctive worldview; they remain bitter toward those who initiated and embody the change. They still hate Jimmy Carter.

And so members of the Old Guard talk about the glory days of the agency as being over, of how lucky they were to work on the projects they did. They describe the agency as one that is now dominated by planners, paper pushers, politicians, bureaucrats; of how the agency has been gutted by reorganizations, reductions, retirements, and sold out by leaders who no longer believe in its mission. They feel sorry for younger engineers who will miss the chance to be part of the "real" bureau. They know that these engineers will likely never experience the thrill of seeing their projects built. They will never know what it feels like to create something powerful, beautiful, and permanent, of having a whole country celebrate their accomplishments, of changing the world. But they relish their memories, sometimes at the lunches they organize every few months, and they still take their grandchildren to see their dams.

~~~~ **Four** ~~~~

The New Guard: Agents of Rationality, Arbiters of Democracy

[Reclamation] culture then was one of the most homogeneous cultures I have ever encountered. . . . It combined high standards and very narrow values. To cope, I pretended I was on another planet.

BR social scientist

What's so scary about letting ordinary people participate in our decisions? I thought we were supposed to be in favor of democracy.

BR planner

There are no incommensurables when decisions are made in the real world.

Stokey and Zeckhauser

It took Jack, a natural scientist, over a year to realize that he was being excluded from meetings that he ought to be attending. Jack tried not to take his exclusion personally, since he thought it was mostly a matter of "habit." In his words, "It just didn't occur to anyone that I should be there. But partly, I think, it was also a reflection of their thinking that what I do isn't highly relevant." Jack's predicament illustrated a problem that many of the new bureau employees confronted. They were new, they were different, and their work seemed unimportant.

In the aftermath of NEPA, federal agencies gradually realized that the courts were taking its procedural requirements seriously. Once courts began delaying projects and agencies begrudgingly began preparing EISs, the question of who was qualified to write them became an issue. BR engineers initially felt no qualms about claiming their authority to do so, but environmental groups, public citizens, and eventually courts began to insist that the new expertise now required by EISs was best provided by people with some training in different fields. Slowly, federal agencies began hiring "environmental specialists," people trained in biology, geology, archaeology, sociology, social psychology, and recreation, whose expressed job was to help write EISs.[1] Con-

---

1. NEPA also added lawyers and economists. Although some of these disciplines had been represented in the past, NEPA increased their numbers and changed people's jobs.

sequently, one of the earliest and most noticeable results of NEPA was that these new sorts of people started showing up to work in organizations that didn't know what to do with them.

This chapter explains how these disparate, initially marginal people forged a common identity for themselves. The engineering ethos that was naturalized in the BR did not seem natural to the New Guard. In reacting against the worldview that excluded them and the expectations of the Old Guard, they expanded their organizational role from EIS writers to decision analysts. In doing so, they developed an "interest" in rationality and planning, a commitment to commensuration and to making the bureaucracy more democratic. As they began to identify with and be identified by rationality, CAWCS, and the procedural and technologically mediated democracy known as "public involvement," their investments deepened and their horizons expanded. The conjuncture of conditions that allowed them to gain control of CAWCS—the environmental movement that spawned NEPA, the Old Guard's mistakes, and the civil rights movement and participatory democracy movements that made Indians and other stakeholders important—offered both legitimacy and the latitude to impose their framework, challenge the status quo, and change a bureaucracy. And so members of the New Guard were both harbingers and handmaidens of the "New Bureau."

Like the Old Guard, members of the New Guard were committed to their version of excellence, and these commitments, too, obscured for them the limitations of their rationality and the shallowness of their democracy. It took time for some to recognize that their rational decision procedures were strategies that both included and excluded. And just as their own exclusion prompted them to reevaluate their relation to the agency, members of the Yavapai community reacted against what their framework left out.

The Bureau's New Pioneers

The NEPA-induced arrivals to the Bureau of Reclamation were a hardy band of pioneers who faced the challenging task of defining their jobs and convincing powerful, skeptical bureaucrats to take them, and their particular expertise, seriously. With their varied backgrounds, disparate training, and sheer organizational novelty, it is hard to imagine a more politically benign assortment of people. As James Thompson (1967:20–21, 67) might have predicted, these new people—hired to perform ambiguous tasks in response to external pressure—would normally be relegated to peripheral organizational positions, their work well buffered from the agency's core technology of planning and promoting dams. Yet turbulent political events, natural disasters, the miscalculations of key actors, and the influence of a growing environmental movement converged to create a unique opportunity for these newcomers. Members of the New Guard were able to exploit this opportunity by forging a loose and, for a time, potent coalition within the agency; they gained control over one of its most consequential projects, and ultimately, their success allowed them to help reconstruct both the agency's decision-making procedures and redefine members' sense of its mission.

But this is not simply an account of one group's surprising accumulation of power. The New Guard, as I named this group, played a crucial role in the resolution of the Orme Dam conflict, the changes they advocated for planning procedures have been broadly adopted inside the agency, and many have risen to prominent positions within the agency over the past ten years. Yet to construe this simply as an ascent to power oversimplifies the group's influence and underemphasizes the effects of a turbulent environment. The New Guard's cohesion derived, in part, from their marginality and from the organizational and political crisis that stemmed from Carter's hit list, the Old Guard's botched EIS, and the three large floods that occurred in Phoenix between March of 1978 and February of 1980. Their capacity to change a bureaucracy, to cajole the organization into adopting its rational decision procedures, was more a symptom of weakness and organizational desperation than a sign of strength. The story of how these newcomers coalesced and grew, how they emerged as champions of rationality and a more democratic process, and their success in brokering the Orme Dam controversy provides a rich text for analyzing the conditions and forms of organizational influence. Embedded within this story, however, is the crucial subtext of how and why conceptions of a rigorous instrumental rationality became aligned with the legitimacy of science and the extension of democracy, and the effects of this alignment on the politics surrounding Orme Dam.

The New Guard: A Coalition of Outsiders

While the arrival of early members of the New Guard in the early 1970s was one of the first signals that things were about to change at the Bureau of Reclamation, for a long time no one very important heeded the signal. These new employees did not arrive all at once, of course, and they were not all centrally located: some worked at the Engineering and Research Center in Denver, which was an important base of the New Guard, some worked in regional offices, and eventually many were deployed to local project offices. Initially, many came from other government agencies, often other Interior agencies such as Fish and Wildlife or the Bureau of Land Management.

Several members of the New Guard had initially been hired to work on a large, interagency planning program known as the Westwide Study, and came to the bureau after Richard Nixon cut that program. Participation in that program was an important experience in the careers of many of its participants. It brought together planners and representatives from many resource-development agencies in a friendly forum to think about how the government ought to develop the western United States. Few were traditional bureaucrats; many were new to civil service and some were former academics. Many held nontraditional views about government service and development. They have been described as a self-selected group of the "best and the brightest," as "visionaries." For some members of the New Guard, it was their first encounter with federal bureaucrats, and, as Allen put it: "We had the sense that what we were doing was important for the country. To my astonishment, bright people worked for the federal government. I suffered from snobbery. I was amazed that bureaucrats were smart and were doing interesting things. . . . [This study] became the place where I began to unlearn old prejudices."

Besides providing a place to meet like-minded people and a stepping-stone to their BR jobs, this investigation was also important in shaping participants' goals and intellectual agendas. It was there that commensuration first emerged as a pressing problem for water-development agencies. As an interdisciplinary, interagency forum, early meetings were described as a Tower of Babel, with participants talking past each another in the jargon and assumptions of their own disciplines and agencies. Some decided that a method for debating the issues of different disciplines and perspectives was needed. Some participants realized that they had what was first defined as a "measurement problem." For Allen:

> It soon became clear to me that we were not all talking the same language. Everyone was a good scientist. We all understood the need for sound methodology. What [the others] did not know was how important it was to find ways to discuss and compare across disciplines . . . that's what my role became. If we started measuring things, we had no way of working across disciplines. . . . We needed ways of getting things equivalent even though they were based on different dimensions. Simply being interdisciplinary prompted a concern for commensuration. . . . The people I was working with were all physical scientists. They were used to concrete variables. I'm a [social scientist]—I'm used to creating metrics. It took me a long time to persuade them this was an important

> problem. I put together a simpleminded questionnaire designed
> to evaluate the significance of trade-offs. . . . We needed a way to
> get some perspective on impacts. For example, if there is soil ero-
> sion of 100 tons of soil, we know that the Soil Conservation Depart-
> ment is going to think that is a terribly significant impact. But what
> about comparing that impact versus the loss of a species habitat
> in acres . . . there was no easy answer for how to make compari-
> sons. . . . We were of such different disciplines and perspectives.
> How do we put all them together to decide which plan is best?

Jack remembers the chronology a little differently. To commensurate impacts, he devised a simple scale to evaluate the quality of a resource before and after implementing a plan. Jack believed his procedure helped spur interest in commensuration and, more broadly, in rational decision making. While priority does not matter much for my purposes, both men agree that for a small group of people representing different agencies, participating in this program helped focus their interest in decision technologies and define commensuration as key to good planning. Since most of the members of this project either eventually returned to, or were hired by, resource-development agencies, concern over commensuration diffused through quite a number of agencies as a result of this project. Within the BR, for Jack, Allen, and other members of the New Guard, commensuration would become a recurring theme.

Unity from Marginality

Although it may have taken Jack, a biologist hired as an environmental analyst, some time to notice the meetings he wasn't invited to at the BR, other symptoms of his marginality were obvious. It had taken a while to locate an office for him, and "it was not exactly centrally located." He remembers going for days without having a work-related conversation with anyone, and he felt baffled about what he should be doing, other than trying to look busy. "Let's just say," he now chuckles, "I wasn't very closely monitored." "There were some days," Jack recounts, "when I felt like shouting down the hall, 'Hey! I'm here! Does anybody care?' "

For Jack, getting hired by the BR was the easy part. Being noticed and being taken seriously were the real challenges. As was true for most of these post-NEPA newcomers, their most urgent need was to invent themselves bureaucratically. The rules, procedures, and regulations of bureaucracies are so taken-for-granted, members who perform them (and scholars who emphasize their capacity to control behavior or hamper efficiency) often forget their constitutive effects. You may show up eager to work, but without the bureaucratic scripts detailing your responsibilities, the protocols by which you should enact these, the rules you are to follow, and your formal relations to other departments and other organizational members, you do not practically, or legitimately, exist. Although bureaucratic scripts are always subject to improvisation, they nevertheless confer a location, a status, a nominal visibility, and a defense against dismissal that makes them the premise of bureaucratic action.

And so the early work of the New Guard quite fundamentally involved creating the positions they already filled, as well as designing and staffing the positions of other environmental specialists who would work under them. This involved writing job descriptions and hiring and evaluation criteria, and translating legal mandates into bureaucratic procedures, scientific methodologies, and local terminology. It also required finding ways of inserting these tasks into the routines of other bureaucrats. Peter arrived in the early 1970s as one of the first "environmental types": "It was clear they didn't know what to do with us. Heck, we didn't know what we were supposed to be doing either. All of a sudden we were in charge of promoting something called 'environmental quality' in an agency that had been building dams for seventy years. How the heck do you even measure 'environmental quality'?"

Environmental quality, social well-being, regional economic development, and national economic development were the four "accounts" to be evaluated as required by the new principles and standards (P&S) guidelines issued by the Water Resources Council, the federal advisory board created in 1965 and comprised of leaders of major water agencies and other professionals. Early members of the New Guard were charged with determining, in the abstract, how social and environmental impacts would be assessed in these accounts and incorporated into BR planning. Part of defining their jobs for the early New Guard members also involved creating the internal review process for the EIS and other planning documents.

Early members of the New Guard faced daunting problems. One concerned how to integrate themselves into the organization while not completely compromising their own values, their professional training, or their credibility with the outside groups that would be scrutinizing their work. Another practical problem was to find a way to integrate the demands of NEPA with the P&S guidelines, which became the planning guidelines for the agency, so efforts to meld NEPA and P&S guidelines were seen as the means to ensure that environmental and social issues were incorporated into the crucial early stages of decision making.

How to do this preoccupied planners for more than a decade. Timing was important, because if EIS preparation were not incorporated into the normal planning process, the EISs would be relegated to the equivalent of an institutional afterthought, a situation in which they would have little chance to shape projects and influence decision making. By the time an EIS was written for a project, it was often too late to change the project or to create less damaging alternatives. Members knew that as long as they remained mere EIS writers or reviewers, they would have little influence and few chances to shape BR policy.

Members also agreed that good decision making depended on the capacity to make careful, controlled comparisons between proposed policies. But devising ways to organize these comparisons was a complicated task. For example, the "social account" was supposed to summarize the significance of the accumulated social impacts, both good and bad, of each candidate plan so that these could be compared. This meant finding a way to reconcile things like the flood protection provided by Orme Dam with the forced relocation of the Yavapai community. A second set of comparisons involved how to compare constructively the social, economic, and environmental impacts for each plan. Such comparing "across accounts" would involve, for example, reconciling the loss of archaeological sites with the creation of new jobs, or the destruction of bald eagle habitat with the benefit of improved transportation. Finding a way to make comparisons like these sustained the New Guard's interest in commensuration and eventually led to first contracting with, and later hiring, decision experts who helped introduce rational decision protocols in the BR.[2]

Because of their shared marginality in the BR, and partly because they were trying simultaneously to solve parallel problems of how to define, measure, and compare abstractions such as "social well-being" or "environmental quality" or "efficiency," members of the New Guard turned to each other for support and guidance. Much has been made of how marginality produces a distinct capacity for innovation, whether in science, art, or social theory. Members of the New Guard did, over time, come to appreciate their differences as a source of inspiration, their distance as a virtue.[3] Early on, their status as outsiders

2. Decision experts were hired to write a report on commensuration (Lord, Deane, and Waterstone 1979). This was the first in a series of reports written by consultants, visiting academics, and, later, employee specialists that identified problems and proposed techniques for commensuration, scaling, and other techniques related to rational analytic decision-making.

3. For example, Matthew attributes CAWCS's success partly to the New Guard's distinctiveness: "Most involved with designing and managing CAWCS were different sorts of people," and by virtue of their "not being invested in business as usual," they were

seemed a problem, a political and organizational liability, something to shed. Even so, their marginality prompted them to seek reassurance in each other's company, to forge a common interest.

As a source of solidarity and cooperation, the New Guard's sense of difference warrants unpacking. Although many had more professional training than did agency engineers, without seniority, powerful internal allies, or a recognized political constituency, they seemed likely to remain isolated and ineffectual. Their biggest problem was that they and their work were suspect to many traditional employees, who valued and nurtured organizational loyalty. How could suspect environmental specialists be organizationally rehabilitated when their jobs seemed to revolve around criticizing the objectives of the agency that hired them. If the uncontested mission of the agency was to "store and move water," as one man described it, what natural alliance could there possibly be for those whose job it was to document all the harmful of effects of doing one's job?

Defining Difference

As organizational misfits, members of the New Guard were more invested in making sense of their difference than were other employees. Simply not being engineers meant that the newcomers were often lumped together, both by the more traditional bureau employees and by one another. One older engineer referred to these employees collectively as the "all the 'ologists' we had to hire after NEPA." For Allen, "Anybody who wasn't an engineer was suspect. It didn't matter if you were an economist, a biologist, or what. At the core of a lot of things was a value set of how decisions were made. It was really a way of perceiving the world." When forced to attend to them, the engineers viewed their "otherness" as homogeneous and conceived and treated them as a coherent category, as "those people they had been forced to hire" or as "environmental types." This, of course, shaped how these employees thought of themselves and their ties to one another. Early members of the New Guard were uniformly surprised by the depth and scope of what they called the "bureau" or "engineering" culture they encountered. BR engineers' distinctiveness was pronounced enough to warrant a cultural tag. How else to convey this powerful difference?

Members of the New Guard described these differences in both prac-

---

"freer to be innovative, to take chances, to question old assumptions and think in new ways. And God knows that's what was needed in CAWCS."

tical and theoretical terms. Several described their early experience in terms of the "culture shock" they encountered. For Allen, "They couldn't figure out what the hell I was about. . . . That didn't necessarily make me feel uncomfortable. It takes a long time. You gotta learn the language. You have to learn the values of the culture you're dealing with . . . [here,] engineering values. To go solve engineering problems in very good ways, with a high level of excellence." Susan, who worked at the bureau in the late 1970s, also described the divide between engineers and environmental and social analysts in cultural terms: "The hardest part was learning to think and talk like engineers—figuring them out enough so that you could get them to pay attention to you, to convince them that you know useful things. This took a long time, since at first I found them rather bizarre. I mean these guys just love to build dams, and they've managed to create a whole little world, a culture, devoted to that. When I first arrived, I felt like an anthropologist plopped in the middle of some exotic tribe." Sometimes this difference was made manifest in small details, as when Ben noticed at his first meeting that he was the only one in the room not using graph paper for note taking. (He jokes about how, after he adopted this device, his doodling improved, becoming more symmetrical and precise.)

For Faye, one of the hardest features of the BR's "engineering culture" was its unremitting maleness. Simply being female made her visible and different, and she remembers longing for the company of other women. She complained of how tired she became of "all the sports talk, the tool talk, the hunting talk" that dominated coffee breaks and lunch hours; her fantasy, never enacted, was to interrupt "the boys" with a good cookie recipe or an announcement that she had just run her stockings or started her period. On days when she had important meetings scheduled, knowing she would be the only woman present, she would wear a conservative, navy pin-striped suit, her designated "man-eater suit," to command respect.

Sometimes New Guard members conveyed the distinctions between themselves and engineers in general professional terms. Gary, for example, spoke of the early seventies as "the lawsuit days. . . . Those were the planners versus the engineers days. I was on the side of the planners." Members often described themselves and similar people in other agencies as "decision experts," as "rational analytic types," or as "planners." Initially, I was surprised at how many identified themselves and their goals in terms of their commitment to rational planning. For Matthew, "We're planners. Number one, we care about good decision making. That means we don't have a particular agenda to impose other than trying to force people to be rational and explicit about what they decide. I mean, we care about the quality of the environment, and we care about not having some people bear all the costs of water development, and we care about efficiency. But overall, we want to force people to be more explicit about what they want, how much they're willing to sacrifice to get it, who it is that is making the sacrifices, and what alternatives there might be for getting what they want. What we're about is not really so abstract."

Others are conceptually quite sophisticated when they describe their values. Ben represented himself as "a real Stokey and Zeckhauser type." Stokey and Zeckhauser wrote an influential text promoting rational decision making and commensuration in public choice. More than simply showing allegiance to rational choice decision methods, however, Ben was referring to their famous aphorism, which appeared as an epigraph to one of the reports they commissioned, "There are no incommensurables when decisions are made in the real world." In making this connection, Ben was signaling his faith in the ultimate commensurability of public values.[4]

Members of the Old Guard were typically referred to simply as "engineers," "construction guys," or "dinosaurs." Scott described one man as "a construction type. He had to write something for this new EIS thing. He was typical of other kinds of other federal agencies and non-planning reclamation types. He didn't understand planning. We had to formulate alternatives. This didn't make sense to him. Orme was there before there was planning in the project offices. There were just construction engineers. Their idea of planning was deciding which was the best construction site." Gary described their differences:

> We were rational; they were irrational. . . . That's not quite fair, I suppose. Maybe I was too strong. We had different values. They cared about efficiency and building good structures. They just had a completely different value system than we did. They were rational about how to do best what they valued. They valued building. Building was good. Period. They felt like if they got something built, that was good. These are the guys who show their grandchildren the dam they built. . . . Another [such value] is reliability. This system must never break. It must always work. I want to know, "What is an acceptable failure rate, [e.g.,] being down one day a month or one day a year?" To ask this question of them is heretical.

Ben described as an "intrinsic value" for the Old Guard: "the beautiful engineering solution."

4. The document (Anderson 1981) begins with a decision fable, the moral of which is that "sometimes you have to compare apples and oranges."

The Old Guard's commitment to dam building as the solution to any problem was frustrating to planners who believed that, in some cases, early-warning systems, redistributing water, water conservation, or re-negotiated releases modifying the way water was released were viable alternatives to newer, bigger, stronger dams. As Susan put it: "Selling nonstructural plans around here is like spitting into the wind." A man investigating dam safety, a critical issue in light of the aging infrastructure of BR projects and the collapse of Teton Dam in June of 1976, confirms this. He is only half joking when he claims that for some engineers, the safety of dams is taken literally to mean they are not concerned with human safety but with protecting their structures. Even more frustrating for planners who framed decisions as choices among alternatives was the Old Guard's attachments to particular structures. Since these attachments were never acknowledged as such, the superiority of the loved dam was defended in engineering criteria that were hard for planners to counter. In lyrics that would do Tammy Wynette proud, one decision analyst commemorated this devotion in a devastating parody entitled "Stand by Your Dam."

Part of what defined the New Guard were conspicuous characteristics they did not share with other bureau personnel. As newer employees, they were less invested in the traditional mission of the agency. Less convinced of the intrinsic value of building dams, they did not identify with the agency's legacy, as did other employees. Nor were they as intensely loyal to the organization, its constituents, or most important, to particular projects, as were older employees. They did not endorse the engineering ethos of the agency, with its faith in the ability and appropriateness of technology to exploit natural resources.

Not being engineers also meant that the traditional career trajectory and professional socialization the BR cultivated and celebrated were unavailable to these new employees. BR engineers understood the agency as the world's preeminent engineering institution, and the specialized training and frequent promotions they received were not extended to other employees. New employees who did not receive this same type of education and socialization were disadvantaged by their more limited knowledge of the agency. It took them much longer to develop a cognitive "map" of the organization and to make broad contacts within the agency.

Being new was an important organizational liability, and newness was often used to exclude the New Guard, since their inexperience and lack of traditional socialization precluded knowing "how things were done" within the organization. Their newness was also a political liabil-

ity. The BR is deeply dependent on close relationships with key political allies, and these are a source of power inside the agency. Relationships with their "clients" and with political supporters are carefully
cultivated over years of interactions and alliances. It is not easy for a
newcomer to insert herself into these powerful and protected relationships, and not having them was a liability.

Members of the New Guard also tended to be politically more liberal
than other bureau employees. Some members thought Carter inept or
misguided, and some supported his environmentalism. Unlike the Old
Guard, most were unhappy with Reagan and were deeply worried
about James Watt's influence on the Interior Department. Members of
the New Guard were typically highly trained: most had M.A. degrees;
a few had Ph.D.s. Since environmentalism was often part of their education, they saw environmentalists as having legitimate "water interests," not as the "radicals," "tree huggers," and "bugs and bunnies
crowd" that the Old Guard loathed. Many had hobbies that reinforced
their environmental values: they were bird-watchers, mountain climb-
ers, wildlife photographers, hikers, cross-country skiers, campers, and
fly-fishermen. This greater sympathy for environmentalists made them
suspect within the agency. Serge Taylor's (1984:127) superb analysis of
the Army Corps of Engineers and the U.S. Forest Service reveals a similar pattern. He describes the new environmental specialists as "boundary spanners." Their bind was in being dependent on two competing
constituencies—their employers and environmental experts and
groups—while trying not to be co-opted by either.[5]

Trained in either the natural or the social sciences, members of the
New Guard strongly believed in the potential of science to resolve dis-
putes and improve decision making. Like the Progressive founders of
the BR, members were convinced that specialized knowledge could
become a powerful, neutral adjudicator of interests and conflict. Now,
of course, it was planners, not engineers, with the expertise needed to
collect and organize this knowledge.

An even more striking difference between the BR founders and the
members of the New Guard, however, was that the latter wanted to
make this knowledge available and accessible to members of the public
so that they could influence decisions. Whereas the Progressive engi-

5. Often, the environmental specialists' natural sympathies with environmental interests, and their need to work with environmental interest groups, made them suspect
to traditional corps employees. They were suspected of leaking critical information to
environmentalists to aid their attacks on corp projects EISs. As Taylor notes, sometimes
this suspicion was well founded. One member of the New Guard helped environmental
groups critique other agencies' EISs. He reported that his boss approved this arrange-
ment, but he would not tell me if his critiques included BR EISs.

neers asked that the public and the politicians cede to them, as enlightened elites, the discretion to make decisions about irrigation and developing the West, the New Guard was committed to more inclusive decision making as NEPA required. They saw the public's role as providing the values and shaping the goals used to evaluate projects.

How members of the New Guard characterized the differences between themselves and the Old Guard varied over time. These changes sometimes reflected more refined distinctions as members acquired allies and knowledge of the organization and as new kinds of people became attached to the New Guard. Early on, newcomers described themselves as aliens who landed on a planet of engineers. This sharp distinction between engineers and planners was blurred as nontraditional engineers became affiliated with and champions of CAWCS. These engineers differed from the Old Guard in important ways: they included women, they were usually younger, and their careers were unconventional, with shorter tenure in the BR, and a broader range of experience both inside and outside the agency. New Guard engineers were interested in planning as process, and their main concern was to resolve a controversy, to arrive at a decision that would stick. They did not share the Old Guard's strong, personal ties to local Orme constituents or to the dam.

During CAWCS, New Guard engineers were also closer to the action than were members of the Old Guard. As project managers, assistant project managers, or principal investigators, they had to figure out how to apply the new planning guidelines to CAWCS. New Guard engineers supported public participation; they believed in expanding the traditional constituency of the agency to include environmentalists, taxpayers, and those bearing the costs of water development as having legitimate water interests. Other members of the New Guard who were not engineers looked on the nontraditional engineer as "one of us," "a good guy," "someone who believes in public involvement," or someone who "doesn't think like an engineer." Another important group that became attached to the New Guard was the consultants, who gradually became invested in the aims and values of the New Guard and were incorporated into the coalition.

Their common qualities may not have been enough to foster the organizational alliance of early members of the New Guard. Since many members were representing disciplines and expertise that were new to the BR, the need to act as partisans of their disciplines might have overshadowed their common interests in a different context. Instead of banding together, some might have sought instead to ingratiate themselves with the more powerful BR employees. That this did not happen is partly attributable to their experience of the monolithic quality of the BR's engineering culture. Also important was the timing of the New Guard's arrival, which coincided with a chaotic period for the BR. The impact of NEPA, with its directive to involve the public in agency planning, the emerging environmental movement, and the proposed changes in the planning protocol generated uncertainty within the agency, which enhanced the New Guard's authority. Members of the New Guard, rather than cater too slavishly to old interests, chose to focus on the new skills and resources they could bring to the bureau.

The New Guard was always a loose coalition, one that was perhaps strongest from 1978 through 1982, a time span which just predates and postdates CAWCS. Even at their most cohesive, the boundary between themselves and members of the Old Guard was just one of a number of relevant boundaries. There were situations where other classifications or loyalties overrode the New Guard's allegiances to one another. More parochial loyalties might intervene during budget battles, for example, when social analysts might argue with economists or biologists over which impacts mattered most and warranted more funds, or when external consultants defended their bills to BR administrators or auditors. Nevertheless, the cohesion that most members felt despite different training, traditions, and the public-private distinction between consultants and BR employees was exceptional. The solidarity among members of the New Guard was strongest when they perceived some other group as a threat, or when there was conflict which united them. This explains why, during CAWCS, when members often felt embattled and some were spending most of their waking hours together, being a member of the New Guard was an especially potent group identity.

Some of the New Guard resented their marginality and the privileged status of the engineers. Gary told me: "Engineers at that time were so in demand, right out of college they were [job grade] sevens and we were fives. They got promotions every six months; we had to wait a year. We hated it 'cause we knew we were smarter." When asked if he thought things had changed much since NEPA, Gary replied that a divide still existed between planners and engineers in the BR but that it was not as wide as it had once been. He singled out design engineers from Denver and "front office" engineers in local offices, with close ties to their constituents, as two types who gave planners the most trouble.

The hostility between the Old and New Guard went both ways. Allen believed that part of the Old Guard's unease with the New Guard was that they blamed planners for all the unwanted change that was being imposed on the agency:

[Reclamation] culture was feeling besieged and under attack all the time. There wasn't an environmental movement at the time. That wasn't it. There was the perception that all of the political pressures were [toward] not doing the quality engineering work that most people were so proud of. These were the people who designed and built Grand Coulee and Hoover and Glen Canyon. . . . They felt . . . "What we've stood for and what we have done was being attacked. Our mandate was to make the West a place for people to live. To bring water to it." BR people have closely identified with this traditional mission of the BR. . . . There was sense that [this] mission was slipping away. What they were understanding at a gut level, something not yet articulated, was that the value consensus surrounding water resource development had gone away, and this was very scary for them. It evoked defensive feelings.

Over time, some people's accounts of the divisions between the Old and New Guards softened, and they emphasize the support and training they received from supervisors who were sympathetic engineers. Yet even when downplaying the animosity between planners and environmental specialists, and engineers, the distinctions were preserved simply by being noted. Despite the New Guard's more generous retrospective accounts about their conflicts with the Old Guard, and a consensus that the divide had lessened, distance remained between the groups. I observed elaborate strategy sessions where members of the New Guard would carefully plan how to "manage" effectively people they perceived as unsympathetic to their goals of adopting rational decision protocol. Such people were called "dyed in the wool engineers," a label never intended as a compliment. As Ben put it: "With some types, the best you can hope for is early retirement."[6]

In addition to their common feeling that they were marginal and underappreciated, their troubles with traditional engineers who resented their presence, and the resentment that some felt toward traditional engineers, members of the New Guard were also united by their shared desire to resolve some of the conflicts that surrounded water development. When asked what he liked about his job, Gary told me a story about how he had successfully found and sold a compromise to a proposed project that satisfied what had initially been hostile groups. He concluded the story by saying that "it's days like that [that]

6. During the late 1980s and early 1990s, Ben's wish came true when draconian "reductions in forces" were imposed on the agency; natural attrition and the lure of early retirement dramatically downsized the BR, and the ranks of design engineers and "construction types" were radically thinned.

make you feel good about your work." Other New Guard members echo Gary's sentiment. In describing what they find fulfilling about their work, they often mention two things: the importance of finding ways to incorporate the values and opinions of the public into agency decision making and their role in helping to resolve conflict. Most believe that the two tasks are closely linked.

Perhaps because they were more sympathetic to a wider range of interest groups, members of the New Guard saw conflict as inevitable, as endemic to the organization's mission. They criticized the Old Guard for failing to notice or acknowledge that their assumed consensus on water development no longer existed, if it ever had. Since the BR, like other Interior agencies, makes decisions about physical resources, its decisions often receive more publicity and generate more controversy, especially locally, than many agencies. This is partly a legacy of the environmental movement, but as one man put it, "Dams are hard to ignore." The importance of water has produced long-standing interest groups, whose skillful, well-funded lobbyists expertly monitor water policy and its effect on their interests. Their attentiveness may exacerbate conflict, since even small effects on some group's interests will result in its mobilization. Also, lobbyists, like engineers, become committed to particular policies and are reluctant to abandon plans they have long supported.

Given the New Guard's view of conflict as inevitable, public, and protracted, it is easier to appreciate why procedures for mitigating conflict would be so appealing, its resolution so satisfying.[7] The inevitability of conflict over natural resources, the need to take seriously environmental interests, and the New Guard's faith in the potential of science to help resolve conflict all reinforced their interest in making agency decisions more rational.

The Allure of Rationality

The New Guard's adoption of rational decision models as a way to implement NEPA and organize CAWCS was rooted in their organizational, political, and intellectual commitments to it. These mod-

7. The New Guard's view is similar to that of Cyert and March, who see conflict in firms as omnipresent. Members of the New Guard believe that science, in the form of rational analytic models, can help resolve conflict by identifying both the source of conflict and consensus, and by providing useful and well-organized information. In contrast, Cyert and March (1963:116–17) argue that organizational conflict is best only "quasi-resolved," since any real attempt to reconcile differences formally would exacerbate them. In making explicit both the presence and magnitude of conflict, these models would undermine organizational strategies for managing it that rely on minimizing and obscuring conflict.

els helped the New Guard solve the pressing intellectual puzzle of how to organize and integrate the information NEPA now required agencies to collect. Assessing impacts for a study like CAWCS meant including, along with engineering and economic data, data drawn from over a dozen disciplines, ranging from archaeology to zoology. NEPA also required that the opinions and values of the public be included. Rational decision-making models offered a strategy for collecting, using, and reconciling such disparate kinds and forms of information.

In addition, members came to see that the intellectual promise of this rigorous form of rationality could help redress the BR's political problems. The legitimation crisis that followed the botched 1976 EIS, and the problem of integrating and organizing the disparate information now required by NEPA, including public opinion, could be resolved by a retrievable rationality. A rigorous technology would assure people that reliable and relevant information was systematically included, that appropriate methods were used, and that the study was "objective." Based on well-established, public procedures, their methods could be easily reproduced and defended if their credibility were challenged. Science could solve both the cognitive problem of organizing disparate information and the political problem of repairing the BR's damaged credibility.[8]

Rationality may seem an unlikely prescription for ameliorating marginality, but the New Guard's investment in rationality also reflected their precarious organizational status. Part of the appeal of rationality was its capacity to include; rationality that is premised on commensuration is a strategy for inclusion, for integrating diverse phenomena, linking different systems of knowledge. Also, a commitment to rational decision making also gave heterogeneous people something in common. Rationality, like motherhood and apple pie, is hard to oppose. The abstractness of rational decision making fosters this inclusion; it offers diverse applications and makes it easy to endorse generally, without having to negotiate particular applications. It functions like the vague goals in the "quasi-resolution of conflict" (Cyert and March 1963:116–17), where vague consensus is accomplished without requiring the detailed trade-offs that reveal or exacerbate conflict; endorsing

8. An example illustrates how "science" can be mobilized against "politics." The draft EIS produced during CAWCS predicted that the stress and despondency that would attend Orme Dam would increase the mortality and morbidity rates on the reservation. According to one manager, "people in Washington" couldn't release a document that said the agency would "kill Indians." Several members of the New Guard were pressured to "tone down" the language. They refused to do so, successfully invoking the authority of science to block these censors.

rationality does not generate the same conflict that using rational procedure does.

The New Guard's commitment to rationality is also linked to symbolic dimensions of organizational decisions. Decisions need not necessarily or exclusively be about choice. Sometimes decisions are opportunities to signal commitments to certain values (including rationality),
allocate responsibility, legitimate power or status, or devise strategies
for mobilizing action (March and Olson 1976; Meyer and Rowan 1977;
Feldman and March 1981; DiMaggio and Powell 1991; Dobbin 1994;
Brunsson 1985). The decision to adopt rational procedures had these
dimensions. It signaled that the New Guard should be allocated responsibility for decision technology. It demonstrated that the agency
was "doing something" about resolving the controversy, complying
with the law, and responding to its critics. And it was a way to buy
time. The flexibility and generality of these technologies provided
members of the New Guard with the organizational equivalent of a
universal tool. By being able to solve any problem, their technology
placed members of the New Guard in the bureaucratically desirable
position of always having relevant expertise.

Yet, even for a group eager to prove its value to skeptics, rationality
stood for something bigger than organizational survival. Rationality
was a means to accommodate a changing world, to comply with a
worthwhile law. It was a way to mediate and represent difference—in
interests, values, and stakes. It was a way to incorporate environmental
values, improve decisions, and help people do their jobs better. Rationality could make government more effective and more democratic.
However organizationally useful, politically expedient, and intellectually defensible these decision technologies were, the promise of rationality was also deeply personal. For people who wanted to do good,
rationality was both a useful idea and an ideal against which anxieties
about being a bureaucrat could be assuaged, the nobility and possibilities of government service could be defended, and the potential of
democratic participation could be realized.

Pitching Rationality to Skeptics: Fear and
Loathing in Boulder City

Once members of the New Guard understood their contributions to the
agency as both environmental specialists and decision analysts, they
needed to convince others of this. NEPA and the new planning guidelines provided a powerful argument that the status quo in decision
making was unacceptable. Having both raised the stakes and tarnished
the agency's credibility, the 1976 EIS convinced some superiors to give

rational decision-making procedures a test. Some believed that it was time to bring in new experts, people not publicly identified as Orme supporters, and to give them the resources to do an exemplary study and the time to "get the science right." Consequently, they authorized contracts and in-house research on decision analysis and later hired staff with backgrounds in decision analysis.[9]

More difficult to convince were local project managers. Agreeing on the usefulness of abstract policy is relatively easy, but closer to the ground, where investments are deeper and consequences more directly felt by participants, there was greater suspicion. A different kind of sales job was required to get the techniques used on specific projects. But the dissemination of information within a large bureaucracy is so convoluted that it took a very long time for the New Guard's capabilities as decision experts even to become known within the agency, especially in project offices.

Most project managers had no idea what was meant by rational, analytic decision making or multiattribute trade-off schemes. Educating them was a tough job. One man was almost a full-time spokesperson for a time. In dozens of meetings, conference calls, and memos, he would patiently explain the conceptual background and virtues of rational decision-making models. Expressing his frustration in heroically neutral language, he characterized the objections of BR managers as devolving from "atheoretical concerns."

People with long experience in making policy resented the implication that they did not know how to make good decisions. They were skeptical of outsiders who knew a lot of theory and little politics. Several members of the Old Guard argued that, compared with their experience and expertise, "fancy [decision] theory" would perform poorly in the "real world." Some argued that it wasn't necessary to fix what wasn't broken, an implausible interpretation in light of recent events.

To illustrate the nature of the "atheoretical concerns," the New Guard spokesman described one manager's objections as illustrative: "I had to explain to a regional planning officer . . . why we should do this public values assessment. He had plenty of arguments of why we shouldn't bother: it was expensive, it would take too long to do, even if we do it, we won't learn anything new, and what if we learn something we don't want to know or don't want others to know? There is always resistance to something new. . . . Expense and feared loss of control are the two issues that really cover [the resistance]."

---

9. The men who approved the money for these projects were engineers with extensive planning experience. As sophisticated readers of the political climate, they were among the first to take seriously the threats posed by environmentalists.

This exchange captures the sophisticated response of a savvy bureaucrat who understands the political and economic cost of explicit
information. He argues that more information is not always good,
which is partly an economic argument: Sometimes the marginal utility
of the information is not worth its cost. But the trouble with information goes beyond its cost and uncertain usefulness. What if you learn
something you don't want to know? Information, once obtained, may
be hard to suppress or control, especially in a politicized environment.
Information is a political gamble, and surprising information is especially worrisome. It may jeopardize a preferred plan, be hard to interpret, aid an enemy, or compromise a friend. The loyalty that project
managers work so hard to cultivate among supporters cuts both ways,
and employees want to protect their constituents' credibility. Efforts
to suppress damaging information can backfire, both legally and politically. As every politician knows, ambiguity is a valuable strategy for
protecting interests and avoiding conflict.

Since the new decision process was unfamiliar, it was hard both to
understand and to manipulate. This increased bureaucrats' anxiety
about being surprised and losing control. To address this concern, New
Guard members emphasized how seldom the process produced surprises. As Ben explained: "Some people view the methods as if the
stuff is going into a box and then there will be some big surprise. You
start by formulating objectives. That is itself a new process. By the time
you formulate your objectives, arrange your alternatives—that is also
a new thing—and figure out what your impacts are and contact the
relevant people, you already know what you are going to 'be surprised'
about. . . . Surprises [don't] happen often."

The procedure evoked contradictory responses, sometimes in the
same person. On the one hand, it probably would not provide any new
information, wasting time and money; on the other, it could lead to
unexpected results that might make people look bad. Both things happened during CAWCS. During the early stages of the study, a lot of
time and money were spent studying things which turned out to be
irrelevant. This is hardly unusual. A memorable "surprise" occurred
when Barry Goldwater, Arizona's senior senator and long-time Orme
advocate, received a private briefing from the project managers. When
informed that an Orme alternative performed equally well on all the
major objectives, with fewer harmful environmental and social impacts, and appeared to be the superior alternative, Goldwater became
enraged.[10]

10. Several days later, when Goldwater had finally become convinced that Orme Dam
was politically unsalvageable, the adroit politician happily announced his support for

For critics worried about the investment required to learn rational decision techniques, the New Guard stressed their universal applicability and adaptability. Once developed and learned, these techniques can quickly be used to structure and improve any type of decision that needs to be made; however public or invisible, controversial or mundane, these techniques help people make better decisions. Sometimes members emphasized the continuity between what their decision models did and what ordinary people did when they decide things. They argued that most people make decisions based on fact and value judgments, and consider the consequences of different courses of actions and how these relate to their goals; most of us recognize that doing something often precludes doing something else and that most options have advantages and disadvantages. What was different about using their rational models, the New Guard would say, was that the analytic models, unlike intuition, force people to be more explicit and rigorous in their choices. The models require them to clarify their objectives and preferences; to be precise about how much they value some things in relation to other things. It forces consistency in beliefs and choices. Also, the procedures allow testing the sensitivity of various assumptions for their importance in determining final outcomes. And this sort of self-consciousness and rigor leads to more honest decisions.

Of all the arguments used to convince skeptics of the value of the decision-making strategies, none was as effective as the example CAWCS provided. The Orme controversy placed a critical project in jeopardy, and members of the New Guard created a study, and a process, that seemed to solve the problem. CAWCS became the ultimate test of their procedures, of their expertise, of their value to the organization.

Creating CAWCS

CAWCS was the BR's public, if unacknowledged, response to the crisis that Orme Dam had become. Carter's hit list, the favorable response that NEPA lawsuits were garnering from courts, the public's greater interest in environmental issues, the Old Guard's bungled EIS, and recent floods had all raised the visibility and the stakes of this decision. The time, money, and attention devoted to, and the willingness to experiment with, CAWCS, which included unusual managerial autonomy and a willingness to hire nontraditional employees, testify to the magnitude of the crisis for the BR. Ceding responsibility for CAWCS

---

the new plan at a news conference, where he chastised the agency for taking so long to arrive at such an obvious solution.

to the New Guard was also a testament of agency faith that Orme's superiority would make it the preferred choice, as well as a sign that some older bureaucrats were content to let others take the heat for a while.

Shortly after the BR went public with the draft EIS, a new regional director was appointed. His introduction to the Orme controversy was abrupt and unpleasant: at what had seemed an innocent function in Arizona, he was publicly "hung out to dry" for the bureau's handling of Orme Dam. After this experience, which he made clear to subordinates should never to be repeated, the old project director, an Orme devotee, was removed and a new man with a background in planning and public involvement was brought in to serve as acting director. His mandate became "fix the mess," and he was told that whatever resources he needed would be made available.

Members of the New Guard lobbied the new regional director and the new acting project manager. They argued that a completely new, objective study was needed to restore the agency's compromised reputation and that much of the Orme controversy resulted from people's not having the right information needed to understand the decision's implications. Allen told the new director: "[Orme supporters] were not informed supporters. They had only been exposed to one alternative and believed it would perform in ways that we later found out it wouldn't. And they had political clout [but] it was the agency's fault they were badly informed. They weren't doing public service properly. They weren't providing the kind of information people needed. . . . What was needed was to step way back and conduct an objective, scientific analysis. We need to get outsiders. . . . We needed a strong public involvement process to support the study. Well, they bought it, and that's how CAWCS was invented."

Matthew, an engineer who advocated public involvement and "good science," systematically recruited people who were new to the BR, or to CAP, or who were otherwise not invested in the status quo. He is still proud of the team he helped assemble. The controversy surrounding Orme and its association with the Central Arizona Project made CAWCS a high profile assignment, and it attracted bright, ambitious, risk-taking people. As Matthew explained, "Early on, we all knew our necks were on the line." For employees who had felt excluded, CAWCS was also a chance to retaliate. For one man, "When we created CAWCS, we knew we were trying to create something new. . . . We planned it to be a test case. You have to understand that part of this was personal: there was the revenge factor at work. . . . I wanted to pay back some of those who gave me so much grief by creating this incredible study that would completely leave them out in the cold."

CAWCS began formally in 1978 when a diverse committee . formed to decide which parts of the study would be conducted internally and which contracted out to consultants. Members wrote the "Request for Proposal" (RFP) soliciting consultants to bid competitively for the study.[11] How to make project impacts commensurable was a hot topic among members. Writing the job description for CAWCS was itself an extraordinary process, because participants decided early on that this would be the first occasion for members of the New Guard to rehearse some of the decision strategies they were advocating. Members of the New Guard saw in CAWCS the acid test for their procedures. If they could generate a good decision on what to do about Orme Dam, they believed their procedures could work anywhere. The situation was complicated, since not all of the procedures had been fully developed yet, and none had been soundly tested before. As one man described it:

> We began to invent the process we were to use in CAWCS. It was godawful. . . . We demanded consensus on every single significant decision, including what constituted a significant decision. . . . We decided if we couldn't do decision making [in the committee] in a rational, open, consensus model, we didn't have a chance to pull it off with the public on something as hard as Orme. It was amazing that any of us survived. We were literally ready to kill each other at some points. . . . It made a decision seem almost impossible. We needed first of all to figure out a decision model for this whole thing. The commensuration question came back at us. How were we going to put this all together?

The resulting document, according to participants, was "the most elaborate RFP ever prepared for a water project." Commemorated in a signing ceremony, it represented three long months of long days, "hundreds of arguments," and "intensely fulfilling work." Participants were surprised at how invested they became in the project and one another. Allen remembers the experience as "one of the more fascinating, exquisitely intensive, group processes I have ever been through. . . . What a sense of accomplishment! We felt like family when it was over."

CAWCS proceeded in three stages, with the public participating in each stage. First, study objectives were identified and a broad range of elements, both structural (e.g., dams, levees, bridges) and nonstructural (improved floodplain management), for meeting these were

11. An RFP typically describes a problem or piece of work, the types of services required to solve the problem or do the work, and the standards that will be used for evaluating proposals.

screened. The original goals of flood control, improved water supply, and additional regulatory storage were supplemented with an attempt to address public concerns over social and environmental impacts, dam safety, and cultural resources. Second, these elements were combined into plans and evaluated further. These were winnowed down to the eight candidate plans, which were evaluated in great detail in the final phase. These plans included three versions of a confluence dam, Plan 6 (the alternative eventually selected by Watt), and a "no-action" plan approximating the status quo.[12]

The process that created CAWCS generated the same strong commitments, loyalties, and identification that came to characterize the bigger study, and many of the people who worked on this committee worked on CAWCS as well. New employees, both consultants and agency people affiliated with the New Guard, found it an overwhelming first project. Denise, a novice consultant, was hired by the prime contractor during the final phase of CAWCS. She described the experience as "learning to swim in the ocean during a hurricane." The publicity surrounding the study was such that during critical periods, reporters would court inexperienced team members in their efforts to obtain unreleased information or an intemperate quote.[13] Especially during the final year of the study, when impacts and interests took on human faces, the stakes of the decision weighed heavily on members of the New Guard. Some of them came to believe that lives and communities were at stake. It was hard to sleep some nights. The vindication of the new procedures became a less important goal than making a good decision, even though many remained convinced these were closely linked.

Implementing Rationality

Different rational decision-making techniques were used in different parts of the investigation. As the EIS required, impacts for each plan were summarized and compared. All impacts were ultimately expressed quantitatively, as numbers or ratios summarizing both the good and bad consequences attending each alternative, and all techniques made a sharp distinction between the factual judgments made by "experts," for example, the social, economic, or environmental "im-

12. Brown (1984:148–49) gives more detail on CAWCS' organization and objectives. Reservoir capacity that is dedicated to conserving and storing water to balance water supply and demand is known as regulatory storage.

13. One man unhappily found himself the subject of an scathing newspaper editorial, the result of his suggesting to a reporter that, with a cost-benefit ratio well over one, the "big" Orme dam might not be the most efficient alternative.

pacts" attending various plans, and the evaluations of those facts concerning whether these were good or bad, for example, their "effects."[14]

The economic analysis incorporated cost-benefit analyses for each plan, assuming a range of operating conditions. In these market-based models, commensuration was accomplished by either estimating or simulating prices. The agency deployed standardized methodologies for estimating the prices of most costs and benefits. For values where there were no reliable data for estimating prices, contingent valuation methods were used. These used surveys to elicit the willingness of respondents to pay for hypothetical activities or public goods without prices (see Portney [1994:3–17] for a useful overview of contingent valuation). But these did not always produce robust results.

Economists tried valiantly to incorporate environmental values into their cost-benefit analysis; one example involved deriving a dollar value for some forms of recreation that existed outside a formal market. Tubing down the Salt River is an extremely popular form of recreation in Arizona, one the confluence dam would eliminate. Economists tried to derive a demand curve for tubing by comparing data obtained from a willingness-to-pay scale with the estimated costs of tubing obtained from "experiential" data gathered from tubers. The problem was a common one: attitudes and behavior simply did not align. One economist described the results:

> We tried so hard to measure the value of tubing as an economic value. We hired graduate students to live on the river and interview people. We gathered a whole bunch of data. We spent lots of time and money. We'd run the data through models and try to come up with a dollar value, but the data failed all reliability tests. We built a regression model trying to synthesize a demand curve for the experience and the willingness-to-pay data. We wanted to correlate expressed willingness-to-pay with how much tubers really did pay, in travel expenses, etc. . . . The curve didn't work. It didn't turn out to be measurable. We never did come up with a dollar value for tubing. It's easy to put a dollar value on waiting to cross a flooded river, or fixing a building, in comparison. I want to believe that a lot of things [that some New Guard members] want to quantify are quantifiable, but that didn't work. I think it

---

14. Conflict ensued over which "decision factors" to use to capture the important dimensions of the decision, to distinguish between the plans. Analysts used their discretion in selecting the evaluation factors for their specialty, but more controversial was how to winnow the list of factors that would be used by the public to measure their preferences in the Public Values Assessment. It was widely understood, however, that some factors were proxies, or even euphemisms, for other goals. For example, "flood control" meant dams, and most people understood this.

was more a failure of methods than of theory, but you couldn't
prove it with our experience.

As often happens with things that are hard to measure, the value of
tubing was excluded from the economic analysis. This economist felt
ambivalent about this failure. As he said: "Tubing must have value.
Every weekend in the summer the river is packed with thousands of
people down there doing it. I just don't know how to accurately capture
that value." As a result of what he described as a "methodological failure," he felt a conflict between what he called his "professional and
environmental values": "I want to be a hard scientist and I want to be
an environmentalist. Sometimes [I] can succeed at doing both. When
I wear my professional hat—the values [the environmentalists] assert
do exist—but the techniques for measuring are poorly defined. They
are hard to measure, and when they are measured, the values are small.
And [the environmentalists] don't like this. But as an economist, what
can I do?"

The general structure of the social account was similar to that used
by other disciplines, consisting of defining the "baseline" or "present"
condition, making causal projections about future conditions with each
one of the alternatives and saying whether these changes or "impacts"
would be good or bad for the people affected. The definition of the
baseline condition and the projection of the future state with each alternative were also structured by "impact factors" which, for relocation,
included: stress, morbidity and mortality rates, personal autonomy,
satisfaction with lifestyle, family interactions, informal support networks, and community viability and community cohesion. The communities of those who faced possible relocation were described according to these factors, and then projections were made about each
of these factors for a range of future conditions assuming that each
plan—including the "do-nothing" plan—was implemented.

The impacts associated with each plan were then evaluated by the
analysts. This evaluation was termed rating the "effects" of the plans,
and these were ultimately expressed using an ordinal scale. Commensuration did not take place explicitly until the Social Well-Being Account was constructed. This account represents the "culmination" of
the social assessment and summarizes quantitatively the impacts and
effects for each alternative.[15] This was the first time that such an account

15. The procedure for devising this account is described in detail in USBR (1982a). First
the plans were plotted on a scale representing the range of impacts for each category, e.g.,
relocation at Fort McDowell or at Roosevelt Lake and flood-damage reduction. Then
numerical weights were assigned to each impact category. On the basis of these weighted
ratings, an overall score was calculated for each plan, and the plans which maximized
"social well-being" were designated. The rationale for the weights given to impact cate-

had ever been constructed in a social assessment for the bureau. Like the Public Values Assessment and the Economic Accounts, the "findings" of the Social Account were not then formally incorporated in commensurate terms into the findings of the other disciplines. Commensuration ended with the designation of the "socially preferred plan": the plan that the social analysts, on the basis of their analysis and calculations, determined was the alternative that maximized social benefits (positive effects) and minimized costs (negative effects).

The social analysis culminated in the construction of a "Social Well-Being Account" that quantified all social impacts associated with each plan. Projected social impacts were displayed as precise differences between the present and future conditions. Sometimes carefully defined ordinal scales were constructed for particular social impacts, but the cumulative social impacts associated with each plan were always quantified.[16] For example, analysts believed that forced relocation would undermine the political efficacy of Yavapai leaders who would have fought and failed to prevent it. This "impact" had to be described as a specified difference (e.g., substantial, moderate, or insignificant shifts, or no change) in the political efficacy of community leaders for future conditions with and without forced relocation.

Analysts were far more confident of their predictions than they were of their scaling; they disliked being put in the position of having to explain why something was really a "9" instead of a "8," or why political efficacy would decline "substantially" as opposed to "moderately." Most social analysts would have preferred to make projections about the social impacts associated with various alternatives, and then defend these projections with their primary data and the relevant social science literature. As Susan explained, "You get used to working backwards. You figure out what you think is important, what you think is going to happen and then find a way to make it look like it was all measured." Susan believed the projections, which were firmly grounded in social science research. What was arbitrary for her was how to translate these into the qualitative terms dictated by the decision framework.

The Public Values Assessment (PVA), part of the program for incorporating citizens into the decision process in CAWCS, relied on a judgment-based model to commensurate public preferences about the

gories is based on the number of people affected, their duration, whether or not they are reversible, and the estimated probability that the projected impacts will actually occur.

16. The efforts of social analysts to describe impacts in terms they thought more accessible were not always appreciated. One project manager, an engineer, wanted to know what "all these words" were doing in the chart that summarized social impacts for members of the public.

various plans. The PVA was a technique for constructing utility functions for individuals based on their judgments of the relative importance of the various decision factors.[17] Decision analysts developed a
user-friendly computer program (dubbed MATS, for Multi-Attribute
Trade-Off System) that provided the framework for the PVA. Incorporating measures that technical experts (e.g., economists, sociologists,
hydrologists, archaeologists, etc.) placed on the performance of each
alternative, MATS would, through a series of questions and comparisons, elicit preferences from the public, measure these, and then mechanically identify for people the plan that maximized their measured
preferences. The combined ratings of the various groups were used to
calculate a "desirability score" for each alternative. The analysis included sensitivity tests and a series of comparisons between different
groups across different decision factors to show how much agreement
there was about these factors. Average differences in factor weights
were also compared across all the groups to pinpoint precisely where
consensus did or did not exist. The findings of the PVA were included
in the EIS and its supporting documentation; they were provided to
all groups that participated and to all those involved in making the
final decision, for example, the Governor's Advisory Council, BR leaders, political figures, and Secretary Watt.

This decision technology was controversial with some members of
the New Guard. Some worried about the artificiality of the commensuration techniques and the arbitrariness of devising quantitative measures for social impacts. Ann argued that quantifying social impacts
made them harder to interpret and less meaningful for most people.
She was deeply skeptical of such "scientism," believing that the "false
precision" conveyed by these techniques obscured more than it revealed and left their analysis vulnerable to critics who might fixate on
the numbers or on the scaling and ignore the findings. They also worried that commensuration required disposing of too much critical information. A consultant experienced in controversial public decisions was
also skeptical at first of the decision technology. He believed that decisions like this were fundamentally political and typically irrational and
that imposing a rational decision structure would lessen the odds of

17. Fourteen factors were included in the PVA: Cost, Net Economic Benefits, Historic
Resources, Prehistoric Resources, Flood Control, CAP Regulatory Storage, Indian Relocation, Non-Indian Relocation, Lake Recreation, Stream Recreation, Threatened and Endangered Species, Lake Habitat, Stream Habitat, and Water Quality. These factors were
selected by analysts after extensive consulting with experts and affected groups. They
were chosen for their capacity to discriminate between plans, be carefully defined, reflect
just one idea, and be measured. Factor definitions included a range of impacts linked
to alternatives that performed best or worst for this factor.

making a decision. Despite these doubts, both social impacts and public values were expressed in commensurated terms.

This emphasis on the technical evaluation of the "performance" of plans left outside the PVA analysis the worth of the goals that these plans were designed to accomplish. Whereas members of the public or study participants would talk about whether this sort of water development was a good thing for Arizona, and whether more flood protection was really needed, there were no formal mechanisms within these analyses for incorporating such concerns over project goals. Instead, alternatives were described as performed poorly or well, causing some kinds of impacts and not others, and people's views were summarized about how much they cared about these. The models that informed these investigations represented rigorous refinements in conceptualizing rationality that stimulated innovative applications. But underneath their technical sophistication, the basic logic of instrumental rationality lay intact: the evaluation of means for accomplishing ends that are formally exogenous to the framework, and therefore logically indefensible.

Retreats from Commensuration

It is interesting to note where commensuration stopped in CAWCS. In the PVA, commensuration ended with the display of numbers generated for each group for each alternative. The PVA was the only (documented) instance during the investigation where trade-offs were formally made among different types of impacts. Instead of somehow aggregating or integrating these trade-offs, the PVA merely presented the results of public's evaluations of the plans as a series of "snapshots" of the preferences of the participating interest groups. Making trade-offs between the various interests would required weighting the "value" of the values of the respective groups; this was judged inappropriate and politically dangerous by team managers.

The potential for conflict became evident when shouting matches ensued between the environmentalists, developers, and water lobbyists brought together to test the techniques. As a way to eliminate the conflict, members of the New Guard decided to segregate the public into groups based on similar values and interests when conducting the actual procedures. No effort was made to make the findings of the PVA commensurate with any of the results of the other "accounts." These each culminated with a number, but these numbers were never formally or publicly integrated.

The only occasion during CAWCS when the use of the rational trade-off procedure was successfully rejected by study participants involved the influential Governor's Advisory Committee (GAC). This group was appointed by Governor Bruce Babbitt to represent and monitor the state's interests in the decision and to make a formal recommendation to the governor. GAC was also envisioned as a way to buy time and create a forum where a consensus might emerge. Composed of representatives of various, often influential stakeholders, the group's recommendation was a turning point in the decision.

Despite the urgings of CAWCS managers, GAC rejected the multiattribute trade-off technique as a means for arriving at its recommendation. Those GAC members most opposed to using these techniques included the head of the state's largest utilities and the mayor of Phoenix, two ardent and powerful Orme supporters. Their stated objection to the techniques was that they were unnecessary for such savvy, experienced decision makers, and their influence was enough to quash their use. Privately, investigators believed that these Orme supporters sensed that public opinion was turning against their dam, and they hoped to hide this (accurate) impression from committee members and the press. They also probably regarded these techniques as harder to manipulate.[18]

There are several reasons why commensuration was limited in this way. First, the procedures imposed by NEPA and by the principles and standards issued by the Water Resource Council did not require a framework where the impacts and effects were integrated across all disciplines or accounts. Also, it was long unclear who would be responsible for making the final decision; estimates of how far up the agency and, eventually, up the Department of the Interior the decision would be bumped kept changing. Nor was it known how much influence various parties, including the GAC, would have. Providing information about a decision in a way that already appeared "decided" to powerful political actors seemed inappropriate.

The political packaging of the decision, which included not making the Secretary of the Interior look as if he were rubber-stamping a made decision, was something that concerned both local managers and agency leaders.[19] Yet Watt's reputation for unpredictability made such an accommodation riskier; even after the endorsement of the Arizona congressional delegation and the GAC (and the governor), there was

18. GAC members quickly ascertained that a strong consensus around Orme Dam was impossible and made a nearly unanimous recommendation for a non-Orme alternative. The ardent Orme supporters who had opposed the trade-off techniques eventually voted for the alternative.

19. This shows tacit recognition of the symbolic significance of decision making, an awareness that choice is not exclusively about deciding something; as their action implies, a choice can also be a signal about one's status or power.

still uncertainty about what Watt would do, even though the Orme alternative seemed such an obviously superior choice. Just what information to "send up" to him to inform his decision was something carefully deliberated within the agency. It was finally decided to have Watt select from three "candidate" plans, with the heartiest agency endorsement going to the best non-Orme alternative. This decision also reflected participants' concern with facilitating face saving for long-time Orme supporters. Allowing Orme to remain a "contender" for longer as the decision traveled up the hierarchy, rather than excluding it as a suitable candidate earlier, was taken as a signal that supporting Orme had not been such a poor decision.

Unlike the Old Guard, members of the New Guard came to the final phase of the project divided in their assessment of alternative plans. Some had initially supported Orme Dam, some were undecided about which plan was best, and others thought Orme was a bad idea. As more became known about the performance of the alternatives, more members of the New Guard came to think that a non-Orme alternative was technically viable. A small but important group became convinced that Orme was an unnecessary and politically disastrous solution. But it was only after tests of the new rational analytic decision revealed that the goals of the project were best satisfied by Plan 6 that some members were persuaded to switch their support from Orme to that plan.

For those who had first supported Orme Dam, their confidence in the legitimacy of these procedures and the credibility of the investigation allowed them to switch their support to the plan identified by the procedure as the best outcome. Among the New Guard, disagreements would center on the appropriate weighting of factors or the language used to convey the significance of decision factors. These disagreements decreased when sensitivity tests (which required commensurated input) showed that preferences were quite stable, that even if some more marginal attributes were thrown out and new ones added, the weights that individuals attached to the various factors would have to be radically changed in order for another alternative to emerge as maximizing utility. For the New Guard, the procedure worked the way it was supposed to. It increased their rationality.

Also persuasive were the findings of the Public Values Assessment. Representatives of over sixty groups or communities participated, and its results showed that values of most people would be maximized by an alternative to Orme Dam. One virtue of this procedure was that it allowed people who had formerly been excluded from participating in the debate over Orme Dam now to be incorporated into the process. Most notably, the Yavapai community was consulted and involved.

NEPA, in forcing the BR to develop a range of alternatives to evaluate (where different plans were distinguished by more than the dimensions of the proposed dams) decisions now involved real choices between plans rather than simply affirming (or occasionally rejecting) a single plan. The PVA procedures showed the political viability of a compromise plan, one that accomplished the policy goal of improved water supply and better flood protection, without forcing the relocation of the Yavapai community and without the most harmful environmental consequences. This, along with documenting the breadth of opposition to Orme Dam, allowed political leaders to shift their support from Orme Dam to an alternative plan.

The way that people were incorporated into the PVA portion of the public involvement program merits scrutiny. Public involvement in CAWCS included an enormous number and broad range of activities, ranging from newsletters sent, opinions solicited by response forms, public meetings held, presentations given, and the creation of special advisory groups like GAC. Although expensive (estimated costs were $1,000,000 [Brown 1984]), thousands of people participated in the program, and it was widely credited with helping to create the compromise that emerged. The PVA was a major component of the public involvement program, and although heroic efforts were made to be as inclusive as possible, participation in it was highly structured and restrictive in other ways. It was limited to representatives of groups or organizations that had demonstrated prior interest in CAWCS. Two characteristics are especially notable. First, participation required "interest groups"; the assumption was that if people cared about an issue, they were involved in some formal group that corresponded to their interest.[20]

Second, it was assumed that the individual utilities of participants were somehow indicative of their groups, that groups were homogeneous in ways that made members' values comparable and allowed representatives to be proxies for the groups' "collective preference."[21]

20. The Yavapai were represented by tribal council members and others designated by community members, by an advocacy organization found by sympathizers, and by people affiliated with religious or political organizations that supported their claims.

21. A detailed account of all CAWCS public involvement activities is found in the 1982 summary (USBR 1982c). The PVA is described in (USBR 1981b). There were many forums in which interested individuals could participate as individuals rather than representatives, but not the PVA. Requests to participate were sent to 112 groups representing the gamut of stakeholder interests. This list was culled from previous contacts, the efforts of CAWCS personnel to locate groups with a possible interest in the decision, and the recommendations of all those invited or those who participated in earlier meetings. Sixty groups agreed to participate. Groups with like interests—e.g., environmental,

Interpersonal utility comparisons remain theoretically controversial among decision theorists, but one way to finesse the problem is to create a "bigger" person by proxy, where the values and utility of a group's representative encompasses all members. The group-behind-the-individual enhances the importance and relevance of the "representative" person's values; the "solidity" of the group for members is also facilitated by the formal standing that is granted the group by this process. The authority of the procedures is also bolstered by tacitly incorporating all those "represented" and by appropriating the legitimacy and normalcy of interest-group politics.

These participation requirements were, in part, practical strategies for controlling the scope of an analysis that could have easily included thousands of individuals, and ensured that the entire range of interests was represented. But they also reinforce some powerful ideas about interest groups as the appropriate political units of analysis, first by linking participation to membership in these groups, and then by transforming members of these groups, by proxy and by procedure, into "rational subjects." The conjoining of rationality, and all that this connotes, with interest groups valorizes both.

The Symbolic Significance of CAWCS

For the New Guard, CAWCS represented the triumph of rationality and democracy: The people spoke, the leaders listened, and instead of Orme Dam, a better alternative was built. Their rational decision models provided members of the public with the appropriate information, which was organized to ensure a reasoned response. In complex decisions involving difficult technical information that taxed the limits of even expert knowledge, these models could structure participation in ways that allowed ordinary citizens to make sophisticated decisions in accordance with their values. The New Guard's commitment to public involvement and to rational decision making was linked, both reinforcing their commitment to rational choice models. The New Guard wanted to include the public; they wanted to trust citizens to help them make good decisions that reflected citizens' values and concerns. But they could not simply let them vote on policy. For members of the New Guard, their procedures were partly a means for vindicating the quality of decisions made in a more democratic process.

The New Guard's commitment to something as abstract and intangi-

---

flooding, Indian, and water-development concerns—met together in an effort to minimize conflict in ways that did not affect the procedure.

ble as "rational procedure" meant that work was needed to reify their values and accomplishments. Susan described the problem as the "kid predicament," which confronts parents who have trouble "explaining to your kids what it is you do when you're away from them all day. Implicit in their question is the assumption that in order to justify your absence, it had better be pretty good." The New Guard could not simply take their grandchildren to see their dams. Instead, they had to find other ways to make their work tangible to themselves and to others.

When we reify ideas, we simplify and organize them in ways that give them weight, eases communication, and makes them tangible. One powerful way to do this is to create symbols that give form to abstract ideas or relationships. These symbols allow us to interact with ideas, to become emotionally involved with them, and to create ties among those who use or respond to them. For the New Guard, the most available and accessible symbol for their work and their commitments to rationality was CAWCS. The successful public study that first embodied their ideas and their contributions to resolving a persistent, embarrassing political problem came to stand for who they were. It signified to them, that however abstract one's job might seem, it can make a difference in people's lives. As one man put it:

> When we started [CAWCS,] I wouldn't have bet a quarter on the chances of us pulling this off. It was such an incredibly improbable set of things. I was talking about social impacts—something only a few obscure planners thought about. We were talking about Native Americans. No one cared about them; they were just a bunch of "Apaches." The idea that you would look for an alternative to a dam that was in such a perfect dam site, when there were so few of those things left, it was almost as though we were being sacrilegious—to interfere with this perfect dam—from the perspective of the engineers. . . . When people say, "The hours you put in, is it really worth it?" Every once in a while, you better believe it. That's what public service is all about. It's about every once in a while being on the right side with the right tools when it really counts.

In forms as varied as the stories they told, the official logo they created, the celebrations they attended, and the glass paperweights some were awarded from grateful participants, CAWCS became the symbol the New Guard needed. It was their "dam." Although it cannot be toured or photographed, in the New Guard's stories, it does have one quality that would appeal to children: a happy ending.

CAWCS, as a symbol, gained currency as it was mobilized. A man trying to convince his supervisor to fund an expensive public involvement program used CAWCS to exemplify what might be accomplished.

> [What's needed] isn't just dollars, time, or staff resources that are
> critical. . . . It's the devotion of people and their lives to a process;
> I gave as an example the ten-year reunion of CAWCS, and how it
> represented a profound professional experience in the lives of all
> of the people that worked on it. It was so engrossing and so all-
> encompassing, it was almost like a combat experience that we all
> shared. . . . We developed the camaraderie, the unity of spirit—
> even though we fought like gangbusters; it was us against all the
> odds, against everyone. We won. But it wasn't in the winning; it
> was in the doing that gave that experience. That's not something
> you go buy. It isn't sellable. You have to arrange the conditions
> and hope that it works. . . . This isn't a job. You can't think of it
> like that. It's a commitment—of time, effort, energy, enthusiasm,
> and a very big chunk of people's selves. That is what you have to
> have.

Members still talk about the day they learned of James Watt's decision, of Wes Steiner's conversion, or of whatever signaled to them that a successful resolution was in sight. The significance of "the day that Orme died," as some have described this epiphany, is revealed in people's precise recollections of what they were doing or thinking when they heard the news, the familiar way that we personalize important public events. When Steiner announced that he no longer supported Orme Dam, an Indian activist recalls shouting for joy as she was vacuuming. For Allen, it was Watt's press release: "I will never forget until I die the day Watt made the famous announcement. He basically decided we were alright. I never heard of any other good decision Watt made. The guy was a loose cannon. We didn't know what to expect. It seemed so clear what the right choice was, but you didn't know with him. That was one of the days I always look back on."

The intensity of CAWCS left its mark on those who were part of it, and even now it is hard to miss the emotion when participants talk of it. During its height, many felt consumed by it, unable to think of other things. Project loyalty became a basis for association, since it was easier and more fun to be with people who understood. The bond among members of the New Guard was forged from adversity and uncertainty, from having to trust one another, from sharing, for a time, a common fate. Virginia, a CAWCS consultant, describes it as a life-transforming experience:

> There was an excitement around CAWCS. We knew we were do-
> ing something new. We were creating a new process, inventing

much of it as we went along. And it was so challenging. People were routinely putting in 70, 80, even 100 hour weeks. . . . God, was I tired! We knew we were doing something important. The stakes were high. We believed then, and I know I still believe now, that people's lives were at stake. We had to learn to trust each other. This was especially important since we were all so different from each other. . . . Even our politics were different. Yet there was great esprit de corps and intimacy among the team, partly because we created a process that enabled us to talk across all those boundaries. And that's pretty rare. . . . You don't get many opportunities in life to participate in something like CAWCS. It is something to savor. . . . I hope that the process we created continues, because I believe in it. I'll never forget the experience. It sounds corny but it changed my life.

Despite diverse professional backgrounds, this group was united by having worked on something that mattered, personally and politically. They had become invested not just in each other but in the process they helped devise and test. Although, after CAWCS, their lives had taken them in dramatically different directions, they still felt linked. It was still reassuring to be with the only people who could understand what the experience meant to them. And that is why, ten years later, their reunion was so satisfying.

Reinterpreting Rationality

Time and experience have prompted some reappraisal of the New Guard's rationality. Ben, who helped create the procedures adapting rational choice models to bureau planning, the man who earlier described himself as a disciple of Stokey and Zeckhauser, as someone who believes there are "no incommensurables in the real world," admits that maybe not all relationships in public choice should be subjected to commensuration. Ben now believes that some relationships should be defined in absolute terms, as unequivocal obligations, or as rights. He cites approvingly laws like the Threatened and Endangered Species Act that use language like "you must" and "you shall not."

Ben has also come to think that it may be better to define decision searches more narrowly and then "monitor the heck out of their performance." He concedes, in what he describes as "reflective moments," that maybe a "satisficing" decision strategy is better than the maximizing rational choice models he adapted and promoted.[22] At first glance,

22. Satisficing, as opposed to maximizing, decision models involves comparisons of alternatives with a set of aspiration levels set for the various dimensions of choice. It is not necessary to make trade-offs among different dimensions, since all that matters is whether or not some threshold is met for each dimension. Instead of evaluating alterna-

this seems a small concession, one acknowledging the uncontroversial cognitive limitations of human beings. But Ben, trained in decision analysis, knows well the assumptions underlying these models. In advocating satisficing as a decision strategy, he is relinquishing the requirement for commensuration. After all, he says, "No one has ever done a really good job of predicting the future, and maybe our time and money is better spent in devising plans that can be closely monitored and easily adapted." Ben's criticisms of commensuration are primarily cognitive, not cultural. His apprehension is not that he believes commensuration distorts or is somehow inappropriate but that it responds to normal cognitive biases intruding on the process, the imperfections of our knowledge, and the limitations of resources available to decision makers.[23]

Another man who helped develop commensuration techniques for biological impacts has also become more sensitive to how these processes can be abused. Much of Paul's career has been spent grappling with the problem of commensuration. He helped to develop the Habitat Evaluation Procedure (HEP), a widely used system for making projected biological impacts commensurable. When asked to reflect on the consequences of the procedures used to commensurate environmental impacts, he is both philosophical and pragmatic. He sees commensuration as fundamental to planning. To critics, he quickly points out that without commensurated impacts, nonquantified impacts are often excluded:

> [Commensuration] is always a problem with planning. Before [NEPA], we did it as an economic model—we assigned dollar values. It was hard to get environmental values included since they weren't easy to translate into economic terms. We would do it by deriving some trumped-up value for irreplaceable resources, or by getting local people to say they won't accept the plan without that environmental resource. . . . Principles and Standards, which fit with my philosophy, provided a framework for benefit-cost ratios in dollars and, in another scale, for nondollars. It said you were supposed to quantify [both ways] . . . you were supposed to de-

---

tives simultaneously and selecting the one that maximizes one's preferences, as more rigorous rational models require, in this strategy, search is sequential. The first alternative that satisfies minimal thresholds is selected. See Herbert Simon (1945, 1955).

23. Ben's other criticisms of the rational models that he helped develop and promote are unrelated to commensuration. He worries about the appropriateness of using the values of contemporaries to make choices whose impacts will be felt most acutely by successors. He notes how difficult it is to devise a decision framework that adequately represents highly valued resources. In his words, "The bias of most systems is to pull impacts toward the middle."

velop a single bottom line for each account according to those in-
structions; to say which is the best plan as a result of the planning
procedure. People have trouble doing it. I'm not sure we always
do it, because it's hard.

Paul, like others, is unsympathetic to those who do not appreciate the
zero-sum quality of natural resource planning, to people who will not
accept the need to make difficult trade-offs: "People say you can't trade
apples and oranges. Well, I can. . . . People say you can't trade squirrels
for deer, but to me, you do that everyday. If I were a farmer, I have
to decide what to plant. If I plant corn, I don't plant hay. As a manager,
I have to decide to keep water in a reservoir or run it down a stream.
That's life. Some people don't think that way. They believe you can't
trade 'their' resource for anything else. Well that's a political strategy
or a lack of understanding about resources." Yet Paul is well aware of
how commensuration can be misused in the BR:

> I don't think people necessarily do things dishonestly. . . . If you
> want to play the system to get something done, you can manipu-
> late things. You can find a way to assign numbers to get what you
> want and then righteously defend those numbers. It's hard to dis-
> prove somebody's adoption of some number. They know if I assign
> a nine, I get what I want, and if I assign an eight, I won't. I have
> trouble dealing with that . . . scaling is really an indicator rather
> than an absolute number. I find people get locked into an answer
> when they shouldn't. In HEP, [assessing] stream flow is a proce-
> dural requirement. Theoretically, you do all the accounting in
> terms of assigning number values and then you look at how flows
> effect species. You look at all the different effects for the same flow
> for different species. Then you draw a graph. Some fish benefit;
> some fish are hurt. There are lines all over the graph. Fishery peo-
> ple have learned to cope with that. They say, "Here's the guide-
> lines. The flow that works best for the species we want to benefit
> is about this." HEP people in the bureau haven't learned that. More
> often, they use numbers as facts rather than indicators.

This scientist was describing what March and Simon (1958:164–69)
call "uncertainty absorption," a process in which "inferences are drawn
from a body of evidence and the inferences, instead of the evidence
itself, are then communicated." Uncertainty absorption and selective
attention to information naturalize classificatory schemes in ways that
reflect and reproduce organizational structure. Like the bureau analysts' use of HEP, these schemes become taken-for-granted, and their
influence in how information is assembled and attended to is often
forgotten by those who use them. It becomes normal, in Paul's word,
to "fixate" on the numbers and forget that these are rough indicators

based on layers of estimation and projection. Also forgotten is just how much information gets edited. The uncertainty that surrounds the information, and the assumptions and scaling built into these models, are the first casualties of this editing.

In reflecting on the consequences of commensuration, Paul appreciates its symbolic potential. He describes how he used MATS to help him perform employee evaluations, a sensitive task. With a little fudging, Paul can weight people with different job descriptions and "get to a number" to help him decide which jobs matter most and who deserves the most money. Paul uses MATS "mainly to see if it confirms or does not confirm my judgment; I use it to make up my own mind. If I had to defend my decision, I can prove how rigorous I was by showing the process I used to arrive at my decision. [The process] serves as a reasonable, convincing backup." Paul generally finds the commensurated trade-off models a "reliable shorthand. It is a convenient way to express the difference between poor and perfect without having to write a bunch of words. The problem is it is so compelling to play with the numbers. To just multiply two numbers together without doing the background work to really make those numbers comparable. But its certainly convenient and its readily accepted."

Like Ben, Paul now believes that some relationships are best excluded from trade-off schemes. For example, he thinks that the Yavapai's claim to their land is something that ought to be defined as a right and excluded from negotiations. He believes lawmakers, not bureaucrats, should determine those things which should be considered nonnegotiable and legally incommensurate. Even during CAWCS, when zeal for their models was untempered by experience, an example reveals that even devotees saw limits to commensuration. When Bill, a young and slightly weird social scientist, used MATS to help him decide which of his two girlfriends he should marry, he became the butt of jokes. When asked to explain why it was wrong, or at least so funny, that this man should use the models they had been promoting as "universally applicable and adaptable" in this way, most were hard pressed to explain what was wrong in applying them to decisions about whom to marry. People understood, if only tacitly, that there were boundaries around their appropriateness, that spouses ought to be incommensurable entities. Despite their reservations, members of the New Guard remained convinced that rational decision procedures improved decisions and allowed more people to participate in them.

Agents of Rationality

As is true of many experiences, what may have begun for the New Guard as a good idea or a way to solve a problem was transformed into something more. Abstract ideas become symbolized, personalized, and invested with feelings and values by the people who use and promote them. They take on new associations and meanings over time. They also create categories and schemas for viewing and interpreting the world. The New Guard's investment in rational decision making had many dimensions. What had begun as a way to solve a political problem, a strategy for integrating information, a useful organizational expertise, or a set of fascinating ideas or powerful tools became a means of institutionalizing deeply held beliefs about good government, a way to feel good about their work. Some ideas become so compelling to us that our attachments to them become emotional as well as intellectual, our identification with them becomes part of our repertoire for understanding ourselves. (This explains why some intellectual differences become so vitriolic and personal among academics.) Ideas themselves can become intertwined with other values in complex relationships that may not always be clear to those involved.

The New Guard's commitments to rationality and its link to public involvement were like that. For many, their investments were simultaneously intellectual, political, and emotional. While less tangible than a dam, less beautiful than a wild river, rationality was no less powerful or personal to them. What was incommensurable then, for the New Guard, was the procedures themselves—because of what they stood for, because of how they reflected their sense of themselves and the worth of their work. Members of the New Guard gave many speeches about public involvement, consensus building, and good decision making. They did not give speeches about what democracy or good government meant to them. Like with most of us, they found it hard to talk about things that are deeply felt, personal. But when they described what made them feel good about their work, one can hear their feelings. As Susan told me over lunch:

> Now if I go to a public meeting and I see all different sorts of people there, and it seems like people are really taking each other seriously, and trying to understand, well, it just gives me hope. It really does. They might never agree with one another, they might wind up fighting over what they want, they might even wind up screaming at each other, but at least they are all in the same room, talking about the issues. And I believe they have a right to all be in the room. . . . How long did we ignore the Fort McDowell community? . . . I think it's important for [people] to really understand what the stakes are for other people. . . . They need the right information. And they need to look people in the face when they talk about what's going to happen to them. That's what I've worked for. . . . I hope it means something. That's what I want my role to be.

The New Guard's promotion of rational decision-making models meshes with Theodore Porter's (1995) argument about the conditions that propel the diffusion and use of quantitative technologies. Porter argues that the proliferation of quantitative expertise represents a quest for what he terms "mechanical objectivity"—knowledge whose authority is based on explicitly following rules. This type of objectivity is most valuable under particular conditions: when decisions or knowledge affects dispersed, diverse groups, when accounts must be provided to powerful outsiders, when decisions are public, controversial, and politicized so that consensus is hard to reach, and when those making the decisions or creating the knowledge are distrusted and relatively weak. These are characteristics that apply to the New Guard. Recourse to the standardized use of numbers can solve pressing problems for harried bureaucrats like the New Guard, but the legitimacy and distance afforded by numbers come at the price of autonomy, as discretion is replaced by the exacting discipline of quantitative methods. And that is why the extension of quantitative technologies is often resisted by those whose authority they threaten.

The Old Guard did not understand the procedures the New Guard were promoting and did not see for some time that these might pose a threat to their power. They had nothing to offer a deeply divided and skeptical public in their stead. They were too discredited to retain public control over the investigations; nevertheless, their faith in Orme (and in politics as usual) was such that they could not imagine the New Guard's techniques as autonomous methods that might somehow constrain their power in making decisions. One group that appreciated this threat and was able to block the intrusion of the New Guard's techniques was the powerful Orme supporters on the GAC. The GAC members saw these procedures as limiting their discretion, as being difficult to manipulate, as making too public people's differing preferences, and stopped their use.

The New Guard, for tangled reasons, became agents of what Max Weber might call procedural rationality. Like the early Italian merchant capitalists Weber describes, members of the New Guard became an effective interest group promoting rationalization. In this example, "interest group" requires caution and unpacking. Interest and identity, as organizing ideas, were mutual, simultaneous constructions conjoined in subtle ways that make it hard to assert priority or establish neat causal links between them. Members' sense of themselves as a "group" and their understanding of their "interests" were contingent and unfolding ideas. Like Weber's merchants, they were deeply concerned with making better predictions about the future and using these to inform their actions. They, too, worried about the uncertainty of (new) law and the unpredictability of politics.

The New Guard's prescription was to try to make both more rational, more visible, and so they promoted rational decision analysis as a strategy for implementing new law and improving decision making. This commitment to rationality was nurtured by a desire for inclusion: their own, within their organization, and that of the "public," which had been excluded in the past. Commensuration became their mechanism of inclusion. It offered a sturdy, adaptive, universal device for conferring a formal parity in an unequal world. The consequence of this parity was having "the public" defined as interest groups, of having their commitments rendered as preferences that could be mechanically mapped onto outcomes.

The New Guard's investment in rationality became a substantive value. The procedures that they had understood as means became ends, and their commitments deepened, becoming independent of use and closely linked to their understanding of themselves. While Weber noted this capacity, and made it an essential feature of the spread of capitalism, he does not analyze the transformation in much detail. Nor does he describe how once purely practical techniques become invested with symbolic value that can supersede their technical advantage. For the New Guard, the processes by which both things happened are evident and accessible to analysis. An understanding of these processes is essential in explaining not only the diffusion of rational forms but also their power.

The capacity to define frameworks and adjudicate facts, to include and exclude, can be a formidable source of power. When it becomes naturalized in institutions, its links to agents may be hard to apprehend. But the New Guard's power was not that of the Old Guard to build the projects they wanted where they wanted. Because of their commitments and dependence on public participation and what Porter (1995) terms "mechanical objectivity," the New Guard's authority is rooted in technique and accountability. Theirs is a more portable and versatile authority, a more dispersed power than was the Old Guard's, but it is also more constrained. The techniques used by the New Guard must be seen as legitimate to experts outside the agency, and their mechanisms depend upon members of the public offering up their values for measurement. Both dependencies reinforce the autonomy of the techniques in ways that limit the discretion of the New Guard.

The New Guard Now: Reinventing the Agency

The New Guard is a less salient category that it once was, since neither the organization nor the members who composed it are the same. Once CAWCS was completed, members moved on to other projects, other jobs, and in some cases, other careers. The consultants, hungry for new work, left first, to write the proposals that would generate the new projects and new teams. Some members quit consulting after CAWCS, knowing it would never be so good again. A few went to work for environmental organizations.

BR employees lived with CAWCS longer, dealing with what some called the "cleanup" work—lawsuits, EIS amendments, the requisite documentation, and the inevitable political brushfires that occasionally needed putting out. CAWCS did boost careers. Some New Guard members now enjoy prominent positions within the agency, and their stature is such that to provide more details of their accomplishments would be to compromise promised confidentiality. Other members parlayed their experience in CAWCS to different kinds of jobs within the BR, as negotiators of water rights, as policy analysts, as planners charged with reinventing the agency's mission. Some, quite recently, were charged with the unenviable task of overseeing the downsizing of the agency in response to draconian budget cuts and multiple reorganizations.[24] Many left the BR to work on water issues in other forums, as members of regional or local water commissions or other agencies.

Within the BR, the original motives and aims for coalescing no longer pertain. NEPA and the Water Resource Council's Principles and Standards are well institutionalized; guidelines for both have been revised since CAWCS, and the procedures for complying are now established routines. The preparation of EISs typically begins much earlier than it once did and is better integrated with project planning. Rational decision-making procedures, reinforced by these regulations, are used for many different kinds of agency decisions; specific technologies, like MATS or HEP, have also been adopted by other agencies for selective use on key decisions. Occasionally BR decision analysts serve as consultants to other agencies making hard choices. Nonengineers are far better integrated into the agency; the engineering ethos that was once taken for granted has been contested and reshaped.

One key dimension of this change was the battle over the terms and scope of public involvement. Where once the "public" that counted, those who were routinely consulted and briefed, were the pampered political and water elites, the BR's constituency has expanded to include more of those affected by its projects, including environmentalists. Where once public involvement seemed radical and intrusive, it is now much more widely accepted as a normal part of doing business.

---

24. Most members of the Old Guard have now retired, as have several members of the New Guard. I am told that the "reduction in forces" has eliminated 20 percent of BR employees through attrition, buyouts, and layoffs.

As Ben describes it, "I don't have to make the public involvement speeches anymore. Area managers make them. The same types I spent so much time trying to convince are now trying to convince others. It took getting their heads bashed in a few times for them to get it, but once that happens, they start to believe in [public involvement]. It makes me nostalgic, but it is also very gratifying. We have opened up the processes. We now work with diverse groups. Part of it is a function of who is making the decisions. Decisions aren't being made at the high national levels. . . . The money isn't there anymore, so more and more decisions are made by local BR offices, at the community level. This means, by its nature, it's a more diverse set of folks who are almost under the radar scopes of the national leaders. We don't build the big, $5 billion dams anymore."

Democratizing a Bureaucracy

The New Bureau, signified in the revised operations of Glen Canyon that produced the Grand Canyon flood, remains a work in process. It is hard to predict how far the agency is willing to go in modifying the way it operates its structures. Its capacity to change these is constrained by contracts already negotiated, legal obligations already undertaken. As one environmentalist told me, "I'll believe they've changed when they start tearing down dams." Although the relative openness of the decision making within the Bureau of Reclamation still varies, agency employees are now, in general, more likely to endorse the idea that citizens affected by their decisions should be involved in making them, and that the agency's traditional constituencies should be expanded to include a broader range of interests. Public involvement, the umbrella term used for such participation, is now a well-funded, taken-for-granted feature of most projects. It is hard to predict how durable the changes it embodies will be. But it is also hard to imagine that the agency could ever revert to the days of huge, well-funded projects.

It may be tempting to dismiss the changes suggested by the New Bureau as too little, too late, to question the significance of broadening constituencies and sharing power once the fix is in, of deemphasizing dam building only in light of the West's overdeveloped and overallocated rivers. Yet I would argue that these changes are worth understanding. The stakes of water politics remain high. That BR decisions are still closely monitored by powerful interests and that they remain contested suggest that they remain political salient. It is clear that the changes in the agency are deeply meaningful for participants. More fundamentally, changes in the BR might offer some insight into understanding the conditions that prompt a bureaucracy to change, of helping us understand when and what kinds of laws might stimulate bureaucracies to become more accessible, and in what terms.

Whatever one might think of the significance of the New Bureau, it represents a complex response to past engineering feats and to broad demographic, political, and economic changes, what one planner calls "the emergence of the Yuppie West." Even so, the New Bureau, with its emphasis on managing existing natural resources rather than on building dams, and its greater reliance on public participation, is at least partly a creation of members of the New Guard and people like them within the agency. And the New Guard's commitment to commensuration has shaped this transformation in important ways. As a technology of inclusion, commensuration has made it harder to justify ignoring some groups and some issues; it may obscure, displace, or diffuse discretion, making it more mechanical, transferring it from engineers to planners, or from politicians to a broader range of interests. These are the political hazards associated with having a scientifically defensible, universally applicable technology in place, all set to measure and trade off any value. Commensuration in practice may yield a "failure of methodology," or it may be blocked by powerful groups of actors. But when commensuration becomes the premise of decision making, such exceptions must often be accompanied by elaborate defenses.

In constructing new, more ephemeral relations of relevance as it obliterates old ones, commensuration challenges preexisting categories and the social relations that sustain them. In so doing, commensuration helped destabilize the political alliances that undergirded and pro- tected the core technology of a dam-building technocracy. Substantive attachments to dams became harder to defend when dams were framed as alternatives and when a broad array of values could formally compete in their evaluation. And commensuration's link to an instrumental conception of reason has important implications for democratic practice, for who and how people can participate, and for how state policies are made legitimate.

In an influential interpretation of Max Weber's political writing, David Beetham has criticized Weber for minimizing the significance of substantive rationality as a source of legitimacy for modern states (1985:264–65).[25] Weber's analysis of democracy in *Economy and Society* makes some forms of democracy untenable in modern societies (e.g., mass democracy) and paints efforts to make social and political institutions more genuinely democratic as hopelessly unrealistic. The legitimacy of the modern bureaucracy, for Weber, resides squarely in its

25. Beetham's interpretation is indebted to Wolfgang J. Mommsen.

legality and in its procedural correctness; this form of authority cannot be effectively countered by recourse to broader societal values, such as a belief in the substantive value of democratic participation. The best we can hope for is an authoritarian form of democracy in which a political leader is able to wrest control of a bureaucracy and impose her values on it.

In the BR during CAWCS, appeals to democracy as a substantive value, both from outside (a legacy of the civil rights and environmental movements) and from within the agency (from members of the New Guard), were influential in stimulating efforts to devise techniques for making its decision-making accessible to more people—in mitigating some of the technocratic characteristics of this agency. Members of the New Guard had a clear interest in expanding public participation in agency decision making, since this created new constituents and an important organizational niche for them; they also sincerely believed that more democratic decisions were better decisions and that NEPA's substantive goal of protecting the environment was a legitimate ones. But these appeals became meaningful, first because they were backed by the force of NEPA's public participation requirements but also because they were translated by the New Guard into specific, portable, and technically respectable mechanisms of inclusion.

Philip Selznick's analysis of the TVA has shown us both the ideological utility of appeals to democracy and how easily these can be compromised when they must be enacted in relation to powerful preexisting institutions. He argues (1984:ix–x), along with Michels (1949), that ideals not attached to specific criteria about the terms and costs of their enactment, ideals not translated into institutional routines, will inevitably become ideological scripts for legitimating the discretion of those in power. The New Guard, because of the crisis they inherited, the law they were implementing, their investment in mobilizing new constituents, and their authority as scientists and analysts, were able to routinize a particular form of democracy within a very technocratic agency. They translated their belief in democracy as a substantive value into a procedural democracy that was technologically driven, rendering it bureaucratic in ways that inevitably emphasized formal participation and formal equality over influence.[26]

26. The use of these sophisticated mechanisms for analyzing and documenting public values is one thing; their influence over agency decisions is quite a separate question. In this case, they did shape how elites interpreted the political viability of Orme Dam in relation to other policy. But just as documentation of environmental impacts does not obligate an agency to select environmentally sensitive policy, neither does documentation of public preferences always translate into influence or ensure the emergence of some compromise policy, as occurred in this case. The results of public involvement

The result of the New Guard's efforts to make their agency more democratic was a sophisticated, abstract form of instrumental rationality, exemplified in their Public Values Assessment, that shaped who could participate and how they might do so. The terms of democracy, as well as the science that informed it, were still controlled by technical experts who fixed the framework for participation, defined its discourse, decided what counted as a relevant fact, constructed the relationship between facts and policy, and, in defining the range of alternatives under consideration, set the agenda. This procedural democracy reproduced the split between facts and values, means and ends, substantive values and technique that is the hallmark of instrumental rationality. In so doing, those who became committed to a particular means, or those whose relation to the decision could not be properly translated into the terms of instrumental rationality, felt betrayed by the framework, which could not formally reconcile disparate values, express substantive values, or accommodate those whose identity was tied to these. As I will argue in the next chapter, Yavapai residents were wary of the New Guard's rationality.

---

efforts must be included and made public in the EIS. This, and the threat of lawsuits over the implementation of NEPA, make such analyses more influential than they might otherwise be. Minimally, they probably create more political heat for decision makers who ignore public opinion, especially if there exists some consensus. The manipulation of public opinion by elites, of course, is a form of influence not addressed in these analyses.

~~~~~ **Five** ~~~~~

Views from the Reservation: The Politics and Perspective of Yavapai People

[I]f a rigid separation of form and content leads to error in the
analysis of a work of art, how much more in the interpretation of
human feelings.

Max Horkheimer

It's true that we have to consider a piece of land as a tool to produce
something useful with, but it's also true that we must recognize the
love for a particular piece of land.

Bertolt Brecht

The land is our mother. You don't sell your mother.

Yavapai teenager, 1981

Colonization is always a cultural project. Legitimate domination depends on the cultural imperialism that struggles to control categories
of relevance. Sometimes "relations of representation," as a distinctive
venue of power, matter as much as relations of production. Despite its
many, varied guises, colonization often produces ideological battles
waged in terms of cultural difference. Efforts to define difference, to
map its contours, document its inferiority, contain it, romanticize it, or
eliminate it, are fundamental strategies of power. But even in its most
coercive forms, where inequalities are overwhelming, the groups in
question will ascribe motives to one other, react to each other, and react
to these reactions. Although some parties may dictate the vocabularies,
do most of the speaking, and gain most from the conversation, colonization and the construction of difference are always a dialogue. Its
meanings are never completely imposed, never fully established (Hall
1988:53–54, 1992:252; Comaroff and Comaroff 1991:27–28; Espeland,
forthcoming).[1]

These mutual and ongoing interpretations between colonial parties
are shaped by the histories that groups bring to these encounters, by

1. More generally, see Sahlins (1981); Todorov (1982). This is chapter is a revised version of Espeland (1994). I am grateful to the Law and Society Association for permission
to reprint it.

changing material conditions, shifting cultural or legal categories, and the emergence of new audiences. Sometimes their dynamism takes the form of inversions, where the terms that were once suppressed are turned against the oppressor. Difference once defined as inferior can become a source of strength. Sometimes this dynamism is linked to consciousness. Changing awareness of representation alters its effect. As strategic bids for legitimacy become habitual, we forget we ever intended them. Difference can be expressed or erased in bureaucratic routines without the bureaucrat's noticing.

Efforts to colonize Yavapai people have persisted over a long period. Some group has trying to take their land almost continually for the past 150 years. Their struggle to stop Orme Dam, to prevent another forced resettlement, is just the latest in a long series of often brutal encounters with miners, soldiers, settlers, contractors, farmers, and bureaucrats ranging from Indian agents to engineers. Their intimate relation to their land is forged from these struggles. Their ties to those who fought before them are made tangible in this land. And like most colonial encounters, the definition of their difference has been a central feature of these struggles. Yavapai identity, as others portray it and they experience it, has been mobilized in complex and contradictory ways.

As "savages," their difference warranted extermination. As "other," education was required to erase it. As "children," their difference required "protection" in ways that always benefited white men. Yavapai difference was also crucial semantic terrain on which the Orme struggle was waged. This time Yavapai difference was explicitly framed in cultural terms. To trivialize Yavapai claims to their land, some Orme supporters denied that Yavapai culture still existed. For them, authentic culture was immutable culture. Members of the New Guard were charged with documenting, measuring, and projecting Yavapai's difference, with turning culture into a decision factor. In reacting against these depictions of their culture, Yavapai residents defended and reexamined their difference. They argued against the rationality that excluded their history and commensurated their culture; they defined their difference against efforts that they believed distorted them. In doing so, their difference became a source of power.

As was true for members of both the Old and New Guards, the interests and identity of Yavapai people are evolving interpretations that change in relation to each other, and in relation to others' efforts to represent them. For the Yavapai community, their ties to their land, their sense of themselves as cultural beings, and the meaning of the Orme dispute have all been profoundly shaped by earlier struggles over their land. Their years spent resisting removal, explaining their special ties to their land and to one another have intensified these relations and changed their meanings. Knowing this history is crucial for understanding the stakes of the Orme struggle for the Yavapai. It is important for appreciating why residents adopted the strategies they did. And it is crucial for appreciating their response to the New Guard's procedures, for grasping the connections between identity and rationality.

This chapter presents the history that Yavapai residents used to frame the Orme dispute. It describes how Yavapai people's relation to their land evolved in their many struggles to retain it. It shows how, during the Orme dispute, Yavapai identity became explicitly politicized. It includes an analysis of how efforts to represent Yavapai interests and identity were shaped by the New Guard's decision procedures and the conception of rationality embedded in these. In reacting against the terms used to evaluate their interests, Yavapai residents devised political strategies that put back into the political process what the New Guard's procedures had edited out. In this way, the New Guard's rationality helped both to produce an effective political strategy and to elicit a collective reappraisal of the terms of Yavapai identity.

Trail of Tears, 1981: History as Reenactment

During an unusually hot Arizona September in 1981, members of the Yavapai community at Fort McDowell began a thirty-two-mile desert march from their reservation to the state capitol in Phoenix to protest Orme Dam. Launched with prayers and singing, the marchers walked along the side of busy highways for three days in temperatures reaching 110 degrees, carrying signs protesting Orme Dam. Nearly 100 Yavapai (about one-quarter of the reservation community) participated in the march, including some frail but determined Yavapai elders and toddlers in wagons pulled by parents. Louisa Hood, a woman in her sixties with crippling arthritis, marched despite her doctor's admonitions. "The doctor said I should stay home," she said quietly. "But I wanted to march with the crowd" (Tulumello 1981:A1). Those who were too sick or weak to march drove alongside in cars and pickup trucks, offering support and water to the marchers. John Williams, a quiet, serious man in his seventies, told one spectator he was walking for his grandmother.

Each night, as the marchers camped, they sang, told stories, and encouraged one another. The march culminated in large political rally at the capitol, where tribal leaders delivered to Governor Bruce Babbitt's top aide a handwritten bark scroll, designed they said, to make it hard for bureaucrats to file away and forget. The scroll proclaimed in simple, eloquent language, their deep attachment to their land, the harm its loss would cause them, and their determination to retain it.

The march was a successful political protest, garnering broad, sympathetic media coverage. It generated powerful images, the kind that television loves, that linger in viewers' minds: a small group of older women walking together in long camp dresses and new tennis shoes, a sensible accommodation of old to new; an old man with a walker; parents fanning the hot, sleepy babies in their arms. These were some of the scenes that made the evening news. But this march was more than a well-executed protest. Named by participants "The Second Trail of Tears," this march was cast as a reenactment of the earlier, brutal Trail of Tears that is a centerpiece of Yavapai history.

Trail of Tears, 1875

Over a century earlier, in February of 1875, about 1,400 Indians, most of whom were Yavapai, began a long, brutal resettlement march from the reservation at Camp Verde, Arizona, to the Apache reservation at San Carlos, Arizona, some 200 miles away (Mariella 1983:96–99; Espeland 1992:266–69). This march was instigated by a group of well-connected, corrupt contractors who sold reservation supplies to the government. Known as the Tucson Ring, these contractors worried that the Yavapai at Camp Verde were becoming too self-sufficient, thus reducing their profits (Mariella 1983:88–90; Bourke 1891:217–24; Bronson 1980:42). Through heroic efforts, which included digging a five-mile irrigation ditch using sharpened sticks, buckets, and even spoons for tools, the Yavapai had managed to develop agriculture so that they could almost feed themselves (Corbusier 1971:17).[2] They had worked so hard, because, after having been forced on the reservation in the first place, they were promised they could remain at Camp Verde forever. Now, just five years later, Ulysses Grant ordered their removal to the San Carlos reservation, the mountainous Apache reservation where poor land made farming difficult, and where the Yavapai were a small minority unable to speak with most other inhabitants.

The march lasted nearly two weeks. Despite the protests of the Yavapai and their ally, William Corbusier, the camp doctor, Camp Commander Alfred Dudley conducted it with deliberate cruelty. Instead of waiting till warmer weather, he initiated it during the cold winter months, when snow covered the mountains and rivers and streams were full. Instead of using the road around the mountains for their

---

2. One eyewitness was so impressed by the Yavapai's labors that he called the "digging of that ditch by hand with every conceivable sort of implement . . . worthy of a place in the greatest annals of the west" (Corbusier 1971:17).

removal, where horses and wagons could be used, Dudley insisted that the Yavapai be forced to go through the mountains, saying, "They are Indians: let the beggars walk" (Corbusier 1971:263).

We have four eyewitness accounts of the march. According to Dudley, "Of course the Indians were opposed to going, but when told it was the order of the President, that the move was intended for the purpose of placing them in more healthy and better country, that the move was to be peaceable and that they were not to be driven by troops, their consent was obtained" (Corbusier 1968:261). On the basis of Dudley's account, John P. Clum, the Indian agent at San Carlos, reported that "the removal . . . was effected with comparative ease and great satisfaction, nothing more serious occurring than a fight among themselves while en route, in which seven were killed and ten wounded" (U.S. Department of the Interior 1873:10). Corbusier accompanied the Yavapai on the march and kept a journal of his experiences; he noted that the army quickly ran out of supplies and how heart-wrenching the cries of hungry children were. He wrote that more than twenty-five babies were born during the march. Some were delivered dead by exhausted, malnourished mothers. Some babies froze to death when their mothers were not given blankets to cover them or allowed to rest after giving birth (Corbusier 1971:273). Maggie Hayes, a child on the march, left her account: "We had to walk all the way. The soldiers had ponies to ride. There was no road, very few trails. Many had no moccasins, but those who did, gave them to others who needed them more. Our clothing was torn to rags on the brush and cactus. With bleeding feet, weary in body and sick at heart, many wanted to die. Many did die. Rations were meager. It was winter time. We were not allowed to take the time and strength to bury the dead, and who would want to bury the dying? We waded across many streams. The river was running strong. . . . We were forced to cross the best way we could. Some of the weaker ones washed away" (Bronson 1980:42).

John Williams's retelling of his grandmother's account of the march describes the gratuitous cruelty of the soldiers, who maimed his grandmother and cut off one woman's ears, another's fingers: "The soldiers make them go straight over the mountains. The people don't have a wagon or horses. . . . Just walk. My grandmother had babies, children to take along on that trail. . . . One old man, he carried his wife in a burden basket. That woman was too old to walk; real old. Her husband is old, too. They make it to San Carlos, but don't live very long there. Some of them were real sick. The soldiers just poke them with the gun to make them walk faster. But some of them just went down and died. They leave them there, like dogs. Like killed flies they leave them there. . . . My grandmother was sick after that. . . . I don't know why white people hate Indians so much. . . . My people around here, they kill them and kill them. My God, that is awful for me" (Mariella 1983: 96–97).

The Trail of Tears is a pivotal event in Yavapai oral history. (Yavapai is not a written language.) It is a story that all Yavapai know and is often told as a reminder of the senseless brutality of the white man, of the unreliability of promises that government officials make, and of the pain of losing your land. In casting their protest march in 1981 as a reenactment of this original Trail of Tears in 1875, the Yavapai were clearly emphasizing the parallels between their earlier forced resettlement and their impending one. They were trying to convey—to decision makers, politicians, and their neighbors—the deep cultural and psychological importance of their land. They were also trying to express their difference, their distinctiveness, in a dramatic, public way. But the second Trail of Tears was more than an example of clever political strategy, an astute manipulation of potent images and symbols. This march was part of a complex process of the symbolic reappropriation and reinterpretation of their past. Reflecting their distrust of the government and an implicit critique of the New Guard's rationality, the march was a powerful assertion of Yavapai identity at time when it was being challenged by outsiders and misconstrued by well-wishers.

Before white encroachment, the Yavapai lived in what is now a large section of central and western Arizona. Spanish explorers, arriving in the late sixteenth and early seventeenth centuries, provide the first documentary evidence of the Yavapai (Spicer 1962:265).[3] The Spaniards described a group they encountered as hunters and gatherers living in "primitive conditions," and historians and anthropologists have concluded that these were Yavapai (Schroeder 1982:A-2). The Yavapai had little direct contact with the Spanish, although the Spanish slave trade exacerbated conflict among tribes. It was not until the mid–nineteenth century, after gold and copper were discovered in the area, that non-Indians began moving into Yavapai territory in significant numbers (Coffeen 1972:347). Though the miners did not require much land, military camps were established to protect them and their trade routes. The Yavapai were badly treated by the miners, some of whom formed a paramilitary group to fight the Indians. By 1864, more than one hundred miners and settlers had joined. Its leader, King Woolsey, under the auspices of negotiating a peaceful settlement, invited a large group of Yavapai to his camp. After offering them food, his men opened fire,

---

3. At least four distinct subtribes existed, characterized by some distinctive dialects and cultural practices. According to Mariella (1983:44), Yavapais alive in the 1980s could distinguish among Northeastern Yavapai (Wipukpa), Western Yavapai (Tolkepaya), Central Yavapai (Yavepe), and Southeastern Yavapai (Kewevkepaya).

killing thirty Yavapai in what became known as the Pinole "Treaty" (Schroeder 1974:38–39).

During the 1860s, the federal government built several army forts in the area, intending to move the Indians onto nearby reservations. Since so much land formerly used for hunting and gathering was now controlled by white settlers, some Yavapai, facing starvation, moved onto several small reservations within the boundaries of their aboriginal land (Mariella 1983:36). One of these reservations included Fort Mc-Dowell, the site of the current Yavapai reservation. Most did not remain on the reservations for long. Abused by the soldiers, these Yavapai could not sustain themselves with the rations allocated, and they were not provided with the water or irrigation facilities needed to grow their own food (Khera and Mariella 1982:162). To keep from starving, those living on the reservation were forced to hunt and gather and plant crops outside the reservation boundaries (Mariella 1983:73–75). Overall, these early attempts at relocation were abysmal failures.

The next few years were brutal ones for the Yavapai. With more white settlers moving into the territory and taking the best farmland, the conflict between the groups intensified. Vincent Colyer, sent by President Grant to manage Indian resettlement, describes his meeting with Soulay, a Yavapai chief, in October of 1871. Sick and starving, Soulay was too weak to stand and was unable to talk for several hours. Pointing to the Verde Valley, he finally said, "Where that house stands I have always planted corn and the white man told me to go away or he would shoot me; so I could not plant corn there anymore" (Bronson 1980:39). He described how white hunters had killed or frightened all the deer; for the Yavapai, unable to gather enough food during winter months, death was their only alternative. They were refused food at the military post and scolded for stealing farmers' crops. Soulay asked how he could possibly stop them when they were starving to death.

In 1871 the army sent General Crook, a famous Indian fighter, to Arizona. By employing Indian scouts who were superb trackers, Crook increased the frequency and efficacy of the army's raids on the Yavapai. In 1872 he issued a decree that all roving bands of Indians either enter reservations or be shot on sight. He also ordered that any gardens or food caches found by the military be destroyed (Mariella 1983:75–77). The starving Yavapai living off the reservation now faced the constant threat of military attacks led by the more competent Indian scouts. Having few weapons, they were virtually defenseless. While reliable estimates are hard to make, it is clear that many Yavapai died during this period and that the condition of those who did not was desperate.[4]

---

4. Bronson (1980:40) reports that one year, over fifty Indian raids were conducted, and forty isolated murders occurred. A Yavapai leader was reported as saying, "In the

The final blow to their resistance to resettlement came on December 28 of 1873, when a group of Yavapai hiding in a cave were massacred by the army. Skeleton Cave, as it is known locally, is located about twenty miles northwest of Fort McDowell in beautiful Fish Creek Canyon, a popular site for nature lovers. Few white people know the history behind the name of the cave, but Yavapai people know it well. Relatives, including some grandparents, of many Fort McDowell residents were killed at the cave. Military accounts refer to the event as the Battle of Skeleton Cave. The Yavapai's designation, the Bloody Salt River Massacre, more accurately reflects what happened. After finding a large group of Yavapai hiding out in a cave, Crook's soldiers kept firing rounds of ammunition into the cave, slaughtering those inside. There were no military casualties (Khera 1978:4–5).

Homothaya, also known as Mike Burns, witnessed the massacre as a young child after he was captured by the officer who led the expedition. In a manuscript he wrote as an adult, he describes how soldiers "were ordered to pour continuously buckets of lead against the walls of the caves behind those big boulders so as to scatter the glancing bullets [until] there were no more war cries or songs. Some were partly alive when the Pimas and Maricopas [traditional enemies of the Yavapai] rushed in and pounded their heads and then announced that they were all killed" (Corbusier 1968:77). Mike Burns's father, two siblings, his aunt and uncle, five cousins, and his grandmother were killed that day. (His mother had already been killed by soldiers.) Corpses were left lying in the cave, something deeply offensive to Yavapai people.[5]

Camp Verde: Forced Resettlement, Broken Promises

The military accomplished its mission that spring, when nearly all Yavapai were forced to move to Rio Verde, a military reservation near Camp Verde, Arizona. According to Corbusier, by 1874 there were 2,000 Indians at Rio Verde: 500 Western Yavapai, 1,000 Eastern Yavapai, and 500 Tontos (Apache) (Corbusier 1968:32). Initially, things were almost as bad for Yavapai on the reservation as off. With too little food

---

spring we started with 125 warriors; now we are 25. We used to be able to hide but now the rocks turn to soldiers and seem to be soft, leaving our footprints. We cannot sleep at night—every sound makes us think of a soldier" (Thrapp 1964:115).

5. Burns reports that over 200 were killed, all save one girl left for dead. His figures may include dead from other massacres (see ed. note, Corbusier 1971:77). Official reports state that seventy-six were killed and that eighteen women and children were captured. However, government reports of Indian casualties are notoriously unreliable. What remains indisputable is that a terrible massacre occurred. In 1922, a party of Yavapai led by Carlos Montezuma retrieved some of the bones. These are now buried in the cemetery that Orme Dam would have flooded.

and medicine, disease was rampant among the vulnerable Indians exposed to new diseases in crowded conditions. Corbusier wrote that
worst off were those Yavapai who resisted removal the longest: "They
were exhausted from fatigue, weakness, and lack of proper food; the
troops having harassed them to such a degree that they had but little
time to search for food . . . deaths were so frequent, that many of the
dead remained unburned on account of the inability of the relative to
carry the wood necessary for a funeral pyre" (Corbusier 1968:277). In
spite of their hardships, the Yavapai worked hard to improve conditions at Camp Verde, believing Crook's promise that it would become
their permanent home. They were told that if they cultivated farmland,
they would be paid promptly for any crops they raised. Their hand-
dug irrigation ditch soon yielded fifty-seven acres of crops, and prepa-
rations were made to plan more corn and barley. Indian agent W. S.
Schuyler reported that irrigated crops grown by the Indians at Camp
Verde were "as fine looking as any I have seen in the Territory" and
that the Indians understood they needed to "become self-supporting"
soon (U.S. Department of the Interior 1874:299).[6]

Their success at farming was even more remarkable in light of their
recent experience: forced resettlement after years of conflict, malnutri-
tion, high morbidity and mortality rates, and being forced to adjust to
a stationary life on a much smaller land base and to shift from a subsistence to productive economy, all this without adequate provision of
food, medicine, or farming supplies (Mariella 1983:81–82). Their re-
ward for their extraordinary accomplishments at Rio Verde was the
Trail of Tears, their most brutal relocation.

Starving, sick, grieving, the Yavapai were in desperate condition
when they arrived at the San Carlos Reservation, and many soon died.
Before leaving Camp Verde, General Crook had assured them that once
they "learned the white man's ways," they would be allowed to return

6. It is hard to exaggerate the broad influence of Bureau of Indian Affairs (BIA) policies
in the day-to-day lives of Indians (Cornell 1988:56–58; Champagne 1996:80–84). Founded
in 1824, the BIA was first located in the War Department. It was transferred to the Department of the Interior in 1849, when that agency was created. At various times it has been
referred to as the Indian Service, Indian Department, Indian Bureau, Office of Indian
Affairs, and the Office of the Commissioner of Indian Affairs. To be consistent, I will
refer it as the BIA, although in the late nineteenth and early twentieth centuries it was
more commonly referred to as the Indian Service. During the last half of the nineteenth
century, the agency was led by the Commissioner of Indian Affairs, who reported to the
Secretary of the Interior. Indian agents assigned to individual tribes were charged with
implementing federal policy. These powerful and poorly supervised agents controlled
food rations, jobs, and land use. They could use troops to enforce their decisions and
were the principal agents in the federal policies to acquire Indian land and "civilize"
Indians by irradiating traditional cultures and undermining traditional leaders.

to their homeland (Iverson 1982:43; Mariella 1983:99). With this in mind, a number of young Yavapai men enlisted as army scouts, hoping this would improve their chances to go home sooner. Dishonest contractors, corrupt and inept administrators, and conflict between BIA agents and military personnel resulted in inadequate, often adulterated supplies on the reservation (Bourke 1891:333–38; Thrapp 1967:176–77; Bronson 1980:43). Unable to subsist on the rations provided, the Yavapai again tried to cultivate the land. With few, primitive tools, insufficient seeds, poor soil, and the periodic flooding that destroyed their ditches, self-sufficiency was beyond their reach this time (Mariella 1983:98–104). When Crook was called back to Arizona in 1882 to investigate conditions on the reservation, he proclaimed that "no military department could well have been in a more desperate plight" (Bourke 1891:433).

All told, from 1875 to 1903, some 4,500 Indians, representing many tribes, were relocated to San Carlos, some of whom had long been enemies. Maggie Hayes remembered their predicament: "All of the tribes were dumped on the San Carlos Indian Reservation together, unable to understand each other's languages and temperaments" (Bronson 1980:43). The Yavapai and the Apache typically lived in separate camps, and while some did intermarry, the Yavapai continued to consider themselves distinct (Winchell 1982:95). Although the Yavapai remained at San Carlos for twenty-five years, they never gave up hope of returning to their homelands. Finally, beginning in the late 1890s, they were allowed to leave. By 1901, most Yavapai had returned to central Arizona, either to the Camp Verde area or to Fort McDowell. Some settled on another former military post, Camp Whipple, near Prescott.

Returning Home: Creating the Fort McDowell Reservation

The Yavapai who returned to their homelands found that white settlers had illegally moved onto the former reservations and cultivated the best farmland. Relations between the two groups were tense, especially since Indian agents had done nothing to prepare white settlers for the Yavapai's return. Since the Yavapai were told that their permission to leave San Carlos was contingent on there being no "unfavorable incidents," the onus was on them to keep peace. Given the settlers' hostility toward them, this was difficult.[7]

7. Patricia Mariella quotes what she calls a representative petition sent by these settlers: "Something [is] wrong when these Indians have set apart for their sole use a tract of land in this territory . . . and they should be permitted to stray away far from their reservation . . . and inflict their disgusting persons and practices upon our citizens. The San Carlos Indians have been accumulating in this valley [and] soon they will outnumber

Once Fort McDowell was abandoned as a military camp, the land was given to the Department of the Interior to manage and dispose of. The department directed in 1901 that lands not settled by whites be reserved for Indian use. This provoked a bitter response by the illegal settlers, who succeeded in defeating the bill establishing this policy. Fearful of being returned to San Carlos, the Yavapai had not challenged the settlers who illegally settled on the best land, and they were forced to live in the arid hills. In 1902, the Yavapai, under the leadership of Chief Yuma Frank, sent a petition to President Theodore Roosevelt asking that the land at Fort McDowell be given to them for their exclusive use. They described their urgent condition: "We are now in a starving condition but for three years we have been living in miserable rush tepees on the barren hills obliged to shift for a poverty stricken existence while white and Mexican trespassers upon reserved public lands have occupied and enjoyed all the harvest from the only fruitful lands on the reservation" (Mariella 1983:128).

The petition, signed by fifty-seven Yavapai, was accompanied by a letter from the Indian Service agent McDowell, who wrote that the Yavapai's "desire to be self-sustaining amounts to a mania." Roosevelt sent Frank Mead, a special emissary, to Fort McDowell to report on the tensions developing between the growing Yavapai population and the white settlers. Mead was impressed by the Yavapai, who were "manly, honest, upright, [and willing to] walk 50 and 60 miles to find work, were obedient and law abiding." The Yavapai repeatedly requested Mead for land that would allow them to support themselves (U.S. Department of the Interior 1905:98; quoted in Iverson 1982:43). Mead believed the Yavapai deserved the government's assistance and recommended that they be granted their own reservation. His report to Roosevelt on September 15, 1903, concluded that those settlers at Fort McDowell with legal claims be bought out and those living there illegally be removed. Just three days after receiving the report, President Roosevelt issued an order to begin acquiring land for the reservation (Iverson 1982:43–44).

In spite of the vigorous opposition of white settlers and local political leaders, Fort McDowell was established in 1903 by executive order of President Roosevelt.[8] Although small compared with other reserva-

---

the whites. . . . While a few will work a little, the majority are worthless vagabonds. . . . Please remove them as soon as possible. They belong to the San Carlos Agency" (1983: 114).

8. A small reservation was also established at Camp Verde in 1910 for the Apache and Yavapai who settled there. During the next sixty years several noncontiguous parcels of land were added. The Yavapai who settled on the former Fort Whipple near Prescott obtained reservation status in 1935. Today, about 765 residents live on the Fort McDowell

tions, it was the first and largest Yavapai reservation created following the relocation to San Carlos. The Yavapai were overjoyed. W. H. Gill, a local missionary charged with helping to settle the Yavapai, wrote on October 26, 1903, that "this beautiful valley 10 miles long by 4 miles wide had been turned into an Indian Reservation. . . . There is great joy here in our Indian camps" (Iverson 1982:44–45).[9]

The Yavapai once again laboriously began cultivating farmland, thinking they would finally be left alone. With a sizable land base, fertile soil, a nearby regional trade center with a growing market, and with the Verde River offering an ample water supply, the conditions at Fort McDowell seemed ideal for farming (Iverson 1982:75). But white settlers who had opposed the reservation quickly started scheming for the Indians' removal. The settlers found powerful allies among those who wished to limit the water rights of the Yavapai.

Once the reservation was established, the Yavapai designed an irrigation system composed of brush dams and ditches that allowed them to divert water from the Verde River. They soon realized, however, that without some sort of permanent flood protection, they would continually have to repair or replace their brush dams and redig the ditches and canals that were destroyed annually when the spring runoff flooded the river. This was so exhausting and time intensive, it left little time for farming (Mariella 1983:138). One BIA agent reported, "If only we could stop repairing ditches long enough to farm a little, this would very probably become a prosperous community in a few years" (U.S. Department of the Interior 1906; quoted in Mariella 1983:134). The

---

reservation, with its land base of about 25,000 acres. About 600 people live at Camp Verde, which contains about 1000 acres. About 150 people live on the Prescott reservation, which encompasses about 1,400 acres. During the 1980s, these three Yavapai groups began sponsoring joint cultural events (Mariella and Mitchell-Enos 1996:710–12). For additional details on the differences among these reservations, see Mariella and Mitchell-Enos 1996.

9. In many respects, the Yavapai's experiences were comparable to those of other Indian groups during the nineteenth century. As Stephen Cornell (1988:40) points out, how to gain control over Indian resources formed the core of what was commonly referred to as "the Indian Problem" by whites. Whether this problem was more narrowly defined as protecting settlers from Indians, or Indians from unsavory influences; keeping peace among tribes; promoting civilization, Christianity, or education; or negotiating treaties, all these goals derived from "U.S. expansion over Indian lands and Indian resistance." As for the Yavapai, their early removals stemmed from settlers' wish for their land and contractors' desire to prevent them from becoming self-sufficient. But water is what drove the almost continuous pressure for their resettlement that dominated their relations with both local and federal governments during most of the twentieth century. Water is why the Yavapai community at Fort McDowell continued to be haunted by the threat of resettlement, long after many other Indian tribes had secured some measure of stability over the parcels of land they were allocated.

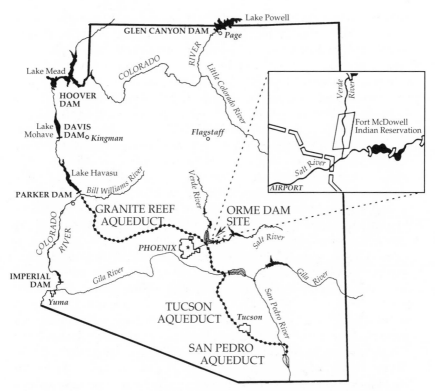

Fig. 3. Fort McDowell Indian Reservation and the proposed Orme Dam site, *USBR Fact Book*, 1981.

Yavapai asked the federal government to help them build a small dam on the Verde River. This request was rejected as too costly. Instead, siding with opponents of the reservation, local representatives of the BIA and the Indian Irrigation Service recommended that Fort McDowell be abandoned and the Yavapai removed to the nearby Salt River Reservation. Established in 1879, this reservation was the home of the Pima and Maricopa tribes, the Yavapai's traditional enemies. The Yavapai bitterly opposed this new effort to resettle them. For the next thirty years, the government, under the auspices of the Indian Bureau and the Indian Irrigation Service, kept pressuring the Yavapai to resettle at Salt River despite their strong, persistent objections.

Persistent Threats, Sustained Resistance

During this period, Indian water rights were deeply politicized in southern Arizona. The creation of the Reclamation Service and rapidly increasing demand for water put pressure on the government to adjudicate water rights on the Salt River. In 1903, local white farmers formed the Salt River Valley Water Users Association to lobby for more irrigation water. This group lobbied the federal government to build two dams: Roosevelt Dam on the Salt River and Granite Reef Dam near the confluence of the Salt and Verde Rivers. Before these dams could be built, the region's water policy needed sorting out, so this group filed suit in 1905. Five years later, the Kent Decree, a complex document establishing the priority of water rights for the entire Salt River Valley, was issued. The decree granted the Yavapai rights to 390 "miners' inches" of Verde River water annually, roughly the amount need to irrigate 1,300 acres. This figure, considered a temporary allotment, assumed that the Yavapai would be resettled on the Salt River Reservation in 1910, after which their water rights would be rescinded and given to white farmers and ranchers. The Yavapai would then be granted a low-priority right to water from the Salt River, which meant that it was likely that once others' rights to water from the Salt River were met, there often would not be enough water left for the Yavapai (Chamberlain 1975:28–29; Khera and Mariella 1982:167).

Once again, the Yavapai faced forced relocation, this time because local farmers and ranchers wanted their land and their water. Many of the Yavapai, including Chief Yuma Frank, were illiterate and were ill-prepared to do battle with the politicians and bureaucrats who dictated Indian policy at that time. The government, especially its local representatives, was happy to exploit the Yavapai's inexperience and often withheld information or misrepresented the facts to them. Local officials also misrepresented the Yavapai's position to their Washington superiors. Desperate not to lose their reservation, the Yavapai enlisted the help of Carlos Montezuma (or Wassaja, his given name): Yavapai, physician, former Indian Bureau employee, and national Indian civil rights activist. His help was crucial in retaining their reservation (Khera and Mariella 1982:169; Iverson 1982:85).[10]

Carlos Montezuma's familiarity with the white and Indian worlds made him an invaluable ally. Born sometime during the 1860s, Montezuma and his two sisters were captured by Pima Indians when he was about seven. The Pimas sold him to Carlos Gentile, an Italian immigrant photographer, for thirty dollars.[11] Gentile was kind to Carlos,

10. See also the letter from Montezuma to Robert G. Valentine, Commissioner of Indian Affairs, Mar. 11, 1911, The Carlos Montezuma Collection, 1898–1922, Arizona Collection, Hayden Library, Arizona State University, Doc. Box 3; hereafter cited as CMC. This section relies on Peter Iverson's helpful biography of Montezuma.

11. His sisters were sold to someone else, and Carlos never saw them again. Carlos's mother tried to find her children but was killed by soldiers before she learned of their

doing his best to raise him, but was forced to relinquish his ward when his business failed. Carlos was eventually sent to live with a Baptist minister in Illinois. He graduated from the University of Illinois and earned a medical degree from Chicago Medical College. After working as a BIA (Bureau of Indian Affairs) physician for seven years, Carlos became bitterly disillusioned with the agency. He believed that the BIA's control over Native Americans, almost absolute in this period, demeaned and subordinated Indians, increasing their dependency on the government.

Montezuma became a powerful advocate of Indian self-determination. Among the causes he championed was the right of Indians to vote, something that he did not live to see.[12] He also advocated abolishing the Indian Bureau and established *Wassaja,* a national Indian newsletter devoted to that end. He also helped create the Society of American Indians, an important pan-Indian organization. Montezuma became interested in the plight of the Fort McDowell Yavapai after visiting the reservation in 1901, when he became reacquainted with relatives recalled from his childhood.

In 1909 tribal Chief Yuma Frank sent Montezuma a letter telling him of the threatened relocation and asking for help. For the next fourteen years, Montezuma led the Yavapai's struggle to retain their land. They appointed him their official representative (a role the BIA refused to acknowledge), and he advised them, publicized their problem nationally, wrote endless letters to various government agents, and successfully lobbied for a congressional investigation of the Indian Bureau's treatment of the Yavapai. (Montezuma was an effective witness at these hearings.) Predictably, Indian agents were furious with him.

Under Montezuma's leadership, in spite of tremendous pressure, the Fort McDowell Yavapai kept resisting repeated attempts to remove them. This pressure took many forms. They were told that if they did not leave voluntarily, soldiers would be called in to remove them. For people with vivid memories of violent encounters with the army, this was a frightening prospect (Khera 1978:14). The day school at Fort McDowell was closed, and the children were sent to boarding schools in Phoenix without the consent of their parents and sometimes even without their knowledge. The miserable children kept running away, and the Yavapai were promised a school if they agreed to move to the Salt River Reservation. Local BIA agents tried to prevent reservation resi-

---

fate. His father participated in the march to San Carlos, where he died soon after arriving (Iverson 1982:5).

12. Indians were granted suffrage in 1924. Montezuma died of tuberculosis at Fort McDowell in 1923 and is buried there.

dents from corresponding with Montezuma.[13] When the superintendent from the BIA learned that Yuma Frank was planning another trip
to Washington to protest their proposed relocation, he threatened to
jail him (Khera 1978:11). Government agents also refused all aid for
housing and agriculture, and condemned the existing dams and
ditches; this forced residents to work secretly at night to repair the
irrigation system.[14] After floods damaged the irrigation system so severely the Yavapai could not repair it themselves, farmland shrank
from lack of water. Indian agents took this as proof that the Yavapai
were poor farmers, undeserving of their land and water rights (Khera
and Mariella 1982:168–69). Despite all these threats and hardships, the
Yavapai's resolve to keep their land did not waiver. After Montezuma
died, his lawyer and friend Joseph Latimore continued to support the
Yavapai's struggle.

During the 1930s, resettlement threats took new forms. The Verde
River Irrigation Company launched a new, and ultimately unsuccessful, raid on the Yavapai's water allotment in 1930. The City of Phoenix
repeatedly tried to acquire portions of the reservation in order to gain
access to Verde River water. On several occasions, Senator Carl Hayden
introduced legislation, with the approval of the Indian Office, authorizing the sale of 120 acres of reservation land to Phoenix. Yavapai residents sent a petition protesting the sale of their land, and Congress
eventually defeated Hayden's bills (Mariella 1983:183–84). The city had
already built a water pipeline at Fort McDowell and dug several test
wells without consulting or compensating the Yavapai. Local bureau
agents were unaware of the construction, although a permit had been
granted to the city by the Department of the Interior. Those charged
with representing and protecting Yavapai interests were performing
poorly (Mariella 1983:177–84).

The Yavapai's long struggle to retain their land and water took its
toll. The time, money, and energy absorbed by the conflict were diverted from more productive things, and the struggle reinforced their
deep mistrust of government (Chamberlain 1975:32). Each time the Ya-

---

13. Charles Dickens, a Yavapai living at Fort McDowell, wrote to Montezuma that
"Superintendent Coe and the Inspector [of the BIA] took your letter from my pocket
and tore it up. They say they want to read all letters you send. They have no right to
do this" (Charles Dickens to Montezuma, Feb. 9, 1911, CMC, Doc. Box 3). Yuma Frank
also complained of tampering with his mail. Letter from Yuma Frank to Montezuma,
March 13, 1911, CMC, Doc. Box 3.

14. Secretary of the Interior R. A. Ballinger wrote to Montezuma in 1911 urging the
Yavapai community to move to the Salt River Reservation. He argued that the government, having spent over $9,000,000 on Roosevelt Dam, was unlikely to fund either a
new dam or repairs to the reservation's existing irrigation system (Iverson 1982:87).

vapai thought the issue was finally resolved, promises were broken, the stated policy was never implemented, or threats emerged from a new quarter. After all this time and effort, the condition of the Yavapai was virtually the same as it had been 1903. They retained their reservation, and the limited water rights on the Verde River, but still did not have a reliable irrigation system that would allow them to exploit their water rights. Meanwhile, the Phoenix area was growing quickly, many new reclamation projects had been built or launched, and the local economy was booming.

As early as 1913, in a report prepared by an engineer in the BIA's Irrigation Service, the secretary of the interior was advised to retain control of the Fort McDowell Reservation for potential future reclamation projects. He wrote that the reservation "contains a reservoir site, with a dam site just below it on the Salt River Reservation. Both of these have been investigated by the U.S. Geological Survey" (Mariella 1983:153). This appears to be the first time a federal agency expressed interest in a confluence dam. Feasibility studies for the Orme site began in earnest in the early 1940s, when Orme Dam was included in the BR's Central Arizona Project. For the next forty years, Orme Dam was the impetus for forced resettlement.

There was no relief for Yavapai people. Since the reservation was established in 1903, there has virtually never been a time when some group was not trying to take their land or use their water. Before that, they endured forty years of starvation, massacres, and abuse. They cannot look at a map of Arizona without recalling the events that occurred at places like Skeleton Cave, Bloody Basin, or Skull Valley. The stories behind the names are persistent reminders of their brutal treatment and of the sacrifices that were made to stay with their land. No wonder Yavapai residents remain deeply suspicious of the motives and promises of white people. No wonder that resettlement and resistance are central to Yavapai identity.

Their distrust, the bitter product of their history, informs their understanding of official government. It has seldom been misplaced. The Yavapai's capacity to keep fighting for over 150 years is remarkable, especially in light of the events that took place. Like the citizens of Owens Valley, they sustained their resistance in their historical narratives, in tradition, and in their capacity to adapt it to new threats and changed circumstance. Yavapai residents have a practical appreciation of their history. They use it to understand the present, anticipate the future, offer warnings and teach lessons (Khera 1978:6).

Hope was harder to sustain than resistance. For a long time, residents were so poorly informed about Orme Dam that they did not understand how serious a threat it posed. When this finally became clear, many Yavapai despaired. They knew how powerful the forces behind the Central Arizona Project were; many felt doomed. For Patty, a leader in the battle against Orme, "We kept hoping because we had to. We had no choice." But here, too, their history guided them. Kept alive in the voices of their ancestors, it could inspire hope. For Charles, history could restore his resolve: "Sometimes when I think at night, tears come into my eyes when I look back on history, how my people were treated, how my land was taken. Today that land is worth billions. But to the Indian it is worth more than that. It was their home, where they were told to live by the Great Spirit. Our ancestors were slaughtered in the cave; they look down on us with tears in their eyes, and they say 'Stay with it; Stay with it.' We *will* stay with it." (USBR 1982a:2-94).

"Participating with the Land"

Land is an integral part of life on the reservation. The struggle to retain their land, the leitmotif of Yavapai history, is reiterated in the lives of contemporary Yavapai. Beliefs about land are not abstract ideas but relationships that are enacted daily on the reservation when residents swim in the river, wander the desert, watch the eagles, or wake up to the sight of the mountains. Land is their bridge to ancestors who came before and descendants who will come after; land defines their difference, and its familiar contours offer reassurance, competence, and sustenance for body and soul.

One beautiful April afternoon in 1989, I was sitting with Patty at her kitchen table, talking with her about her role in the Orme struggle eight years earlier. It was clear that she still savors the victory. When I asked her to describe what it meant to her, she pauses a long while. "It's about still being here," she says quietly. "It's about this land." She elaborates by gesturing at the landscape outside the window: "A lot of things have happened here. The people lived here. They lived off the land. They died here. We all remember that so and so used to plant here, or sit over there, walk this way. We go through this all the time. I do that with some of the elderly. They tell what it was like, where people lived. . . . We remember with the land."

When Yavapai residents talk about their land, one hears the difference between their view of land and that of most white people: in their hesitancy to speak of what is sacred, in the intimate language they use, in their choice of metaphors. Although they savor the beauty of the reservation, they describe land less for its physical attributes than in terms of their relationship to it. As one resident told me: "Most of [my relatives] lived here; they died here. Most of my relatives, they came, and some of them have died here, and those that are being born, they won't be able to participate in this land [if Orme is built] (USBR 1982a: 2-43). This relationship to land is nontransferable; it can only be sustained with the land that one's ancestors also "participated in." As one woman put it: "I couldn't go nowhere [else] and say 'This is where my ancestors lived' or 'I have a culture here.'" (USBR 1982a:B-28). Another resident told a reporter, "God gave this land to us. God promised this land to the Yavapai. He promised no other land. We have always been here, since God made us people. Where would we go? Our ancestors still live here" (*Arizona Republic,* Sep. 12, 1981).

And like other complex, intimate relationships, their relation to the land is hard to generalize from and difficult to talk about, especially to outsiders. One teenager said simply: "[The land] is my life. It's just a part of me." The relation is also a dynamic one. Young people often leave the reservation for a time—to find a job, join the military, go live with friends or relatives, or simply strike out on their own—but I was told that they "always" return. One man who spent five years off the reservation put it this way: "It is only here that I really feel myself, and feel at home. We may go, but we always come back. It's part of knowing yourself, of knowing what this place means."

Yavapai people often contrast their relationship to land with their views of how white people think about land. One man saw this as the crucial difference between Indians and Anglos:

> It basically boils down to the way we view the land . . . and the way they view the use of the land. . . . Indian people view the land as a gift from God, that they're there only temporarily and that God gave them the use of the land to live on, and to function, and to take care of the earth. . . . They don't really own the land. There's no one big title that you can cut out a piece and say 'This is mine and it belongs to me.' Whereas an Anglo person, they come out and build a house and they get a title and a deed and stuff, and they pay off the land and they say, 'This is mine. Nobody else can take it.' An Indian person doesn't view the land that way. The land is forever. The land itself is part of nature and everything around it. Whereas the human beings are there temporarily and there because God wants them to be there, to enjoy himself, to experience life. And from the land, that's where all life comes from. The Indian knows that his land and life is intertwined, that they are one unit. Without the land, the Indian cannot survive and without the Indian the land cannot be land, because the land needs to be taken care of in order to survive life. (USBR 1982a:2-41)

To think that some other parcel of land or some sum of money could somehow be equivalent to their land is to misconstrue the intricate relationship between being Yavapai and being on the land. James described the relationship this way: "You can offer me all the money in the world and I wouldn't trade it for this land. This land to me has so many memories, and inheritance too. And it means so much. You can offer me all the money in the world and I won't take it. This is my land. I grew up here. I know the hills; I go hunting. I know where every waterhole is at. What season it contains water and what not. . . . Like I said, it's more valuable than anything else . . . it is part of us. . . . I care for this land more than anything else. We understand it. It is something you have got and it lasts. Like money, it never lasts. It's just like water; it just goes down the drain" (USBR 1982a:2-40).

The permanence of land is often contrasted with the impermanence of money. Money "flies away," whereas land, if protected and cared for, remains available for future generations. The land's continuity offers continuity and unity for tribal members. As one man put it, "[Our land] keeps the Tribe together" (USBR 1982a:2-40). Other tribes have demonstrated the importance of the link between land and survival. Following World War II, government policy toward Indians was again directed toward eliminating tribal sovereignty and effecting their rapid assimilation. As part of what became known as its termination policies, the federal government relocated individual reservation residents to urban areas in an effort to force their assimilation. The Menominee of Wisconsin and the Klamath of Oregon, for example, were given large cash settlements in exchange for their land. Many were soon destitute, with no reservation to return to, no community to sustain them. Their tragedy, and others like it, framed the Yavapai's passionate defense of their land, their distrust of money.

The land's familiarity offers security for Yavapai. I was repeatedly told of its many practical uses, of its plenitude. One man described the reservation's plants and wildlife: "From these we have survived for many, many years and will continue to do so" (USBR 1982a:2-43). During one outdoor interview, Bill, a man in his twenties, described for me the resources that surrounded us: "If things went from bad to worse, I can survive. I can become that thing we call savage, or that Indians call 'being human,' being 'part of the world.' Just right offhand, I know that there is plenty of food here right now where we are sitting. I know that I will never go hungry. I know that I can eat these things and still be alive tomorrow. And that's what I want to pass on to my kids. It's not the money thing; it's being part of this. There is no other environment like this here." Bill pointed out the bushes that provide tea, the trees that produce berries and nuts, the medicine that comes from mesquite trees. He described how rocks could be used to keep warm, shade for keeping cool. "There's a lot of things here that [you] people don't realize. . . . There is no way you can compensate us for this" (USBR

1982a:2-44). An elder, after describing similar sources of food, proudly produced coffee cans filled with food and medicine for me to try: dried cactus fruit, ground mesquite beans, desert sage. Dinners on the reservation are more likely to feature hamburger than wild berries, but these sources of food and medicine remain important even for those who do not often use them. Appreciating the bounty of the land, knowing that it can sustain you, is a source of comfort and pride. It is also evidence of one's special relationship to land. For those with precarious budgets, it provides a very real sense of security. And mere money cannot compensate for this special knowledge or the comfort it affords.

The land's bounty provides important revenue for both tribal and household budgets. The tribe farms some land and has developed a sand and gravel operation on a river wash. Some residents farm or tend cattle as their main source of income. At least half of the families at Fort McDowell own a few head of cattle, and many have larger herds. Residents do not pay a grazing fee for cattle kept on the reservation, and often treat the cattle like "money in the bank," buying or selling as their relative prosperity dictates (Mariella 1983:224–25). For many others, the land provides critical supplemental income and partial subsistence that, during hard times, can make the difference between getting by and going under. Many residents fish and hunt rabbit, quail, and sometimes deer. Most have gardens that are important sources of food. Basket weavers use the bark from the cottonwood and willow trees that grow along the river banks, as well as other grasses. Many use mesquite wood to heat their houses and for cooking, especially during the hot summer months. Some also cut wood for sale off the reservation. The partial subsistence economy at Fort McDowell was a feature of reservation life that was invisible to most outsiders.

The threat to their land was an important religious issue for Yavapai people. For many residents, religion encompasses all areas of life, including how one makes a living and how one uses the land. One man described the relationship between land and its inhabitants as one of mutual dependence: "The land, we feel, is a resource that's been made available to us, that we are to use to our benefit as long as we live here. We do not commercialize it, see it as a commodity to sell it and move on to another area. We feel that the Creator or the Maker who put us here, put us here for a purpose. . . . That's why we're here . . . and the land that we've had is a resource to us, for us, to use and be willing to share, and to care for" (USBR 1982a:2-44–45). Land plays a crucial role in the practice of the Native American church. Religious observance incorporates sacred sites and shrines on the land and such economic activity as hunting or farming. The religious significance of land is not transferable. As Elizabeth Brandt (USBR 1982a:B-24–25) writes:

"Because of this intimate connection between *specific* sites and *specific* lands, the loss of land generally means the inability to practice one's religion. In short, if the land is gone, there is no church, no altar, none of the ways in which people can address the creator. . . . [If] religious sites are inundated, or access blocked in any way, or sacred sites opened for unauthorized access and viewing, then the right to practice one's religion has been abridged."

Other reservation churches, including more mainstream denominations, are shaped by religious beliefs about land. Cemeteries and grave sites are considered sacred sites by all residents. The remains of ancestors massacred at Skeleton Cave, Carlos Montezuma, and other cultural heroes like Yuma Frank are buried at the Fort McDowell Cemetery. Also buried there are Yavapai scouts who fought in the "Apache Wars," and Yavapai veterans who died in WWI, WWII, and the Korean and Vietnam Wars. The Orme Dam reservoir would have inundated this cemetery, a prospect residents found heart-wrenching even to contemplate. Residents were dismayed at the prospect of flooding or disrupting the cemetery. Even to talk about it was painful and disrespectful to the dead. As one visibly uncomfortable woman explained: "Indian people don't want to talk about their dead people. It's a sacred thing. And anything you do to the dead is the worst thing you can do to the Yavapai Tribe" (USBR 1982a:B-27). A man of about seventy told me: "[The people] are very upset and . . . very sick about it. You hear people crying when you mention that there might be water covering the cemetery. The older people start crying. . . . That's the worst thing they could do is to dig them out and move them someplace. The people that were killed up there in 1872 [Skeleton Cave], you talk about Montezuma's ancestors and my wife's father . . . many Indians killed from that fight up there. People say 'Don't bother them. Don't go out there and bother them. Don't ever mention anything about them.' " Inundating the cemetery, or attempting to move it, as the bureau proposed and as was done in other large water projects, would destroy a sacred site of great importance to all Yavapai. Such sacrilege would offend deeply felt religious beliefs and compromise residents' ability to practice their religion.[15]

The Yavapai's relationship to their land defines them as a people

15. Laverne, a middle-aged mother, said: "This is where I want to die when I do die. This [cemetery] is where I want to be buried, not somewhere else. That's why the cemetery, to us, is so sacred. [We] just don't want the deceased, those that's gone ahead, to be bothered in any way at all. It's just too sacred to talk about." Asking people to talk about the cemetery created my most awkward moments interviewing. I gradually began to appreciate how painful the topic was for residents, how inappropriate it was for them to discuss it with me, and how tolerant they were in their responses to me.

and as individuals.[16] They believe that their land is unique, that its value cannot and should not be expressed as a commodity, or as somehow commensurable with other valued things. Their relation to land is understood to be collectively shared but with particular meanings for individuals that reflect their distinct experiences with the land. This commitment to their land is simultaneously psychological, historical, economic, and religious. (Yavapai people do not often speak of the land in these functional terms, partly because the relationship is not compartmentalized for them.) In threatening their land, Orme Dam threatened them, and its loss represented cultural extinction. In trying to derive a price for their land, the bureau was, in effect, creating a market for their cultural "selves." As Norman Austin, the tribal chairman put it, "If that Orme Dam goes through, my people will be no more" (*Christian Science Monitor*, Oct. 14, 1981, p. 14).

Although they did not use this term, their land was an incommensurate value, and money or other land, regardless of the amount, could not capture its value or compensate for its loss. Land, for the Yavapai, fits Raz's (1986:345) definition of a "constitutive incommensurable." For Yavapai people, land is intrinsically valuable. Understanding and valuing land in this way, as something with which one has a unique relationship, something that should not be expressed as price, help to define what it means to be Yavapai. Believing in the incommensurability of the land is an essential component of knowing how to relate to land, and this, in turn, is critical for knowing how to be and act like a Yavapai. A Yavapai teenager put it this way: "If we took the money, we could not be ourselves . . . and we could not live with ourselves."

Bureaucratic Representations of the Yavapai: The Power of Form

If Yavapai residents' sense of identity and culture depended on the incommensurability of land, the New Guard's conceptions of rationality demanded its commensuration. Three different CAWCS analyses or "accounts" address the impact of this policy on the Yavapai community: the Social Account, Public Values Assessment, and Economic Analysis. The effects of Orme Dam for the Yavapai community were made commensurate in each of these analyses, albeit in different ways and at different stages of analysis.

16. Dick Winchell (1982:78–81) argues that Yavapai identity is directly linked to their conceptions of space and place. Historically, the names of the bands that were the basic social units before the disruption of forced relocation show the significance of place for Yavapai identity. The three subtribes, identified by region, were broken down into bands of twenty to thirty people loosely organized around extended families. The names of these bands, and often their leader, were synonymous with the place they occupied. Changing one's band or residence warranted a name change. See Gifford (1936:249).

The two economic accounts used cost-benefit analysis to express in dollars the values of costs and benefits associated with each alternative. Unlike the other accounts, the economic analysis did not specify a "preferred alternative," nor did it offer an evaluation of the economic impacts. This was deemed unnecessary, since numbers were presumed to "speak for themselves." The CB analysis included the cost of acquiring the Yavapai's land and property as part of the construction costs. The current market value for the land and the judgment of professional appraisers for the nontransferable material property were used to express these values.

The market value of their land and the replacement value of their homes hardly capture their value for Yavapai residents. Such "objective" methods for valuing do not incorporate residents' special knowledge of the reservation's resources, which make them more valuable to them than to others. Nor is the importance of timing in their use, and therefore in their value, captured in standard economic models. If, for example, the sale of a basket sustains a family during a spate of unemployment, that basket can literally keep a family together; its market price is a poor proxy for its worth as a flexible source of supplemental income. The premium placed on uniform methods for valuing in the economic analysis, however defensible to other authorities, systematically undervalued the worth of the reservation's resources to the Yavapai. While such biases characterize much economic analysis, their consequences are most extreme in cases like the Yavapai's.

Bernard Shanks criticizes how poorly market values represent value in a subsistence economy in his analysis of the effects of federal water development on the Missouri River Indians. He writes:

> Environmental perception and ecological adaptation of the Missouri River Indians had evolved out of at least 1000 years' experience with the Missouri River. Overall, they harvested the rich biotic life associated with the river and lived a subsistence life that our white culture described as poverty.
>
> While it is possible to place a dollar on the price of timber lost it appears that the $12 per cord appraised value of firewood is not sufficient if those using the wood have a surplus of time and labor but an extreme shortage of cash. The value of $12 will not transfer from our culture to a natural resources oriented economy.
>
> Deer were valued by economists as worth $100 each and each Indian family used approximately two deer per year. . . . Such estimation of worth seems futile when the animals are virtually free for the taking but once the habitat is destroyed by water impoundments, they do not exist.

Shanks concludes that dams and water development "forced the Indians into a cash economy." He argues that is impossible to compare the cultural and social values between our culture and that of the Missouri River Indians if costs are based on "our economic terms" (1974:576–77).[17]

The Yavapai's special knowledge of the habitat and its resources created what Oliver Williamson (1975) would call high asset specificity, a condition enhancing the coordination and distributive efficiency of organizations relative to markets. As used and appreciated by the Yavapai, the land's value is specific to them, and the market price for the land understates its value.[18] The uniqueness or specificity of the relationship between Yavapai residents and the land makes it hard to capture its value in economic models.[19]

The Public Values Assessment (PVA) (described in chapter 4) involved representatives of various groups being asked to weight the relative importance of fourteen decision factors, one of which was "Indian Relocation."

The Model: Framing and Fairness

The commensurated techniques used to derive and represent the cost, value, and social impact of the Yavapai's relocation imposed a system of valuing that was antithetical to the way that Yavapai residents valued their land, their identity, and their understanding of their culture. In their efforts to save the land, one of the paramount challenges confronting the Yavapai was explaining why their land was, in effect, incommensurable. Their profound sense of belonging to the land is hard for non-Indians to apprehend. Residents became exasperated with how hard it was to convince others that land meant something very different to them from what it did to most white people. As one woman put it: "[White people] don't know how much we love this land. They don't

17. See also Michael Lawson's (1994) investigation of the effects of the Pick-Sloan Plan on the Missouri River Sioux. Developed jointly by the Army Corps of Engineers and the BR, the result was the transformation of the Missouri Basin with the Oahe, Big Bend, and Fort Randall Dams and the most damage done to Indian lands by any federal project.

18. In principle, this is not an irreconcilable problem for economics. In practice, however, devising some "objective" means for determining price is difficult when there is no clear mechanism by which information is reflected in price.

19. Analysts provided "technical performance scores" for the fourteen factors for each of the eight plans. This meant that they judged (on a scale of one to a hundred) how well that alternative performed for that factor. For Indian relocations, the technical performance scores were either 100 for plans not requiring relocation, or 0 for plans which did. See USBR (1981b:App. B, "CAWCS Public Values Assessment"), for more detail on the PVA.

know how much we love this land, how we understand this land. They don't know that we have put all our life into this land. They don't know this and they don't try to understand what we're trying to explain to them, why we don't want to move. . . . We don't want to move because this is our land, and this is our homeland, and we love this land" (USBR 1982a:2-41).

In private discussions with representatives of the Bureau of Reclamation, and with other Orme supporters, and sometimes even in their public speeches, Yavapai residents relied on analogies, often ones that involved intimate relations, to convey the land's meaning for them. The most favored analogy was to described land as their "mother." Analogies often emphasized categories of "incommensurable" relationships that Yavapai residents believed they shared with white people. So, for example, they would ask a negotiator how much money he would charge for his children, or whether he would be willing to accept a "similar" child in exchange for his own child. Religion provided another example of a deeply valued but incommensurate, inalienable relationship.

These analogies, often misconstrued by those who heard them as sarcasm or exaggeration, were rejected by Orme supporters as inappropriate. Land could not, in their view, be valued as children and religion were, and it was not unique in ways that precluded its being priced. When their attempts to define their land as an incommensurable value failed, the Yavapai would sometimes resort to price, the white man's method of valuing. Norman Austin, the tribal chairman, told one reporter, "I have heard my people's answer. I don't care if you give a million dollars to each and everyone of us. Our answer will still be no" (*Christian Science Monitor,* July 14, 1981, p. 14).

The inability of these models to accommodate intrinsic value was not the only way that Yavapai people thought the framework distorted the stakes of the decision. Yavapai leaders argued that the decision they confronted was ultimately a moral decision but that its ethical implications were being excluded from the decision making. They believed that the legacy of broken promises that had characterized their relations with the federal and local governments for decades was directly relevant to this decision. For example, in the executive order signed by Theodore Roosevelt creating the reservation, the Yavapai were promised that they would never again be forced from their land. The Yavapai argued that it was wrong for the government to break another treaty with Native Americans. As one Yavapai man put it: "[President Roosevelt] told us we could live on this land forever. The white man keeps trying and trying to break that promise. Doesn't that matter? Where in all these studies do they say, 'You shouldn't break a promise?' Where? You tell me." Another man described the taking of Indian land by force as "the white man's original sin." "How many times can one commit original sin?" he asked. "You still come to take our land by force—over and over and over. And now, you come again" (Casserly 1981:A-5).[20]

This concern over the morality of broken promises is hard to address within the rational decision-making framework. Information was organized according to a causal logic that tracked change in future states of affairs; impacts were "measured" on the basis of the anticipated consequences associated with each alternative plan. This way of valuing is directly linked to a purely instrumental conception of action, action that causes measurable changes in states of affairs.[21] In the models used in the study, impacts of proposed action are identified, examined, and evaluated. Framed in this way, debate focuses on whether or not future states are likely to bring about certain specific consequences and whether these are good or bad. It is hard to say how the relative "wrongness" of breaking another promise to the Yavapai, or violating a trust, will alter the future in any direct, meaningful way. This is one example of how the consequentialism embedded in rational choice frameworks serves to select out from consideration those attributes which are not directly, causally, or literally linked to future states. The overall effect of this was the exclusion of moral concerns in the decision documents and their neglect in the debate surrounding the decision. Some Yavapai residents believed that minimizing the ethical dimensions of the decision not only minimized their claims but, perhaps more fundamentally, also reproduced a way of deciding things that allowed powerful people to disguise their immorality as rationality.

The question of fairness in the distribution of costs and benefits is

20. Religious leaders also emphasized the moral dimensions of the decision and were concerned that these were being neglected. One Lutheran minister said, "I teach a catechism class for young people. . . . I find it very difficult . . . to ask young people to respect the property of their neighbors when, many times, public officials say, 'I don't have to respect promises made by my government many years ago. . . . Society breaks down when covenants are not kept. I appeal to the decision makers to respect something greater than land, something greater than water: it is the spirit of trust" (*Phoenix Gazette,* Sept. 30, 1981).

21. The transitivity of values required in these models is accomplished by trading off units or amounts of different dimensions. The "wrongness" of breaking a promise can be evaluated only in terms of its wrongness relative to other factors, or to how many benefits must accrue in order to somehow override its wrongness. General moral values are exceedingly hard to convey in this framework, because they require, at least in the abstract, continuous variables. Values are made equivalent by determining the comparable worth of some fixed amount for two dimensions. For dimensions that do not lend themselves to incrementalism, this is hard to do.

another moral issue that was neglected within the rational procedures employed. There are usually clear winners and losers in public choice, since those who bear the costs often do not enjoy the benefits. Although fairness was a common theme in public discourse about the dam, within the context of the decision procedures, there was no formal way to represent its distributive effects. Like broken promises, "fairness" is hard to capture in consequentialist terms.[22] The issue of fairness came up repeatedly at public meetings; the Yavapai and their supporters raised it in the media, at rallies, and in other political contexts. One Yavapai supporter said at a public meeting: "The real issue is taking other people's land. We are taking their land to make up for our mistakes. . . . We must consider fairness and equity in making this decision. The problem is that equity is not considered on a par with the profit motive" (USBR 1981a:App. A-6). Supporters of a confluence dam also tried to make the distributive consequences of the decision a political issue. For example, the *Arizona Republic* (Aug. 24, 1975, p. A-4) ran a strong pro-Orme editorial which concluded that "it is inconceivable that any court would fail to place the needs of more than a million people [the current approximate population of the Phoenix metropolitan area] above those of 456 people."

History presents a different version of the same problem for rational choice models. The consequentialism underlying the bureau's rational choice procedures cannot accommodate history in any meaningful way. Just as it is hard to ascertain how moral issues implicate future states in any direct, causal way, it is also hard to incorporate the significance of history into spelling out its consequences in causal terms for future impacts or future states of affairs. History does not lend itself to being carved up into discrete decision "factors" as vehicles for expressing change across future conditions.[23] It is theoretically possible to incorporate the historical significance of the Yavapai by simply attaching a higher price to land or to assume that the factors used to represent the present condition somehow reflect the cumulative im-

22. Within a strict utilitarian calculus, the best plan is the one that creates the overall greatest good. Consequently, even very modest benefits to a large group of people would overwhelm significant costs to a small group of people by increasing the overall utility. As John Rawls (1971:27, 29) points out, the interests of society are not reducible to a big utility matrix, since such a device would disregard "the separateness of persons" (see also Raz 1986:271–87).

23. Two common characteristics of history make it especially hard to incorporate into a rational choice framework: history often emphasizes contingent and idiosyncratic properties of periods and events, and it is often written in a chronological or narrative form, or both. As I have already argued, designating something as unique is impossible within a commensurated framework; the significance of sequence is also obliterated by the reduction of context to discrete factors.

pacts of history. This is, however, an abstract, obscure, and almost uninterpretable representation of history. In practice, it does not communicate what the Yavapai believe is essential to know about them. Since Yavapai history is inextricably linked to their understanding of the land and themselves as unique, incommensurable entities, neglecting their historical significance, or attempting to cast it in commensurated terms by means of some other factor, is, in their eyes, a dangerous misrepresentation. It does not express their values; it is not "right."

The Yavapai believed that their survival was at stake and that this decision threatened their collective. But Orme Dam also threatened their past. Their sense of who they are is defined in relation to who their ancestors were, a relation mediated by land. Without the land, this tie is ruptured. The "cost" of losing their land extends back to the sacrifices of their ancestors and the legacy they have fought to preserve and pass on. The Yavapai are highly self-conscious of this heritage. As one woman said: "This is where our ancestors lived. Where my great-grandmother lived and died here. And she told my grandfather before she died, she said: 'Don't ever let them take this land away. Hold on to it.' So we're trying our hardest to hold on to this land" (USBR 1982a: 2-98). Losing the land that their ancestors fought so hard to preserve would betray these earlier struggles. The sense of failure attending this betrayal would be profound.[24]

The exclusion of history does not affect all the interest groups equally in this decision. The ahistoricity of the decision procedure harms the Yavapai community more than other groups. The Yavapai believed that its exclusion from the framework fundamentally misrepresented the stakes of the decision for them, since past injustices and broken promises were not explicitly part of the decision calculus. Ignoring Yavapai history meant excluding relevant information about which most white people knew little or held wildly distorted views. This was information that was hard for white people to confront. Yavapai residents felt that the exclusion of their history made their relocation seem more comparable to the relocations of white residents.

More fundamentally, Yavapai history helps define for them their uniqueness, including their unique relation to the land. Inattention to

24. At best, in the 1981 Social Assessment, the Yavapai's history of forced resettlement and resistance to resettlement is briefly described. It is used to justify the large negative weight given to their forced relocation and to explain the projected negative impacts. This brief historical narrative appeared only in the final social report and not in the more public EIS. The EIS does not include Yavapai history, nor does the quantitative summary of the social analysis of the alternative plans. At worst, in the 1976 EIS, Yavapai history was ignored except to use past resettlements to justify predictions of their successful adjustment to another forced resettlement.

this history fosters or perhaps even ensures the failure to grasp this relationship. The exclusion of Yavapai history from the decision also left a silence that others felt free to fill with their own versions of the past. Some Orme supporters disputed the distinctiveness of the Yavapai and their special claim to the land at Fort McDowell. In doing so, they were trying to minimize the effects of their forced relocation. For example, in 1975, an editorial in Arizona's largest, most powerful newspaper entitled "Heap Big Offer," exhorted the Yavapai to accept the government's "generous" offer for their land: "There is bound to be opposition from those who automatically assume that the white man mistreats the red man. As a matter of fact, despite lamentations to the contrary, the McDowell Apaches are not being driven off their ancestral lands. The tribe itself is not an ethnological entity, having been formed by stray Mohaves and Apaches a relatively short time ago. . . . They would not live astride the Verde River if the U.S. Government hadn't given them this land . . . in 1891. Actually, the original tribesmen volunteered to give up their natural nomadic life as hunters and raiders in order to take advantage of the government offer" (*Arizona Republic,* August 25, 1975, p. 8).

None of this is true. The "McDowell Apaches" were not Apaches, nor were they some mixture of "stray" Mohaves and Apaches. White settlers were responsible for this misnomer.[25] The Yavapai language is related to the Yuman family of languages, and the Apache language is a member of the Athpaskan, or Dene, family of languages (Khera 1978:2). The first written evidence of their living in the area comes from the sixteenth-century diaries of Spanish explorers, who used several names to characterize the Yavapai but never confused them with Apaches or other existing groups. The Yavapai's entitlement to this land was documented historically and legally established some twenty years earlier during formal land-claim proceedings (Schroeder 1974: 1982). The Yavapai were a nomadic people, yet they relied on agriculture to supplement their hunting and gathering. Agriculture's significance varied over time, but evidence suggests that Yavapai have been farming for centuries. The Yavapai became "raiders" only after whites occupied so much of their land that what remained available to them could no longer support them. They "volunteered" to move to a federal

---

25. This was a sensitive issue for Yavapai people. The federal government's persistent and strategic mislabeling of them as "Apache" or "Apache-Mohave" facilitated their elimination and removal. Apaches used guns to defend their homeland, so being identified as Apache meant that white settlers and the military were more likely to kill them. Killing an Apache was considered a social good during this period (Khera 1978:2); it also made it easier to justify their forced resettlement to the "Apache" San Carlos Reservation. The editorial's mislabeling of was clearly politically motivated.

reservation only after they had been starved and slaughtered into sub-
mission by the army. While such deliberate attempts to misrepresent
their past angered and mobilized the Yavapai community, for many
white readers, such accounts were all they knew about Yavapai history.

The framework's neglect of history also meant that the cumulative
consequences of past government policies on the reservation were ignored. For nearly eighty years, the government, in anticipation of imminent resettlement, refused to help or even allow the Yavapai to develop the reservation. Patricia Mariella (1983:193–212) has termed this
policy pattern "condemnation before the fact." As Mariella insists, current land-use patterns at Fort McDowell can only be understood in the
context of past federal policy toward the Yavapai; the contemporary
social and economic context, or, in the language of the study, the "baseline" condition, reflects 150 years of government intrusion and neglect.
Besides federal policies of resettlement and threatened removal, these
influences include uncertainty over water rights and the allocation of
temporary water rights inadequate for large-scale irrigation, failure to
invest in permanent irrigation or even in basic farm equipment, bureaucratic haggling and incrementalist approaches to perennial water
problems, and prevention of the Yavapai community from developing
their resources. All of these policies are implicated in current patterns
of land use on the reservation, ranging from undeveloped agriculture
to the location of residential housing and tribal offices.

The introduction of Orme Dam as a component of the Central Arizona Project reproduced the same pattern of condemnation before the
fact. Long before Congress approved CAP, the reservation was already
experiencing the "impacts" of Orme. During the period from 1948 until
1981, literally millions of dollars were being spent to subsidize water
for non-Indian farmers and municipalities, and even to aid Indian development on other reservations. But because of the uncertainty about
the Yavapai's future, and because federal agencies assumed that Orme
would be built, the reservation languished while other communities
flourished as a result of federal investments.[26]

Had the Fort McDowell residents been allowed to exploit the resources on the reservation to their full advantage, it is hard to say how

26. In 1981, Dan Shaffer, an economic planner, described the predicament: "As soon
as Orme Dam was planned . . . two-thirds of the reservation . . . was, in effect, condemned
and Federal agencies weren't interested in helping the tribe to do any development at
all within that area. So, it was thrown into limbo. . . . Time and time again, the tribe has
been held hostage to what somebody thought might happen and the same thing happened with Orme Dam. . . . Federal agencies didn't want to have anything to do with
anything within the heartland of the reservation where all of the resources are" (USBR
1982a:2-86).

this would have affected the community. It seems reasonable to assume that the tribe would have been better off. Many of the white farmers and ranchers who received the benefit of federally subsidized water during this period developed lucrative enterprises. While it is theoretically possible to derive some arbitrary number to value the missed opportunities resulting from this policy of condemnation, this was not done; the historical legacy of prior condemnation did not fit within the official time frame of the decision, and deriving such a figure would be difficult to do and hard to defend. The legacy of these policies was not directly addressed in the economic, the social, or the public involvement accounts in CAWCS. The exclusion of economic costs of these missed opportunities did have political ramifications since, once again, the relatively undeveloped state of the reservation was used by Orme supporters as evidence that the Yavapai community was wasting its resources.

The "missed opportunities" created by the Orme struggle were personal as well as economic. Time and energy spent on the conflict were diverted from families, work, and community. One woman spoke sadly of how much her children had missed her, saying: "My children grew up without me. They told me, 'You were always going, always leaving for a meeting. You were always leaving with a suitcase.' I tell them, 'Look at the community first. Then think of yourself and your family.' That's how to look at it. That's how I was taught. That's why I was gone." One man estimated that during 1981, he spent one-quarter of his time fighting the dam. The time spent away from home attending meetings or political rallies was hard on families. The time invested in writing letters, organizing protests, lobbying politicians and neighbors, and granting interviews meant that other parts of life were neglected. The intrusiveness of sociologists, bureaucrats, reporters, engineers, and politicians coming to the reservation all made normal life impossible. The money spent on gas, photocopying, and plane tickets to Washington, as well as money unearned because of lost work days, all diverted scarce resources to the Orme conflict.[27] The stress and uncertainty surrounding the decision, and residents' inability to plan for the future, took their toll, emotionally and physically. As one middle-aged mother told me during the controversy, "Every time I hear the word 'Orme Dam' I shudder. . . . That's such an awful word to hear. . . . My kids say 'Mom, what's going to happen to us?' I hope nothing ever happens. but you don't know what to plan for, what to tell them. The houses—

---

27. Leaders in the struggle represented a diverse group, including current and former elected officials, both men and women, elders and teenagers, housewives and businessmen.

we're still paying rent on these homes. One of these days we're going
to have to buy one. . . . But what if they move us or if they were to
put the dam in? I think you have to live from day to day. You can't
plan for things or look ahead. That's the way I feel. And it's hard"
(USBR 1982a:10). Michael O'Sullivan (1981) has shown how the threat
of relocation created tremendous stress for residents and a sense of
having lost control of their lives, so much so that morbidity rates increased dramatically for residents during the Orme controversy. The
stress associated with Orme Dam continues despite the decision not
to build a confluence dam. Some residents believe, given their history,
they can never afford to let down their guard.

In seeing their history excluded from the decision framework, Yavapai residents believed that much of the context necessary for an informed decision had been stripped away. For them, the relevant history of the decision stretches further back than the bureaucrats wanted
to go. Losing their reservation land was not a question of exchanging
one piece of land for another. It meant losing the last .03 percent of
their ancestral homeland. Orme Dam was part of a pattern and not the
discrete choice that the bureau portrayed it to be. Relocation, whether
enacted or threatened, was a continuous crisis that began when white
men first started appropriating their land. The cumulative costs which
they and their relatives had borne ever since white settlers arrived
should not conveniently be ignored. The inability to develop their own
resources or determine their own fate, the exhaustion that accompanies
perpetual uncertainty, the sadness of having to teach their children not
to be complacent, not to trust, are important consequences of the Orme
Dam decision. The burden of having both the past and the future riding
on one's actions was wearing. All these mattered for the decision and
should not be excluded. Excluding Yavapai history minimized the
harm associated with losing their land and made it easier to justify
Orme Dam.

The consequentialist logic of rational choice models are also poorly
equipped to express symbolic values, and these were systematically
excluded from the decision framework. Just as it is difficult to make
causal connections on the basis of moral principles, it is also hard to
show how the symbolic significance of something implicates future
states. The symbolic significance of the incommensurability of land, of
the cultural boundary that the Yavapai draw around land, and the
other features of their culture they believe to be intrinsically valuable
cannot be captured in consequentialist terms. Incommensurable categories are a specific form of boundary, often signaling which classes
of things or ideas have special symbolic value.

Part of the risk in making incommensurate qualities commensurate is that the symbolic logic of incommensurable boundaries is undermined. Although boundaries we define as incommensurable help to constitute some of our most cherished categories, their symbolic significance largely transcends our capacity to "measure" their "empirical" impact. Often, what has symbolic significance is the very judgment that something is incommensurable. Such beliefs are attached to institutions or forms of life, and their symbolic significance derives from the social conventions and contexts that sustain their meaning. For the Yavapai, land was a constitutive incommensurable, and believing so is closely linked to one's capacity to be a Yavapai. The bureau, in imposing a relativistic conception of value on their land and, in effect, on their culture, violated this symbolic boundary.[28]

The distortions that emerged from the rational procedures of the bureau stem not only from what it excluded but also from the kind of information that was included and the form it was given. Carving up impacts into discrete, imposed categories or components is a forced fragmentation that minimizes the pervasiveness and cumulative experience of the impacts. The unity and the integrity of the impacts are not captured, and there is no mechanism, other than simple quantified aggregation, for expressing their interdependence. Some Yavapai residents believed that the often overwhelming complexity of the decision-making procedures distracted people from the real and relatively straightforward stakes of the decision. As one elder expressed it: "White men like to count things that aren't there. We have a way of life that will be destroyed if that dam comes through. Why don't they just say that?"

For many Yavapai, it was absurd, even cruel, to try to attach a price to land and to their culture. Their land was an incommensurate value, and money or other land, regardless of the amount, could not represent its value or compensate for its loss. The inability of the decision framework to accommodate ultimate or incommensurate values made it an inaccurate, even a dangerous representation of their interests. Since the models did not permit incommensurate values, they could not capture the value of land and the value of their way of life. In transforming what was, for one group, an incommensurate value into a price, as was done in the BR's cost-benefit analysis, or into some weighted value summarizing the social impacts to the tribe, as was done in the social

---

28. Bernard Shanks (1974:576) makes a similar point when he argues that "existing cost-benefit analysis fails to adequately consider cultural costs and values. It is an evaluation device for the dominant culture that can't be translated into the values of another culture."

analysis, or as a component of a preference function, as was done in the Public Values Assessment, the very expression of value given to the Yavapai's land and culture was a contradiction of that value. The consequentialist logic motivating these procedures selects out from formal consideration the historical legacy of the Yavapai, the moral issues surrounding the decision, and the symbolic meaning of the stakes of the decision.

In promoting these decision models, the New Guard did not intend to misrepresent Yavapai values or interests. Some members had become staunch supporters of the Yavapai community. Unlike many members of the Old Guard, the New Guard believed that forced relocation would have devastating consequences for the Yavapai. The New Guard believed that their procedures would improve the quality of decision and that this would help the Yavapai: by including them, by making explicit the consequences of Orme for them, and by making it obvious who benefited and who gained. And the rational procedures used did produce important, positive effects. The decision was more inclusive because of the New Guard's commitment to participation and to making sure that "the public" provided the values. The public involvement program generated tremendous publicity for the decision, educated people, and generally provided a forum for debate. This was crucial for the outcome, for resolving the conflict.

Even more crucial for the outcome was the effect of NEPA's requirement to evaluate alternative plans. Had members of the New Guard not created realistic alternatives to Orme, had the decision been between building Orme and doing nothing, the Yavapai would have surely lost their battle to retain their land. The emergence of a viable alternative that would meet project goals without a confluence dam surprised everyone. As late as March of 1981, the BR commissioner was still convinced a decision to build Orme was imminent (*Arizona Republic*, March 27, 1981, p. C-1). As one planner told me, "We never would have created Plan 6 unless we had been forced to try."

But the defeat of Orme Dam also depended on the Yavapai's refusing to let themselves be represented exclusively by the formal study. Throughout CAWCS, Yavapai residents embraced more direct forms of politics to explain their position and influence the outcome: they courted the media, hired lawyers, and mobilized allies, which included an impressive array of Indian tribes, religious organizations, and civil rights groups. Their threats to tie up the project in court and to take their grievance to the United Nations and, perhaps most feared, their reported negotiations with the popular television newsmagazine "Sixty Minutes" were taken seriously by Orme supporters. Concerns

and threatened lawsuits were some of the face-saving
ısed by Arizona politicians like John Rhodes, Dennis De-
Barry Goldwater to back away from Orme Dam.

other groups involved in the decision, Yavapai residents
derstand the techniques and methodologies used in
CAvv⌣⌣. ieir criticisms of the decision procedures were vivid and
practical rather than abstract and theoretical. Residents argued that
land and money were not, for them, comparable and that money was
an inappropriate expression of value. How could something that is sacred be given a monetary value, they would ask. As one of their leaders
told a reporter: "We cannot compromise our principles, our birthright,
our integrity. How do you negotiate honor? We will never negotiate"
(Casserly 1981:A-5). But the inappropriateness of doing so was something they were unable to explain to many other participants, and their
refusal to negotiate was often misinterpreted as a bargaining strategy.

Yavapai leaders knew that they could not control the framework of
the investigation, because, as one man put it, "white men will do things
their way." Despite their objections, a "fair market price" was attached
to their land, their projected suffering was "quantified," and their culture was "measured." But their history, the symbolic salience of their
land, and the moral implications of the decision were excluded from
the consequentialist decision framework.

In privileging expert knowledge, these models excluded in even subtler ways. The models ensured that only those fluent in their use, those
with the requisite technical skills, could be charged with brokering the
decision. The important dimensions of choice were ultimately defined
by "decision experts." While these decision processes can be (and in
this case were) responsive to public preferences, they must still con-
form to technical criteria known to analysts, and the predictions made
concerning the performance of alternatives must also be defensible according to some external source of authority; typically this means they
must somehow be "certified" by credentialed experts.

This characteristic of the decision illustrates what Michel Foucault
has analyzed as a pervasive, taken-for-granted feature of modern
thought: the elaborate specialization and ranking according to criteria
of "scientificity" that makes "local" forms of knowledge or practical
reason less pertinent, less applicable, and inferior. When these "objective" forms are used, the authority of practical reason and personal
experience becomes less relevant.

Yavapai people understood that frameworks were political, sources
of bias. Their experience had taught them not to trust the government
to conduct a fair investigation, to be suspicious of its numbers. As one
tribal leader told me, "We know that government studies are always

slanted in their favor." Many suspected that even if the formal study supported their position, its findings would be ignored. Despite their distrust, residents did not boycott the formal study. This tactic, they believed, was too risky. Most residents cooperated with CAWCS, politely allowing strangers to enter their homes, to interview them, and to attend community events. But their resolve to work outside the study was fueled by their distrust and their concerns about the study.

Residents may not have convinced the bureaucrats of the narrowness of their framework, but the Yavapai's practical understanding of its limitations informed their resistance. Having to explain why land could not be expressed as price, why their removal from land was different from the relocation of white people, and why the moral and historical dimensions of the decision should not be stripped away required that they reappraise their difference against the terms imposed by the study. They could not control the terms of the decision framework, but their defense was shaped in reaction to its conceptions of rationality, the limitations of consequentialism, and the partiality of science that framed the investigation.

So Yavapai residents adopted political strategies based on representing themselves in their own terms. They understood clearly how politicized their difference had become. Their sense of themselves as a unique, endangered cultural group already presupposed a self-consciousness and scrutiny that reflected the challenges they had faced in their encounters with the government and with other settlers. Culture that is not questioned, compromised, or compared does not require a label; it is naturalized and does not demand the articulate description and defense that the Yavapai had been forced to provide. Being continually placed in the unusual position of having to define what made them a unique people, with ancestral rights to their property, made them sensitive to attempts to commensurate their concerns with those of other parties in the decision. Such public and politically motivated misappropriation of their past also highlighted the importance of knowing and representing their own history.

The Yavapai's repeated and protracted struggles with the government required them to construct a portrait of themselves in categories that made sense to them, that would privilege their experience and authority, and that were defensible and stable and sturdy enough to withstand intense scrutiny. In earlier struggles—to be allowed to leave San Carlos, to obtain their own reservation—Yavapai people were required to prove themselves civilized in terms imposed by settlers and politicians; they were forced to prove they were peaceful, hard-working, compliant. This time, their resistance could challenge the terms that were being imposed. This time, the strategies they adopted reflected their understanding of the political importance of defining and asserting their difference.

The community took great pains to publicize and explain their difference to other groups and to the media. While relying on well-known techniques of protest, they adapted these in ways that highlighted their distinctiveness. The reenactment of the Trail of Tears was one poignant example of this. This march was a dramatic reinsertion of their history into the decision; it was a vivid public and symbolic expression of their cultural and historical distinctiveness, from the style of praying that launched the march to its culmination with the presentation of a bark scroll designed to subvert normal bureaucratic practice. The genre, the protest march, was a familiar part of American politics and so was accessible and interpretable to white audiences. Cast as a reenactment, it was also the Yavapai's public assertion of the continuity of both their oppression and their culture. It was a symbolic response (where symbolic value had been systematically excluded) to the question of cultural continuity posed by powerful white opponents who assumed that continuity was the premise of cultural authority, that change equaled assimilation and negated difference.

The strategies adapted by the Yavapai community reasserted and made public what the rational framework had removed: residents reenacted, as protest, their excluded history; they defended the morality of their claims; and they reexamined the incommensurability of their land. In explaining why land could not be expressed as price, why their removal from land was different from the relocation of white people, and why the moral and historical dimensions of the decision should not be stripped away, they reasserted the political nature of what the New Guard had tried to make technical and defended their substantive values as members of the New Guard were attempting to translate these into the terms of instrumental rationality. They may not have convinced the bureaucrats of the narrowness of the framework, but their practical understanding of its failings informed their resistance. And this was both empowering to them and persuasive to others.

Of the three groups' identities, the Yavapai's was the most explicitly politicized. Forged from struggle, people's understanding of themselves reflected their tenacious efforts to stay together, to keep their land. Their evolving understanding of themselves illustrates the dynamism of identity, how identities both incorporate and react against efforts to contain them, to measure them, to "rationalize" them. The New Guard's efforts to translate the terms of their identity into the strictures of instrumental reason did not suppress the Yavapai's sense of their distinctiveness. Instead, it led to the reexamination and reinvigoration of their difference, through ritual, resistance, discussion.

Being Yavapai Now

The struggle against Orme changed Yavapai residents. One consequence of this defense of themselves and their land is a heightened sensitivity, appreciation, and reinterpretation of what made them Yavapai. The long and painful history of the Yavapai's efforts to stay with the land has irrevocably changed its meaning for them and their understanding of their relationship to it. As one man told me: "What we have, who we are, is something we have fought for, and in the fighting we have learned about ourselves, our heritage, and what these mean to us." After they had spent years explaining their special claim to the land, self-consciously taking stock of the content of their culture and the meaning of their collective identity, their appreciation of these has deepened. Their explanations of their difference are more articulate and are institutionalized in holidays, pow-wows, and pageants. Their efforts to reinterpret, to represent their difference, has made them different.

The Yavapai's struggle to stop the dam generated broad publicity for the community. Yavapai residents became adept at giving interviews and speeches, and they generally became more experienced and sophisticated political actors. Their political significance is now recognized beyond the reservation as well. Politics on the reservation are accorded a new significance and are now seen as legitimate "regional news." Reservation events that before would have gone unnoticed are more likely to be covered. The accomplishments of the Yavapai community have also inspired other native groups. Lawrence Aschenbrenner, an attorney with the Native American Rights Fund, said of their struggle (Blundell 1981:35): "It's pretty amazing. All sorts of well-intentioned people told the Yavapai they were sticking their heads in the sand, that if they'd just negotiate, they could make a heck of a deal. . . . What these people have done is an example to other tribes who can now say, 'By God, if we get together and don't give up, we can win too.' "

The reservation has changed in other ways. As a result of the conflict, some residents have become committed environmentalists. Some believe that, in addition to being more visible, the community has become even more politicized as a result of their success. Residents' response to new federal rules limiting gaming on reservations also supports this view. Several years ago, the community organized another very effective political protest. The tribe built a very successful casino on the land that was once condemned by Orme. When federal agents tried to raid the casino, the Yavapai organized an effective blockade that garnered national attention and eventually led to a negotiated resolution to the conflict. Of the five reservations raided, only the Yavapai mobilized to oppose this intrusion (*Mesa Tribune,* May 14, 1992, p. A-1). Participants in this protest believed that their experience during the Orme struggle helped to provide not only the skill but also the sense of efficacy and courage needed to attempt this daring action. As the chairman told me, "[When] the government raided the reservation for gaming equipment, we fought and prevailed. Our experience with Orme helped us realize that we're going to lose something which is a great benefit to the tribe. We had no recourse or leverage to work with, so we fought and won."

The importance of knowing and using their history, which now includes the "Orme Victory," is stressed even more strongly now. I was told that the community is planning to make films and videos about their struggle to preserve their land "so that young people will appreciate what we've had to do to keep it, why it means so much to us." Leaders in the Orme struggle have been honored with parades, with buildings named for them, and with the pride of grandchildren eager to recount their familial ties to the struggle. The Orme victory appears frequently and prominently in the obituaries and eulogies of those elders who have since died. And the elders are buried, along with the remains of their massacred relatives, the heroes of earlier struggles, and generations of war veterans in the cemetery that Orme Dam did not flood. Now, Yavapai identity includes a sense of being political and being effective.

$\approx\approx\approx$ **Six** $\approx\approx\approx$

Rationality, Form, and Power

You do not expect a rose to smell like a violet; why, then, should we expect the human spirit, the richest thing we have, to exist only in a single form?

Karl Marx

Forme is power.

Thomas Hobbes

How can truth hover between alternatives?

Robert Graves

To make a rational decision is to create a predictable world, one that can be measured, one with well-defined parameters. It involves drawing boundaries around a segment of time and saying that this is the period that matters, these are the people for whom it matters. Like all forms, it stops the flow of life, imposing on it a coherence based on patterns of selection and exclusion, and strict rules of relevance. Imagined futures are translated into competing alternatives. The transpositions required of these forms are hard work, demanding skill, elaborate organization, and discipline.

In rational choice models, the elements of this form are meant to reflect those aspects of the world that matter to decision makers, marking and measuring salient differences and similarities among alternative strategies. Their selection is based on a consequentialist logic that insists that what is relevant is that which is causally connected to carefully defined future states. This heavily edited world can be helpful for its clarity and for the efficiency with which it simplifies what threatens to overwhelm us. In forcing us to define and defend our choices, in displaying our differences, it may help us confront what we otherwise might ignore.

But this form of rationality obscures as well as clarifies. The artifice that is sometimes helpful can sometimes threaten. It requires that we value in a resolutely relative way; the commensuration it demands may violate, even obliterate, other social boundaries that help order our lives and define us. Commitments and preferences are not the same thing. Transforming one to the other can disrupt and distort our relationships to what we value, misrepresenting them and us.[1] The logic of this form can erase or diminish that which is hard to reconcile with instrumentality: thick, messy context, historical legacies, uncertainty, ambivalence, passion, morality, singularity, the constitutive and expressive salience of symbols.

The apparent even-handedness of these forms, the ease with which they can accommodate new things, their seemingly neutral logic, their capacity to integrate, are all qualities that suggest a formal equality. But this formal equality can be symbolic, superficial, even treacherous, blurring important distinctions and hiding power. In deciding things this way, we need to be reminded of the costs of this clarity and efficiency, of whose interests they serve, of its effects for how we interpret our worlds.

My analysis suggests some cautions for those, like members of the New Guard, who believe that their decision procedures were neutral, scientific frameworks for improving decisions made by bureaucrats and politicians. Some participants believed that these procedures fundamentally misrepresented both the stakes of the decision and them. For some, the assumptions built into these models were incompatible with their relation to the decision.

The varied reactions of the New Guard, the Old Guard, and the Yavapai community offer useful insights about the practical consequences of these rational forms. The experiences of the three groups reveal how these forms affect people's participation, the legitimacy of decisions, what people pay attention to, strategies of resistance, and people's sense of their identities and interests. The practical effects of these rational forms, in turn, can suggest useful theoretical insights, ones that can enlarge or challenge existing theoretical explanations of power and rationality.

Legitimacy

The legitimacy of rational procedures is useful to disentangle for these groups. For the New Guard, the compromise plan about Orme Dam that emerged was a vindication, a hopeful sign for those who would rely on science to adjudicate conflict, control technology, and extend democracy. Although politics were never fully reduced to preferences, the political process was improved by defining interested parties and then compelling them rigorously to construct and publicly to confront

1. Amartya Sen (1990:25–43) offers an influential analysis of the difference between commitments and preferences where he argues that commitments, because they are often attached to groups or communities, can help overcome dichotomized conceptions of morality as egoistic or universalized.

their preferences. Members of the New Guard came to this decision agnostic or divided in their allegiance to alternative plans. When their decision procedures identified the alternative without Orme as the most rational, they embraced it. They submitted to the authority of their procedures. Their personal, intellectual, and organizational investments in their procedures, and the stakes involved, made them a group that was eager to be persuaded. For members of the New Guard, their procedures made them rational and the outcome legitimate.

The Old Guard had decided on Orme Dam long before, their commitment to it preceding CAWCS by decades. Nurtured by the agency, energized by years of politicking, sustained by an engineer's faith in Orme's technical prowess, protected by power, this commitment was not easily ruptured. When the New Guard's procedures revealed that the utilities of some members of the Old Guard were maximized by an alternative to Orme, the procedure, not the dam, was discredited. Rather than submitting to procedural rationality, members of the Old Guard rejected its legitimacy. But having been publicly discredited, they could not stop the use of these procedures with nothing to offer in their stead.

Had decision factors been different, had NEPA not required that environmental and social effects be included, had different technical criteria been used, Orme Dam may well have prevailed as the "rational" alternative. If the aesthetic appeal of a big dam, the importance of saving face, and loyalty to friends had been legitimate values, Orme Dam might well have emerged as the "rational" outcome. But "personal" attributes are deemed inappropriate in public decisions, even by members of the Old Guard.[2] As deeply invested as they were in Orme Dam, they believed that their attachment to the dam was "rational," deriving from Orme's superior performance and not from some murky private motives. As engineers, they could not acknowledge an emotional attachment. At the heart of the Old Guard's disagreement with the outcome was the incommensurability of Orme Dam for them. Its incommensurability made their investment antithetical to the New Guard's decision techniques. For the Old Guard, the outcome determined the legitimacy of the procedure.

The Yavapai's response was the most ambivalent. The importance of retaining their land was paramount to their community, and they were overjoyed with the outcome. Reservation residents regard it as a

---

2. Orme Dam might also have prevailed if the safety of existing dams had not also been added as a project goal. Improvements on existing structures both made them safer and allowed them to better regulate water, which enhanced their efficiency for other project purposes. No engineer could claim that dam safety didn't matter.

moral and political victory, which they celebrate annually. But there is something disquieting about this victory for some residents. The Yavapai won because they were politically effective. They won because NEPA required that alternatives be examined, because members of the New Guard, as rational decision makers, were serious about constructing alternatives to Orme Dam, and because this process allowed a workable compromise to emerge. The Yavapai won because NEPA and thirty years of struggle over civil rights had made it impossible to continue to ignore them, because CAWCS gave them time to mobilize, and because they made it clear that building Orme would not be politically expedient. Good reasons. But they did not win because taking their land would have been wrong. Had Orme not been publicly redefined as an inferior alternative, the Yavapai's claims would have been squashed. Although the Yavapai community achieved the outcome they desperately wanted, some still felt misrepresented by the procedures that conveyed their interests. For the Yavapai, the outcome did not determine the legitimacy of the procedure, nor did the procedure determine the legitimacy of the outcome. Although they accomplished their fundamental goal of retaining their land, they did not regard their victory as the triumph of reason.

As Tom Tyler (1990:178) argues, normative issues matter a lot when people are evaluating the legitimacy of outcomes. His work shows that people's willingness to comply with laws and their evaluations of their legal experiences are not necessarily dictated by the favorability of outcomes or their capacity to influence them, as more instrumental approaches would suggest. Instead, the legitimacy of procedures powerfully shapes people's interpretation of justice. The example of the New Guard supports the "normative procedural justice" perspective of Tyler and his colleagues. For the New Guard, the legitimacy of their rational procedures was given, and very directly determined the legitimacy of the outcome.

The Yavapai's ambivalence also supports the position that outcomes do not automatically dictate legitimacy. Their historically informed distrust of government studies and officials made them skeptical of the legitimacy of the New Guard's procedures. As Tyler (1990:174) suggests, prior views about authority can shape people's perceptions of what constitutes fair procedures. The Old Guard's views, however, suggest some possible limits for procedural justice explanations. For these engineers, the outcome clearly discredited the procedures. Prior distrust cannot explain their reaction. Their deep investment in Orme Dam, which I have argued is partly an organizational effect, overrides procedural issues. My findings suggest that when commitments to outcomes are central features of, and symbols for, group identity and loyalty, when outcomes become substantively valued, procedural fairness may be subordinated to these commitments.

Tyler (1990:164–65; 1988) argues that differences in people's backgrounds do not significantly affect the meaning of procedural justice; although people will emphasize different criteria in different contexts, all people use comparable criteria (e.g., the chance to participate, the biases of decision makers, ethical implications, being treated with dignity, etc.) in evaluating the justice of procedures. Deconstructing the meanings of these criteria in concrete contexts would seem a fruitful endeavor: the chance to participate mattered to people, but so did the *terms* of their participation. Likewise, moral issues concerned both members of the New Guard and the Yavapai; however, whereas the former were concerned with the morality of democratic participation, the moral issues that concerned the Yavapai were trust, broken promises, and long-term distributive effects. I have argued that people value things in disparate ways. My findings suggest that the appropriateness of how we value influences our interpretation of what are legitimate procedures and fair outcomes.

Identities and Interests

Identities and interests are helpful, if contested, ideas partly because they reduce complicated relationships in ways that make it easier for us to talk and think about them. But when we use these terms, whether in theory or politics, we tend to forget that they are shorthand for dynamic, dialectical relations among people who are busy doing things and interpreting what they have done. The salience and strength of the symbolic boundaries that we draw around ourselves and others are variable, contingent accomplishments that must be explored empirically and explained theoretically.[3]

The identities of all three groups changed during the course of the Orme dispute, albeit in different ways. For members of the New Guard, the dispute helped constitute their organizational identity. This was a gradual process, as "weird outsiders" became a cohesive group in reaction to their experience of the bureau's engineering culture. Members of the New Guard were clearly concerned with keeping their jobs and cultivating influence, but it took time for these concerns to become transformed into an interest in institutionalizing instrumental rationality, in expanding the constituency of the agency, or in devising mechanisms of participation. The New Guard's organizational interests and identity were mutual, ongoing constructions.

3. See Nicola Beisel (1997) and Michèle Lamont (1992) for thoughtful analyses of these processes.

Nor are they permanent. Now that CAWCS is over, now that members of the New Guard are more powerful and more secure, they no longer think of themselves as a group. Those who stayed with the agency are still motivated by many of the same values and beliefs, but these have become detached from their sense of themselves as a coherent group. Their shared sense of connection is something that is more nostalgia than an active consciousness that informs their work. Now, they identify more strongly with the "New Bureau," the agency they helped to create, than with other members of the New Guard.

For the Old Guard, the defeat of Orme signaled the end of their era in the agency. The New Guard's procedures, in extending the domain and rigor of instrumental rationality, eroded their autonomy. Members of the Old Guard understood themselves primarily as organizational and professional members, as bureau engineers. They saw their interest in Orme Dam as coterminous with the interests of their agency and with those of the broader public. In requiring their agency to incorporate the views of opponents, NEPA forced a new perspective on the Old Guard. They did not think of themselves as participants in an organizational culture, as being somehow distinctive or "biased" until their organizational identities were reinterpreted by newcomers and outsiders. No longer could they take for granted the premises of their engineering ethos. In providing a forum for challenging the Old Guard, and in providing techniques for separating preferences from the person, NEPA demonstrated the relativity of their worldview and offered a much more sensitive barometer of their support or opposition. When others ruptured their neat alignment of professional, organizational, and social interests, members of the Old Guard felt betrayed. It was then that their "interest" in Orme Dam began to feel and appear personal, although they could not explain it in these terms.

The politicization of their identity has also changed members of the Yavapai community. Yavapai leaders were forced to explain their difference from others to skeptics, to experts, to reporters, and to the groups that became mobilized in the decision. In reacting to others' representation of them and their interests, they were forced to grapple with fundamental questions of identity: Who are we? What unites us? Why are we different? The question of "What shall we do?" that was officially motivating this decision, for them, could not be distinguished from "Who are we?" Their political accomplishment was to keep these questions conjoined.

Knowing who they were was part of a complex process of knowing and reinterpreting who they weren't and why they were different. This process was shaped by law, their opponents' claims, their sense of history, and by the conceptions of rationality that informed bureaucrats' representations of them. The Orme crisis, their rejection of the implicit identity conferred by the bureau's procedures, and their victory have all contributed to a reappraised, rejuvenated collective understanding of themselves, one that is projected into the past and forward into the future. Their success meant that their ancestors' earlier struggles were not betrayed, and the future now weighs less heavily on their shoulders.

Relations of Difference

Encounters, in forcing groups to interpret others' behavior and to explain themselves to others, can be venues for the reappraisal and renegotiation of identities. As such, they are theoretically revealing sites for examining how cultures and identities change. In demanding accounts and prompting comparisons, encounters are opportunities for marking and scrutinizing differences. They are also venues for assessing the terms and boundaries of consensus. For some, this takes the form of apprehending as particular, or local, what had been imagined as universal.

Yavapai residents' understanding of themselves as a distinctive and endangered cultural entity already reflected past encounters, prior accounting, and the mediating structures that shaped these. For members of the Old Guard, the Orme dispute was the occasion when they were first forced to acknowledge the relativity of their worldview and the erosion of their power. What the Old Guard had imagined as shared and obvious was proven contingent, contested, and vulnerable. They had faced opponents before, people who did not want their dams, but that opposition had been explained away as politics, bargaining, the necessary sacrifice of the few for the many, or as the treachery and luck of zealots. What was different this time was that explanations based on extremism or exceptionalism no longer held sway in the face of widespread, organized opposition.

Members of the Old Guard were now forced to confront a generalized sense that the consensus over their work had somehow eroded. Their power, their organization, their profession, and the dense, exclusive networks between their loyal supporters had kept them from admitting that the world had changed in ways that challenged their authority and their comfortable assumptions. Their sense of their professional and organizational "selves" was out of sync with recent events. The proud legacy of the agency that had once been so important to the Old Guard's professional identity was now somehow tainted, its monuments discredited; their only recourse, nostalgia.

For the New Guard, the relativity of worldviews was a given. As marginal members of what they experienced as a monolithic organizational culture, they did not presume universal goals or values. Their organization kept them mindful of their difference. Diversity and democracy were, for them, legitimate, and they took conflict for granted. Their marginality and the problem of commensuration helped unite and define them. NEPA helped make them a group. Their challenge was to offer access, representation, and mediation in their efforts to construct a new consensus from divergent interests, goals, and values. Their challenge was to do this in a politicized and polarized public contest.

Relativity was fundamental to the New Guard in more esoteric ways, as well. Their strategy for negotiating diversity, premised on a radical relativity, was quintessentially modern. In their decision procedures, value was a strictly relational dimension, and its integration, by means of commensuration, was required. Something can be valued only in relation to something else, with no conceptual room for incommensurate categories, absolutes, or intrinsic value, in their mode of rationality. What was universal for the New Guard was their version of rationality. Their commitments to this form of rationality became a substantive value. Their zeal in promoting it makes sense only if one understands how their investments in rationality became personal, as well as intellectual and material. Their confidence in its capacity to process diversity fairly and uniformly did not permit them to see, at first, the unequal effects of its procedural equality.

Some Implications for Rational Choice Theory

The effects of the Orme dispute on how these three groups understood their identities and defined their interests offer useful theoretical lessons. Some of these have to do with understanding the limits of rational choice explanations. Jon Elster (1986:36), who is both a proponent of rational choice and one of its most sophisticated critics, argues that understanding the limits of rational choice explanations should be one of the first tasks of rational choice theory. One part of this involves appreciating that not all rational behavior takes the form of instrumental rationality: action directed at accomplishing outcomes. Elster believes that social norms can provide motives for behavior that is incompatible with instrumental rationality, since this action is not oriented to outcomes (1986:113–23; 1989).[4]

4. Dennis Chong (1996) argues that often the distinctions that are drawn between actions motivated by interests and norms (and concomitantly between what he calls economic and sociological explanations of behavior) are exaggerated. In some cases, he argues, people are strategic about the values and norms they embrace; in others, people may continue to embrace norms and values that no longer serve their interests. I agree that both things occur, and my analyses offers some supporting evidence. But Elster is

Elster argues that in some cases the means-ends distinction that is the premise of rational choice explanations seems pointless (1986:23). Efforts to frame the choice between an apple or an orange in terms of maximizing some outcome or sensation seem silly. Choices like deciding whether to work late or visit a friend need not imply some overarching goal under which scenarios are subsumed as alternative options. Choices that cannot be expressed as means-ends relations need not imply that these are irrational. But choices like these can be assimilated into a form of instrumental action by having people or observers rank their options. Pairwise comparisons induce a preference ordering that can be mathematically converted into utility functions. This is how public values were measured during CAWCS. But as the examples of the Yavapai and the Old Guard show, efforts to transform noninstrumental relations into the terms of instrumental action can sometimes generate conflict, misrepresent the nature of people's commitments, and, in doing so, misrepresent the people themselves.

The Orme dispute also illuminates the limitations of assumptions that some rational choice theorists make about people's preferences, tastes, desires, or interests. In what Elster (1983:2–15, 26–33) calls the "thin theory" of rationality, preferences and beliefs are exogenous or taken as theoretically uninteresting givens.[5] What matters for explaining behavior is the formal structure of preferences, not their content. James Coleman, an influential rational choice theorist, has put this bluntly: "In general . . . I assume that interests are unchangeable; in a theory based on purposive action, interest must be taken as a given" (1990:156–57). A famous example of "thin rationality" is George Stigler and Gary Becker's (1977) argument that behavior can be explained by changes in price or income, since people share similar, stable tastes. Advertising, fashion, addiction, and habits are responses to opportunity constraints rather than exemplars of changing taste.

For some rational choice theorists, exogeneity is a virtue, since it leads to a more parsimonious theory. Some appear not to be troubled

---

emphasizing a different relationship to values (comparable to Weber's conception of substantive rationality), where someone does something because it is intrinsically good or bad to do so, and not for the consequences attending the behavior. This distinction in ways of valuing is an important one.

5. Elster's purpose in his investigations of irrationality is to supplement thin rationality with a "broad theory" of rationality that provides universalist criteria (causal relevance and consciousness) for assessing the rationality of preferences and beliefs. See Padgett (1986) for an illuminating assessment of this provocative project. Elster's goal is to broaden our conception of instrumental rationality and is similar in some respects to Jürgen Habermas's efforts to reformulate a conception of rationality that permits the rational evaluation of values. Their "broadening" strategies are, not surprisingly, radically different.

that "decision units" are unaware of their maximizing behavior or even of their motives (Becker 1976:44; Posner 1992:353–54). What this amounts to is a conceptual bracketing of the intentionality that somehow causes behavior. This strikes me as, at best, a superficial and unsatisfying explanation.[6] As many have pointed out, this exogeneity has political consequences by formally removing the goals of action from the realm of debate and explanation.

Others acknowledge that the exogeneity and stability of preferences are a theoretical liability, a regrettable incompleteness (Friedman and Diem 1993:96–99; Hechter 1990:501–2); for them, recourse to behavioral assumptions about individual preferences that "necessarily depart from reality" is the price paid for the absence of a theory of preference formation and development. This theoretical void reflects the hazards of measuring subjective states like values or preferences.

I agree that understanding people's desires, motives, and values is extremely difficult, that these are not clearly "revealed" in behavior, and that people's consciousness of these and how they inform their interpretations of their own and others' behavior is a murky business. Nevertheless, I think that abandoning our efforts at understanding subjective states (or meaning) is abdicating too much. While our theoretical aspirations may be different, I agree with Michael Hechter that being able to account for what people value improves our understanding of people's behavior. Because I think the empirical demands of understanding how meaning is constructed and how it informs action are enormous, I think that what he wants to measure demands interpretation.

"Preferences" is a narrow lens for understanding people's investments, partly because of some restrictive assumptions that some make about preferences: that preferences are stable, prior, complete, or given, are characteristics of isolated or autonomous individuals, and are independent of outcomes. These assumptions are tantamount to trying to hold meaning still, which I believe is incompatible with people's engagement in the world and with one another. My analysis suggests, first of all, that preferences may be expressed by individuals but that they are collective accomplishments. For members of the Old Guard, their deep investment in Orme Dam was a shared meaning, a value reflecting organizational ideology, career incentives, and the duration of their involvement with this project. The value and meaning of land

---

6. One virtue of rational choice theory is its emphasis on preserving human agency in explanation, its refusal to attribute action to reified social constructs. An ironic consequence of this theoretical uninterest in motives is that rational choice explanations often end up emphasizing opportunity constraints, and agency disappears.

for Yavapai residents, about which there was more consensus than I would have first imagined, is derived from the collective interpretations of historical experience, socialization, and contemporary conflict. The value of land is closely linked to people's identities, which encompass not just what to value but how to value. Appreciating where preferences come from entails appreciating how fundamentally social they are.

My analysis also suggests that preferences do change over time, sometimes in patterned ways that I believe are theoretically important. Members of the Old Guard did not begin their careers with the BR because of their commitment to Orme Dam. While some believed that big dams were thrilling, most also believed that developing water resources was a useful endeavor and that it was important to use their considerable expertise to find the best ways to do so. What changed for them was that what they once considered a means became a highly desired end for its own sake. I have argued that this transformation is an organizational, cultural, and political accomplishment. Failing to appreciate this type of transformation limits our capacity to understand bureaucracies, since I believe that these sorts of shifts are common in them and help explain both their power and durability. Max Weber (1978:990–94), his student Robert Michels (1949:390), and other organizational theorists such as Philip Selznick (1957; 1984:258) have all emphasized this pattern as central for appreciating how the power of bureaucratic and technical authority threatens democratic participation.

Another lesson to learn from this analysis is that sometimes people discover what they value, or come to value new things, in the process of choosing. This is not simply a case of learning more about the performance of alternatives so as to improve one's capacity to identify the optimal alternative. As James March (1994:188–92) has argued, both preferences and identities are ambiguous in ways that preclude understanding them as consistent and prior to decisions. Sometimes preferences emerge from decisions, as did the Old Guard's "preference" for Orme Dam. Members of the Old Guard believed that they valued Orme Dam because it was the optimal solution to the problems they were trying to solve. When presented with findings that contradicted this, they were forced somehow to account for or reconcile how poorly what they valued and the way they appeared to value it fit within the boundaries of rationality that members of the New Guard was trying to impose.

Organization theorists have argued that decisions have multiple dimensions and that an important and often unappreciated dimension of decisions is that they are forms of symbolic action. As such, they are opportunities for signaling and defining, as well as for maximizing.

Organizational members often wish to signal their own rationality, whether this is a strategic bid for legitimacy or a more implicit understanding of how to frame "good" decisions. This confounds further the problems associated with disentangling preferences as motives for action. It also explains why it was so awkward for members of the Old Guard to rebut the New Guard's procedures.[7]

Another way that my analysis can inform rational choice theory is to show how cultural processes and power can influence what counts as a "feasibility set." Jon Elster (1979:77, 113) describes human action as result of two filtering devices: the feasibility set and the choice process. Rational choice theory has typically focused on the latter, which for Elster includes the set of actions that satisfy "physical, technical, economic and politico-legal constraints." James Johnson (1989) argues that cultural processes, as part of the "politics of the real," shape the cognitive maps that define what people construe as possible outcomes or alternatives. This represents another effort directed toward making endogenous what was formerly exogenous. This effort is compatible with organizational theorists like March and Simon who have emphasized how the cognitive categories of groups within organizations shape which information is attended to and which is ignored, and how information is edited in patterned ways as it travels through organizations.

The "feasibility sets" that characterized the BR before NEPA and before the New Guard's arrival were powerfully shaped by the engineering ethos and structure of the agency. Criteria of relevance were engineering criteria, so that decisions revolved around the location and design of dams. Defining alternatives in these terms made some outcomes irrelevant. Not building in floodplains, using less water and power, or even limiting growth in arid regions was organizationally unimaginable. But it is not only the feasibility set that is shaped by these processes. Such criteria also shaped who was "real," defining some groups as central and others as invisible. Loyalty to constituencies was also an institutional accomplishment. The cultural and institutional processes that define the relevant and the real are crucial for reproducing power.

---

7. This is a crucial insight of the neoinstitutional theory of organizations and approaches to decision-making that emphasize ambiguity. See, e.g., Meyer and Rowan (1977); Brunsson (1985); March and Olson (1976); Feldman and March (1981); and Dobbin (1994). Susan Hurley (1989:3) makes a similar point when she criticizes what she calls the "subjectivist view" that values are determined by preferences that are prior to and independent of those values. Hurley argues that values play a constitutive role in interpreting behavior and that this undermines efforts to use preferences as the "unproblematic building blocks" of theories of values.

The Significance of Not Choosing and the Costs
of Commensuration

The differing reactions of the Old and New Guards and of the Yavapai community also reveal patterns in what might be called the "costs" of commensuration. I have argued that understanding something as incommensurate can be a special form of valuing, a distinctive way of investing something with meaning. Just as choosing to do something can be a way to create or express commitment, so too can removing something from the realm of choice and comparison. One of the costs of commensuration was the incapacity of these models to accommodate meaningful incommensurable categories. This turned out to be politically costly during the controversy, but I think this incapacity remains theoretically costly for rational choice theory.

Members of the three groups I have described all, at various times and in different ways, expressed their awareness of the importance of incommensurable categories. The Yavapai were the most eloquent in expressing the importance of incommensurable categories, partly because they were most experienced in doing so, and partly because the incommensurability of their land was a constitutive incommensurable, one directly linked to what it meant to them to be Yavapai. For them, the incommensurability of land was as straightforward as not trading one's children or not selling one's mother. For members of the Old Guard, the incommensurability of Orme Dam was unambiguously expressed in their "not needing a computer to tell [them] what [they] want[ed]," and in the vehemence with which they defended Orme.

For members of the New Guard, those most fluent in the technology of commensuration, recognition of the salience of incommensurables was more elusive. When their techniques for commensuration failed to derive a price for tubing down the river, something they knew people valued, it was a "failure of methodology." When a young man with a romantic dilemma used their rational decision model to help him decide which of two women to marry, he was teased.

Some members of the New Guard gradually became more circumspect about the power of their techniques. Some began to question the universal applicability of their version of rationality. Some became convinced that some things, like the rights of Indians to their land or the right of a species to exist, ought to be excluded from trade-offs. Over time, some members also came to see that rationality can exacerbate conflict as well as ameliorate it. For some members of the New Guard, the struggle over Orme prompted a recognition of the limitations of rational procedures in representing at least parts of the world. Their belief in the universal appropriateness of instrumental rationality became tempered by their gradual appreciation of the power attending these forms and of the incommensurability of cultures.

The New Guard's circumspection, forged from practice and politics, can usefully be extended to more theoretical realms. James Coleman, who was an eloquent spokesman on behalf of rational choice theory, made what I think is an interesting admission. In trying to understand what accounts for living arrangements where the rights of the collectivity supersede the rights of the individual (his examples were the military and religious orders), he wrote in a footnote: "The existence of the psychic benefits arising from a restriction on choice is a phenomenon that is inexplicable using current rational choice theory" (Coleman 1990:63).[8]

In my view, the inability of rational choice theory to account for these "psychic benefits" stems from its broader failure to appreciate the symbolic properties of choice, its uninterest in understanding how and when choice is defined as socially or morally appropriate, and its inability to comprehend how boundaries around the appropriateness of choice are constructed and maintained. Appreciating the significance of incommensurable categories is important, since sometimes these categories help constitute our identities and our relations to things and others. An understanding of how restricting choice informs our relations can enlarge rational choice theory by locating it within a broader understanding of its relation to other modes of valuing, other ways of investing. Such an understanding might also mute the universalizing claims that some of its proponents make.

The meaning of commensuration partly derives from where it directs attention. Owing largely to Pierre Bourdieu's influence, many have begun to appreciate how it is that subtle distinctions in the acquisition and use of "cultural capital" become a means for reproducing class power. The Orme dispute also suggests the obverse: how commensuration, in blurring distinctions of all sorts, can also be a means of exerting power and how a defense of distinctiveness, the ultimate form of which is an incommensurable, intrinsic value, can be a means of resisting control. One paradoxical effect of commensuration may be that the homogeneity it imposes, in forcing common units onto diverse values, creates a new form of distinction: a finely calibrated homogeneity that meticulously tracks small differences while obliterating big ones. Another paradoxical effect is that under some conditions, efforts to impose

---

8. Elster (1979) investigates precommitment, an example of people who, in anticipating their own weakness of will, choose to restrict choice for rational reasons. The classic example is Ulysses tying himself to the mast to preclude his giving in to the irresistible power of the Sirens. Precommitment differs from the restriction of choice that derives from believing in incommensurable categories.

commensuration, in highlighting the importance of forms of value, can revitalize for people the salience of incommensurable categories.

In a monetized, bureaucratized, rationalized world, asserting that something is an incommensurate value can be a powerful act of resistance, as the Yavapai demonstrated. Our capacity for resisting commensuration is also evident in Viviana Zelizer's (1989; 1994) analysis of money. For women denied the power to control money, the ferreting away of "pin money" can be a means of resisting patriarchy, just as trivializing woman's money can be a means of reproducing it. Gender, class, and power become encoded in incommensurable categories of "special" money. Zelizer shows how money, the ultimate metric, can become an important cultural resource in negotiating meaning and resisting economic rationality. Zelizer argues that as commodity forms proliferate, so too will people's capacity to create new strategies of "earmarking" currencies, infusing them with new meanings that render them incommensurate.

Incommensuration as a strategy of resistance, of course, presumes a fairly commensurated world; understanding the symbolic significance of rational forms is key for understanding the interpenetration of cultural and economic worlds. Cost-benefit ratios, double-entry bookkeeping, risk analysis, decision trees, as well as formal organizational structures, may become as important as symbols of rationality or efficiency as they are as techniques for producing it. The legitimacy they signal is tied to the authority of science, our belief in the possibility of keeping values and facts distinct, our faith in calculation, and the power to routinize uncertainty that comes with living in a rationalized world. Understanding the appeal, cost, and limits of commensuration will depend on understanding the nature of this broader, inchoate authority.

Identity Politics and Interest-Group Politics

"Identity politics" have become a fixture of contemporary politics. One of the most interesting features of the Orme dispute is in the ways that identities became politicized and mobilized in the decision. I have argued that for Yavapai residents, their difference had been politicized since their first encounters with white settlers and miners who wanted their land. What changed was how their difference was represented, what intervention it warranted, and eventually, whose authority was bolstered by defining this difference.

As CAWCS demonstrated, sometimes identities can become politicized in abstract ways, for example, in the general, seemingly "benign" categories that are used to portray value, measure impacts, or frame debate and in assumptions about what it means to be rational or to "have" a culture. Yavapai opponents sought to diminish their claims by contesting their distinctiveness, by blurring the boundaries they had drawn between themselves and others, by interpreting evidence of change and accommodation as diminished authenticity, of compromised cultural authority. However, once people believe their collective selves are threatened, the politics of identity can be a potent form of resistance. The Yavapai's reinterpretation of their collective identity prompted them to adopt political strategies that emphasized and articulated their distinctiveness as a source of power and authority. The irony is, of course, that once the mobilization of their difference, of their cultural identity, is understood as strategic, its logic approaches the instrumental rationality they were defending against.

Members of the Yavapai community responded, and are still responding, to the categories of value, interest, and, implicitly, identity that were assumed within the rational decision framework of the agency. But rather than resulting in some neat, commensurated closure, the effect of the imposition of the categories and assumptions of the rational decision framework was to sharpen and make more evident incommensurabilities between some groups and between arenas. The controversy evoked competing sources of authority for the bureaucrats and the Yavapai. In so doing, it sharpened distinctions, repoliticized, and destabilized some of the signs and practices that rational choice theory presumes can be made to stand still: in the use of commensuration as a technical strategy for inclusion, commensuration became exclusionary; in the attempt to measure culture, culture was transformed; in the effort to integrate value, value was revalued. As the Yavapai's response shows, legal and bureaucratic categories are not simply static impositions on those whose lives they touch. Once the Yavapai reacted against these categories, troubling contradictions were revealed that shaped the political contest and influenced its outcome.

For members of the Old Guard, the defeat of Orme Dam threatened their professional identities in ways that prompted them to reinterpret their ties to the agency. No longer a means for accomplishing some desired end, Orme Dam had become a substantive value for them, one that informed their understanding of their work. But members could not describe it or defend this substantive value as such. They did not have recourse to identity politics. As engineers and bureaucrats steeped in the language of efficiency and bureaucratic rationality, they could not claim to love a dam as the Yavapai could claim to love their land. Although others would portray their investments as "irrational," as engineers "standing by their dams," members of the Old Guard refused to acknowledge that their attachments were substantive, that they were anything but "rational." The Old Guard found themselves in the awkward position of trying to defend what had become a substantive value in the language of instrumental rationality. As Weber has argued, this is impossible to do when there is conflict about those values.

And so the Old Guard could not resort to the language of affect, faith, or other nonrational means of defending Orme Dam. Occasionally, they would invoke tradition as a way of justifying their claims: the proud legacy of the agency, its past triumphs, and the success that been achieved through the old ways of doing things were all sometimes raised as a means of asserting their authority. But as bureaucrats whose careers had been spent constructing "rational" accounts of what they did, even they could not be convinced by arguments rooted in the virtues of habit. With dams everywhere, the West settled, the dictates of NEPA, and the emergence of the environmental movement, it was just too easy to show that the world had changed.

The only legitimate discourse available to them was within the terms of instrumental rationality. And so they attacked the causal connections that investigators made in predicting the "performance" of the alternatives, or in the significance of the distinctions the models discerned, or in the appropriateness of some factors or the weights assigned to them. For example, the Old Guard had to know better than the anthropologists and the sociologists (and the Yavapai) that the interests of the tribe would be better served by getting money and a reservoir than by retaining possession of their land; they had to know better than the biologists that eagles could survive with a reservoir instead of a river. It was hard to discredit other certified experts given that their own authority depended on their expert knowledge. This placed them in the difficult position of having to discredit the methodology of disciplines that they did not understand, disciplines in which they had no training or experience.

Another strategy for defending Orme Dam was to argue that it was inappropriate to attend to environmental and social values when making a decision; however, this, in effect, forced them to argue that a technocracy could best serve a democracy. Following the civil rights and student movements of the 1960s, which had helped make political inclusion and the scope of democracy national issues, such an argument was a hard sell. Furthermore, the Public Values Assessment provided rigorous (scientific) proof that the values they wished to dismiss were important to large segments of the public. The contradictions that the Old Guard experienced could not be articulated within the hegemonic framework that they endorsed.

The New Guard, having appropriated and enlarged the vocabulary of rationality, left the Old Guard no discourse with which to defend their dam. Their position illustrates why it is so difficult to limit the extension of instrumental rationality. Once you accept its terms, it is hard to defend against its extension except in the domain of substantive value, which, as Weber argued, is formally outside its realm. No wonder the contradiction still haunts them.

One of the central insights of recent social movement theory is that not all movements are directed toward narrow economic interests and that class affiliation is not always the basis for mobilizing. Sometimes people are motivated to participate in movements less for instrumental goals than for their concerns about identities, ways of life, or ethical issues.[9] While the emergence and novelty of identity politics are still under debate in this literature, my analysis of the Orme dispute can suggest some fruitful ways to disentangle the relations between interest-group and identity politics.

One notable feature of this dispute was the role of state actors in creating and legitimating interest-group politics. One powerful legacy of the "old" BR was the creation of water elites and a broad array of organizations, ranging from irrigation districts to project lobbies, dedicated to supporting and monitoring water development. Agency employees were actively involved in creating and supporting these organizations. Loyalties between these organizations and the agency went both ways. For some members of the Old Guard near the end of long and distinguished BR careers, one of the changes hardest to bear was the sense of the agency's having ruptured old alliances, having sold out its "friends." When Daniel, a high-ranking engineer, told me at the end of a lengthy interview, almost in a whisper, that environmentalists and Indians were "stealing water from the farmers" and that the new bureau leadership had "betrayed our true constituents," his face was contorted with anger.

For members of the New Guard, interest groups were also the relevant political units, since these were presumed to be sites of the representative values they needed to inform the decision, values they were committed to measuring. The New Guard's procedures transformed participants into interest groups. In eliciting and measuring the values and preferences of those designated as having "an interest" in the outcome, these procedures implicitly re-created the subjects holding those interests. In treating universalistically "interested" parties, the New Guard's procedures transformed all relationships to the proposed policy into a common standard: qualities became quantities, difference

9. For a useful overview of the new social movement theory, see Buechler (1995). Calhoun (1993) argues that identity politics were a prominent feature of many social movements in the early nineteenth century.

became magnitude. Although NEPA was explicitly intended to empower new groups concerned with protecting the environment, the standing that it granted, and the procedural scrupulousness that it eventually fostered, carried with it assumptions about who could have an interest and how. The New Guard's rendering of NEPA became a means for imposing a particular kind of relationship: identities were reduced to ordered preferences, interests relegated to weighted factors.

It is worth emphasizing that it was members of the public who were charged with providing the values that framed the decision. Members of the Old Guard were not formally or publicly allowed to have an interest in the outcome. Their public role was to be the technical experts who supplied the causal connections between alternatives and their performance. Of course, this formal separation belied the deep investments that men had in Orme Dam and the active role they played in creating public constituencies for their projects. The ideological implications of this separation seem obvious. Nevertheless, the distinction between those who valued and those who measured consequences was built into the framework and constrained how members of the Old Guard could respond. When they, too, felt misrepresented by the New Guard's procedures, when their investment in Orme was not expressed appropriately, they could not publicly use their identity as experts to defend "their" interest.

Efforts to separate identities from interests could be accomplished procedurally but not practically or experientially. The commensuration of interests that was fundamental to the New Guard's rationality was tantamount to commensurating identities for some participants. This elicited varied responses. For Yavapai residents, the commensuration of incommensurables distorted the stakes of the decision and threatened their identities as Yavapai. They mobilized in reaction against these efforts, emphasizing their difference in politically effective strategies. For members of the Old Guard, commensurating Orme Dam challenged their interest in Orme and their organizational identity, although their appreciation of this was less self-conscious than was the Yavapai's. For them, the effect of this commensuration was to silence them, since identity politics were not a legitimate discourse.

My analysis suggests that identity politics can supplement rather than supplant economically motivated politics and that recourse to identity politics is varied. I believe that it is crucial to understand the historical conditions, and especially the role that state agents play, in creating the conditions that give rise to interest-group or identity politics. Conceptions of rationality, especially as these are institutionalized in laws and bureaucratic routines and procedures, can impose directly, or elicit indirectly, interest groups as the relevant unit of politics. Yet efforts to impose or refine the terms of instrumental rationality can also stimulate identity politics. Identities can be reappraised in reaction to the separation of subject and interest, fact and value, and against the homogeneity that commensuration imposes. I believe that there is a dynamic, varied, and important relationship between how we "do" rationality, how we interpret and define interests, and how we understand and assert collective identities. More systematic investigation is needed to better understand the contradictory effects that our efforts to rationalize can produce, whether these effects are to privilege interest-group politics, to fuse interest and identity, or to sharpen the distinctions between what can be disparate modes of engagement.

Form, Power, Consciousness, and Resistance

Power pervades this case in both obvious and subtle ways. Participants knew that billions of dollars' worth of investments, taxes, and potential losses from flood damage depended on the Orme decision. Less obvious was people's faith in their capacity and entitlement to refashion nature as an expression of their will. For Max Horkheimer, Theodor Adorno, and Donald Worster, this is the most fundamental form of domination. Understanding the conditions that promote people's resistance or acquiescence to power requires that we appreciate its many guises, the multiplicity of its forms, and how it structures attention. Before power can be resisted, it must be noticed. The Old Guard, the New Guard, and the Yavapai were attentive to different expressions of power. Explaining this is crucial to understanding why they reacted as they did.

Jean and John Comaroff (1991:27–32) have argued that a more nuanced theory of consciousness is needed to understand better the dynamics of power, to explain how and when tacit power can be contested. They conceive of ideology and hegemony as two forms of power that exist in reciprocal and dynamic relation to each other and are distinguished by consciousness. Ideology is a collective, articulated system of meanings, values, or beliefs; in contrast, hegemony is power that is nonnegotiable, taken-for-granted. Where ideology is power expressed by intentional actors, hegemony need not be experienced as power, since it adheres to the silent, symbolic forms that structure our consciousness. Since the subtlety of power and the possibility of resistance often depend on the middle terrain of consciousness, the Comaroffs argue that our binary conceptions of consciousness need to be expanded to incorporate "the realm of partial recognition, inchoate awareness, of ambiguous perception, and, sometimes of creative tension: that liminal space of human experience in which people discern

acts and facts but cannot or do not order them . . . into articulate conceptions of the world . . . [where] individuals or groups know that something is happening to them but find it difficult to put their fingers on
quite what it is" (1991:29).

If ideology is taken to be a defended worldview of some group with
interests to protect, then the Orme decision is thick with ideology. This
is hardly surprising in a controversial, explicitly "political" decision.
More interesting is what it suggests for how hegemony is reproduced,
apprehended, and resisted, and how this becomes tied to the participants' ideological battles. Most hegemonic in this decision was the
logic of instrumental rationality, which conceived of rationality as the
means best suited for obtaining some end. This logic shaped how lawmakers made policy and judges interpreted it, and how the New Guard
implemented NEPA, the Old Guard justified Orme Dam, and Yavapai
people resisted.

As I have argued, the Yavapai participants were most mindful of
the power attending instrumental rationality and the form of value it
demanded. This knowledge, expressed as distrust and their resolve to
represent themselves in their own terms, was the result of past encounters. Residents of Fort McDowell knew that the forms of debate mattered, although they could not always say precisely how these mattered; they knew that these forms were nonnegotiable and that at stake
was their ability to represent themselves in terms that were meaningful
to them. More than the other parties, they understood that form mattered. The Yavapai could not successfully challenge the framework for
this decision, since in a fundamental way, it is the framework of bureaucracy. Although they cooperated, patiently trying to educate those
charged with representing them, participating in the formal EIS process troubled them.

But the Yavapai were successful in defending the incommensurability of their land, and the immorality of taking it, to other audiences.
If nothing else, their challenges sensitized some members of the New
Guard to the contradictions of what they were doing and sent a strong
message of how important the stakes of the decision were for them.
Even if the costs the Yavapai would bear were not valued appropriately, they were highly valued: in the time and money that were devoted to assessing the consequences of their forced relocation, in the
publicity generated by their possible removal, and in the weight, literally and figuratively, that was attached to these impacts.

Others were less aware of the power of form. The logic of instrumental rationality was so pervasive that it obscured for members of the
Old Guard and for their constituents the character of their investment
in Orme Dam. They believed that their commitment to Orme did con-

form to instrumental logic, that Orme was rational for the right reasons. They used the terms of this logic to defend Orme's superiority. But they did not see how their construction of Orme Dam as the rational means for accomplishing their goals was a function of their strict control over the terms of relevance, of their power to exclude. It was only after the New Guard imposed a more rigorous form of instrumental reason, one used to enlarge the terms of relevance and participation, that members of the Old Guard were forced to rethink their attachments to Orme. Their awareness of the power and selectivity of their worldview, still inchoate and incomplete, came only after others could demand accountability. Some are still struggling to understand what happened.

Their own investment in instrumental rationality was such that the contradiction most apparent to members of the New Guard was the "irrationality" of the Old Guard's substantive commitment to this particular dam. They believed that the former could cure the latter. The local hegemony of the engineering ethos that was invisible to the Old Guard was apparent to the New Guard as outsiders. The New Guard's exclusion helped transform them into agents of instrumental reason, active, articulate advocates for extending the logic that most assumed characterized most decisions. Precisely because of the taken-for-granted quality of both the legitimacy of instrumental reason and the substantive investments in dams within the agency, these contradictions could remain latent within the agency until they were exposed by the New Guard's techniques and challenged by a heterogeneous public that the New Guard insisted on including. What was invisible to most members of the New Guard, especially early on in their bureaucratic careers, was the capacity of their techniques to distort and reproduce power.

The Orme dispute can contribute to our understanding of the relationship between power, consciousness, and resistance. The effects of the BR's engineering ethos on how members understood its mission and defended its projects require that we examine the processes by which intentional acts and defenses become naturalized in institutions. The passionate, articulate ideologies of Progressive reformers and professional pioneers, as they were translated into reclamation law, bureaucratic routines, evaluative categories, and organizational structure, became increasingly invisible to those whose work they informed. But these did not remain invisible to all parties.

The hegemony of the engineering culture was apparent to those who were simultaneously immersed in it and excluded from it. And law, by inserting new information and introducing new audiences and new participants, disrupted the routines of the agency in ways that prompted a gradual awareness that what had seemed natural and universal was vulnerable and distinctive. Also crucial was the capacity of Yavapai people to mobilize their distrust and sustain resistance over time and through extreme hardship. What Aldon Morris (1992:362–63) would call the Yavapai's "oppositional consciousness" was nurtured and sustained by their making history vivid and practical, and by the wariness and self-consciousness that come from repeated threats.

Greater attention to the varied manifestations of consciousness can advance theory on several fronts. It can augment rational choice explanations, first, by locating the boundaries of intentional action within a broader conception of action and, second, by providing explanations for how things become objects of intentional action. Explanations of the dynamism and variety of consciousness can also respond to the critics of instrumental reason who have overemphasized its totalizing character.

Rational Contradictions: Substantive Values, Irreconcilable Values, and the Revenge of Nature

Confronted with the astonishing development and influence of science and technology that characterized capitalism following World War I, critical theorists concerned themselves with revising Marx's critique of political economy in ways that would account for transformations in classical liberal capitalism. Derived from Weber, their central preoccupation was with the consequences of an instrumental reason that was constantly encroaching on new spheres of life, becoming increasingly autonomous, and distorting human consciousness.

While Marx understood capitalism as an unprecedented and relentless despoiler of nature, Max Horkheimer and Theodor Adorno, two German theorists affiliated with the Frankfurt school, believed that the domination of nature was an even more fundamental form of alienation. With deep roots in Judeo-Christian theology, this domination could not be reduced to class conflict or rectified by socialism. Emancipation was no longer predicated on transforming productive forces. Instead, it demanded a reconciliation with nature that would rupture the scientism and technocracy of instrumental reason.

Explaining how this reconciliation might occur was difficult. Whereas Marx saw the inherent contradictions of capitalism as creating the conditions for its transformation, Horkheimer and Adorno did not conceive of instrumental reason as systematically producing conditions conducive to its dismantling. Instead, it produces uncritical, acquiescent people. That is why the prospect for reconstituting reason became a source of despair for them.

As Donald Worster (1985:56) points out, it is crucial to appreciate the distinction between using or manipulating nature and the domination implied by instrumental reason. Growing a garden or clearing a field alters nature but need not be motivated by a desire for mastery. Domination of nature is a totalizing, repressive response that cannot acknowledge any relation but subservience. Nature has no value except as it serves our needs and affirms our power; our efforts to control it are fundamentally irrational and doomed to fail. For Horkheimer (1974:92–127), the price paid for the material affluence obtained by domination is our own subjugation. Just as nature becomes an object, a tool, for us, we become objects and tools to one another, subjects of domination. The violence done to nature is matched by the violence done to ourselves. When we lose sight of ends, we are manipulated by and serve the vast technological apparatus that our commitment to instrumental reason has created. The result is an "administered life" that blunts spontaneity, atrophies individuality, and diminishes our capacity to resist.

Like Horkheimer and Adorno, Worster urges us to value in a new way, to strive for a richer, more humane form of reason that can engage ultimate values and moral questions, define worthy goals, and can conceive of nature as intrinsically valuable, worthy in terms unrelated to our self-preservation. But how are we to reconcile with nature? How do we create a "posthydraulic society" willing to live with scarcity, within the discipline of nature? Can we learn to choose freedom and democracy over wealth and empire?

If we do not, Worster believes, we will pay a terrible price for our hubris. Our dams are aging, their reservoirs filling with silt; our rivers are diminished, our aquifers receding. The water that is loaded with salts, pesticides, herbicides, and fertilizers is delivered to soil depleted by overcropping; we are deeply dependent on growth, on perpetuating the empire that requires increasingly complex interventions. These inevitably toxic by-products of our hydraulic empire, the ultimate contradiction of instrumental reason, may already constitute a fate that may make our choosing irrelevant.

But there are other contradictions as well. At his most hopeful, Worster (1985:323, 325) notes that nostalgia for what has been lost can become a political force. For the first time in history, he says, the American water empire had generated a determined and successful internal opposition to the terms of its conquest, one not rooted in class politics but in "rival ways of valuing nature." For the first time, Americans were rejecting proposed water projects, questioning the ends of the hydraulic empire. "It was as though," he writes, "the American water empire had created, against its will, a dissidence precisely commensurate with its unprecedented technological success."

Worster's language is revealing, perhaps more so than he intended, for I have found that dissent and commensuration can be deeply connected. Commensuration is a prominent characteristic of instrumental rationality, one that is hostile to other modes of valuing. I have argued that one of the ways we express important attachments and cultural boundaries is to define some things as incommensurable, as irreducible to other forms or other values. Efforts to transgress incommensurable boundaries may make us aware of the distinctiveness of valuing in this way; in doing violence to our sense of ourselves and our relations with others, these may motivate and inform dissent, just as the wrongness of commensurating land, culture, and identity shaped the Yavapai's resistance to Orme Dam.

Members of the Old Guard also experienced the contradictions of rival modes of valuing. For them, however, it was dams, not nature or land, that were hard to reconcile with instrumental reason. Their substantive investments might seem surprising to some. For Weber, bureaucracy thrives because it is the perfect tool, impersonal, formalized, and generalized in ways that make it suitable for any purpose, efficient for any end. Like Horkheimer, Worster (1985:57) understands the engineer as the embodied refinement of that perfect tool: the devotee of technology, an expert dedicated to means, the handmaiden of instrumental reason. The hydraulic empire the engineers designed, with billions spent so that burgeoning desert populations might become the world's most profligate water wasters, exemplifies the irrationality of instrumental reason. The perfect conjoining of means to means, the engineer-bureaucrat might seem the emblem of modernity.

But engineers and bureaucrats do not remain impartial tools. They, too, invest their work and their worlds with meanings and attachments that contradict the premises of instrumental logic, that personalize bureaucratic projects and turn tools into goals. Substantive rationality can be an organizational by-product of our efforts to create meaning, and as such it has coexisted with the instrumental reason that Worster describes. Substantive values that transform dams from alternatives into incommensurable, valued ends, and engineers from adjudicators to passionate, partisan advocates, may be ideologically potent. Such commitment helps explain why we have so many dams, why the hydraulic empire is so vast. But as this case also shows, commitments of this form are exposed by, made vulnerable to, the logic of instrumental reason.

As Worster suggests, "rival modes of valuing" may provide sources of fateful contradictions, sites for resisting instrumental rationality. His emphasis on the relentless extension and totalizing domination of nature does not allow him to develop these insights. Nevertheless, they are central to my analysis, which has attempted to explain how these sorts of contradictions emerge and why they can sometimes stimulate and inform social protest. Doing so, I believe, offers a more hopeful counterpoint to the bleak image of instrumental rationality portrayed by Horkheimer and Adorno, Worster, and even Weber.

Under some conditions, efforts to extend or amplify the effects of instrumental reason can be resisted by people who are capable of understanding and criticizing its terms. Sometimes, substantive rationality can provide an alternative logic that informs resistance. And, as the Old Guard showed, sometimes substantive values may arise and coexist with instrumental reason, serving, for a time, as an alternative, tacit logic that becomes vulnerable only after it is exposed. As the conflict between the Old Guard and the New over control of the Orme decision and, ultimately, over the terms of bureaucratic rationality attests, bureaucrats are not homogeneous and bureaucracies are not monoliths. Domination is a relationship that is never completely integrated, never fully legitimated, and never simply imposed.

John Walton (1992:295–307) also emphasizes the contradiction and conflict that inevitably arise within and between governmental agencies as a corrective to the image of "the state" as some coherent system for domination and incorporation. Contradictions, between principles and policies, competing aims and interests, new forms of incorporation and old ones, between divergent claims for legitimation, offer sites and strategies for struggle. State policies and the changing forms of state structures shaped local societies in crucial ways, including their potential for collection action and its form. These struggles can, in turn, transform state structures. The irrigation districts created by the expanding Progressive state were part of its massive efforts to enlist experts to administer economic development; these, in turn, enlarged the public arena, fostered political alliances, and became the organizational vehicles that Owens Valley communities used to press their legal claims in ways that anticipated contemporary environmentalism. Walton's investigation shows just how interdependent, how deeply dialectical, is the relation between collective action and state structure.

Walton's "state" is simultaneously "a relationship of domination and an invitation to protest" (1992:307). His analysis cautions us not to exaggerate either the coherence of "the state" or the acquiescence or impotence of those who become entangled in its projects. The mutual determination of state structure and collective action is central for understanding both. In my case, this dialectic hinges on the contradictions within and between contradictory conceptions of rationality and the identities that become attached to these.

For Max Weber, rationality was partly constrained by what it cannot decide. Instrumental reason cannot be reconciled with substantive reason, nor can it adjudicate between conflicting values-spheres. As he put it, "'Scientific' pleading is meaningless in principle because the various value-spheres of the world stand in irreconcilable conflict with each other" (1946:147). For Weber, one of the most profound effects of the increasing calculation and commensuration attending rationalization is its capacity to reveal deep differences in our orientations. Such differences were deeper than conflict over divergent goals or competing interests, and Weber thought that it was fundamentally impossible to reconcile conflicting substantive values by rational means. The precision of instrumental rationality merely serves to expose the fundamental disagreements that existed among those holding conflicting values rather than to mitigate their differences.

Weber seemed to believe that within well-defined value-spheres, where consensus exists regarding ultimate values, it may be possible to use rational techniques for determining which means are best suited to supporting or achieving those values (Brubaker 1984:61–87). But one characteristic of modernity is that such sites have become fewer, more easily penetrated. Since most rationalized spheres today are overlapping and interdependent, these conditions seldom obtain. The New Guard's goal of using reason, even the rarefied form of instrumental rationality that their techniques embodied, to resolve basic conflicts over substantive values would have seemed futile to Weber. Whether these values were an aesthetic appreciation for the environment, the right to define one's culture, the quest for profit, or even a love of dams, Weber was adamant that no rational means could resolve conflict between substantive values, nor could it provide the rational basis for adopting any one value. Yet I think he might have been sympathetic to the New Guard's concerns; with the motives and resources available to modern bureaucrats, they were grappling with the paradox of modern life.

The sites where commensuration stopped in CAWCS hint at the futility that Weber describes. The ability of the Governor's Advisory Committee to block commensuration was a signal of power. That the New Guard would leave incommensurate the different "accounts" in CAWCS is also revealing. Although the economic, social, and environmental analyses all ended with numerical ratings for each plan, these were never integrated. These endpoints of commensuration reflect a largely implicit set of assumptions about where consensus exists among which groups, or within academic disciplines. How reasonable it is to treat a group like an individual actor depends on assumptions about how similar and how homogeneous members of that group are. In the Public Values Assessment, interest groups were treated as individual actors; in the Social and Environmental Assessments, it was assumed that the analysts possessed some body of knowledge that made it acceptable for them to adjudicate the gravity of harm or benefits that accrued to competing groups or species. Who counts as "agents," and how they count, is one of the important and elusive assumptions underlying this decision.[10] The irreconcilability of values was tacitly recognized among members of the New Guard in the way the Public Values Assessment was conducted and represented. Both the physical and analytical segregation of disparate values suggests that they understood their limited potential truly to resolve conflict.

In the end, the subject of just what could remain incommensurate was not something that was explicitly discussed and decided; no formal policy existed or was invented for addressing this concern. In light of how self-conscious many members of the New Guard were about the salience of commensuration, it may seem puzzling. This may reflect a form of quasi-resolving conflict as a means for managing conflict, but I do not believe this was strategic (Cyert and March 1963:116–17). More fundamentally, I think the limits of commensuration suggest the limitations of instrumental reason.

Weber wrote eloquently of the threat that instrumental rationality posed for substantive values. He showed how sometimes its threat could be stymied by powerful groups with investments in the status quo. But he, like Horkheimer and Adorno, viewed rationalization as an almost inescapable fate. Weber's pessimism was rooted in the irreconcilability of these disparate forms of reason characterizing Western rationalism. With no alternative, no panacea, Weber offered only stoic resignation and the thin hope that such conflict might generate productive "value discussions." But Weber did not fully appreciate how the encroaching threat of instrumental reason might prompt a reinterpretation, a reappraisal, or even a renewal of substantive rationality; that irreconcilable value-spheres and contradictory forms of rationality could also, sometimes, provide the space for freedom.

The contradictions and conflict between the Old and New Guards and the Yavapai community might offer solace to those who fear the "irresistible force" of the iron cage. That the introduction of a new technique representing an extension of instrumental rationality, within a bureaucracy no less, required the vigorous promotion of a partisan interest group suggests that rationalization is hardly an ineluctable process. That it was opposed by groups who saw in it a challenge to their

10. As Foucault has posed the question more generally, How do particular domains of knowledge constitute their subjects? This is a more positive, forceful way of asking not just what conception of the self is embodied in rational choice theory, but rather, How does rationality as practiced create particular kinds of subjects?

power, or to a way of life oriented toward substantive values, is perhaps a reassuring sign of how contested rationality remains, even today. What this also shows is that we continue to value things in pluralistic ways. How we value, and how we defend those values, are deeply important and incommensurable ways of being moral, political, and rational. Value is a basic and often unnoticed cultural form for interpreting and constructing the social world; the forms given to value create some of our most cherished social boundaries, including distinctions we draw between ourselves and others.

Rationalization as a historical force, as the backdrop for everyday life, as an arena for power, must be investigated in the ways that people confront it, make sense of it, enlarge it, or repress it. Weber, for one, wisely and emphatically emphasized the importance of understanding rationalization in its concrete, historically specific forms, urging us to resist attempts to cast it as some universal, evolutionary process. It is only in understanding how particular rational forms are used that we can come to see their differing influences. One of the virtues of keeping the focus close to the ground, close to people's practical experience, is that human agency, and sometimes consciousness, comes to the fore. We can see how cultural and historical actors create, use, and resist different rational forms and why.

One reason why rationalization is not a universal, monolithic process is that people's practical experience can still provide them with reasons and strategies for resisting its particular forms. The processes by which cultural, aesthetic, and moral issues were transformed into the terms of instrumental rationality by lawmakers, judges, and bureaucrats were not static, uncontested impositions of forms. In the contest over Orme Dam, rationalization became the terrain for struggle over powerful material and ideal interests; once cast in these terms, both the interests and the identities of those who shared them were reshaped in ways that affected not only the outcome of the decision but also reappraisals of themselves. Rather than documenting another example of encroaching rationalization, this contest shows how efforts to impose the stringent terms of instrumental rationality on substantive values can sometimes generate new claims, a new defense, and a rejuvenation of substantive values.[11]

In the end then, what I am urging is a greater hermeneutic interest in processes of rationalization and how these generate new interpretive

11. Where Jürgen Habermas (1973, 1972, 1975:36–37) and Claus Offe (1984, 1985) have emphasized how the public sphere has become depoliticized by the efforts of bureaucrats and professionals to transform politics into science or technique, my example shows how this form of mystification can sometimes backfire, resulting in the a repoliticized and, in some cases, a broadened public sphere.

frameworks for confronting and constituting our social worlds, frameworks that destroy old meanings and ways of comprehending meaning, and replace these with new assumptions of what is meaningful and how meaningfulness can be interpreted and represented. Rationalization is a reinterpretation, a reconstitution, of interests and identities. Changing the categories of a decision changes what is meaningful. Defining procedure amounts to defining the terms of the debate, of determining what can be talked about and what cannot and, ultimately, defining how to resist. This aspect of rationalization has been underemphasized in many theoretical accounts.

In part, the power associated with determining the form that a decision will take is the power to determine where attention will be focused. The assumption of commensuration, and the conception of value embedded within it, focus attention in particular ways and, in doing so, has the potential to transform not only the world, but us with it. As Pierre Bourdieu (1985) has argued, "Knowledge of the social world, and more precisely, the categories that make it possible, are the stakes, par excellence, of political struggle, the inextricably theoretical and practical struggle for power to conserve or transform the world by conserving or transforming the categories through which it is conceived."

Commensuration, then, is quintessentially political and may present the most radical challenge that can be made to existing systems of classification, since it makes vulnerable all preexisting categories and boundaries. I have argued that commensuration is a particularly radical form, in its effectiveness in destroying other forms, in eliminating what we define as distinctive or unique. Since one of our most basic ways of investing our selves, our relationships, and our lives with meaning is to make these relationships incommensurate, this form is especially volatile and may be especially powerful. Discerning its influence will always require paying attention to people's lives, since what is most important about categories is how they are lived.

This is the story of a dam that was not built. But it is also a story of the complicated, dynamic interplay between identities, interests, and rationalities. One moral of this story is that we should investigate this complexity rather than assume it away. We cannot understand contemporary politics if we do not. Another moral it suggests is that this complexity may sometimes offer hope.

References ~~~~

Abbreviations

USBR	U.S. Department of the Interior, Bureau of Reclamation
DIOS	Department of the Interior, Office of the Secretary
RE	*Reclamation Era,* a magazine for water users published by the Bureau of Reclamation, formerly the *Reclamation Bulletin* and the *Reclamation Record*
CMC	Carlos Montezuma Collection, Arizona Collection, Hayden Library, Arizona State University
WHPS	Office of the White House Press Secretary
U.S. Congress	Congressional Hearings and Reports
CR	*Congressional Record*

Primary Documents and Printed Sources

Dozens of documents were prepared under the rubric of CAWCS during its five years. Most of these were preliminary reports or documents substantiating sections of the EIS. Preliminary reports included, for example, documents explaining the methods to be used for various investigations such as the social analysis, reports analyzing flood damages, and documents explaining how various plans were devised, evaluated, and screened. CAWCS culminated in the EIS, but this is a highly standardized document with strict page limits, and many reports substantiating the findings presented in the EIS were prepared as supplements to that document. For example, the Public Involvement portion of CAWCS is explained in three separate volumes: "Summary and Evaluation of Central Arizona Water Control Study Public Involvement Program, 1979–1980" (February 1982), "Appendix A: Summary and Evaluation of Central Arizona Water Control Study Public Involvement Program" (1981), and "Appendix B: Central Arizona Water Control Study Public Values Assessment" (1981). Most documents affiliated with CAWCS include CAWCS in their title. While EISs are relatively easy to obtain, this is less true of the substantiating documents. The place to start is the Arizona Projects Office.

Anderson, Barry R. 1981. "Cascaded Trade-Offs: A Multi-Objective, Multiple-Publics Method for Alternatives Evaluation in Water Resources Planning." Prepared for USBR, August.

Arizona Republic. August 24, 1975. "Heap Big Offer."

Brandt, Elizabeth. 1981b. "Yavapai Culture and History and Their Relationship to Proposed Relocation." Appendix B in "Final Report: Social Impacts and Effects of Central Arizona Water Control Study Plans." Prepared for USBR.

Blundell, William E. 1981. "Arizona Indians Win Victory over U.S.: Refuse $33 Million." *Wall Street Journal,* December 17, 1-1.

Brown, Curtis A., Robert J. Quinn, and Kenneth R. Hammond. 1980. "Scaling Impacts of Alternative Plans." Prepared for the USBR, June.

Brown, Curtis A., and Tony Valenti. 1983. "MATS: Multi-Attribute Tradeoff System: User's and Programmer's Manual." Prepared for the USBR, March.

Casserly, J. J. 1981. "Different Drummers: The Indians and Orme Dam." *Arizona Republic,* May 22, A-5.

Christian Science Monitor. 1981. July 14:14.

CMC. 1898–1922. Arizona Collection, Hayden Library, Arizona State University.

Corbusier, William T. 1971. *Verde to San Carlos: Recollections of a Famous Army Surgeon and His Observant Family on the Western Frontier.* Tucson: Dale Stuart King.

CR. 1969. February 18.

Curlin, James. 1973. "National Environmental Policy Act of 1969: Environmental Indices—Status of Development Pursuant to Sections 102 (2) (B) and 204 of the Act." U.S. Senate. Committee on Interior and Insular Affairs. Washington, DC: Government Printing Office.

Devine, Robert S. "The Trouble with Dams," *Atlantic Monthly* (August 1995): 64–74.

DIOS. 1981. Press Release. "Watt Announces Options for Continuation of Central Arizona Project." November 12.

———. 1996. Press Release. "Babbitt Signs Permanent Colorado River Protection: Releases Scientific Report on Grand Canyon Flood." October 9.

Fortune. 1933. "The Dam." 8:74–88.

———. 1943. "The Earth Movers I." 28:214.

Johnson, Lyndon Baines. 1968. WHPS. "Remarks of the President at the Signing of S. 1004, The Colorado River Project Room, September 30."

Lord, William, Donald Deane, and Marvin Waterstone. 1979. "Commensuration in Federal Water Resources Planning: Problem Analysis and Research Appraisal." Research Report 79-2. Prepared for USBR, Water and Power Resources Service, April 6.

New York Times. 1996a. "Artificial Flood Created to Rejuvenate the Grand Canyon." March 27, B-8.

New York Times. 1996b. "Flood is Called Right Tonic for Grand Canyon," April 14. 1-32.

New York Times. 1977. "Carter Asks Senate to Back Tax Rebate."April 8. A-13.

Powell, John Wesley. 1962. *Report on the Lands of the Arid Region of the United States,* edited by Wallace Stegner. Cambridge: Harvard University Press.

Schroeder, Albert. 1982. "Yavapai Land Tenure at Fort McDowell." Appendix B in U.S. Bureau of Reclamation. Final Report: Social Impacts and Effects, A-1–A-2.

Time. 1977. "Water: A Billion Dollar Battleground," April 4:16.

Tulumello, Mike. 1981. "Indians Begin Hike to Capitol." *Mesa Tribune,* September 24. A11.

Udall, Morris K. 1977. "Statement to Departmental Water Projects Review Team." *CR,* March 21.

USBR. 1983. *RE* 66:2–3.

———. 1982a. "Final Report: Social Impacts and Effects of Central Arizona Water Control Study Plans," October.

———. 1982b. "Field Draft, Environmental Impact Statement, Central Arizona Project Regulatory Storage Division, Central Arizona Water Control Study," September.

———. 1982c. "Summary and Evaluation of Central Arizona Water Control Study Public Involvement Program, 1979–1980," February.

———. 1981a. "Appendix A: Summary and Evaluation of Central Arizona Water Control Study Public Involvement Program."

———. 1981b. "Appendix B: Central Arizona Water Control Study Public Values Assessment."

———. 1981c. "Congressional Briefing on Central Arizona Project Status," September.

———. 1980. "Interim Report on Acreage Limitation."

———. 1977a. Memorandum from Manuel Lopez Jr., Regional Director, Lower Colorado Regional Director, to Projects Manager, Arizona Projects Office, September 30.

———. 1977b. Memorandum from Manuel Lopez Jr., Regional Director, Lower Colorado Regional Director, to the Chief of Planning Coordination, June 9.

———. 1977c. "Water and Land Resources Accomplishments."

———. 1976a. "Socioeconomic Study of the Fort McDowell Indian Reservation and Community With and Without the Development of Orme Dam and Reservoir." Prepared by the Natelson Corp.

———. 1976b. "Draft Environmental Impact Statement: Orme Dam Reservoir, Central Arizona Project, Arizona–New Mexico." May.

———. 1972a. "Central Arizona Project Final Environmental Statement."

———. 1972b. "Project Skywater, 1971 Annual Report," January.

———. 1963. "Pacific Southwest Water Plan: Supplemental Information on Central Arizona Project," December.

———. 1947. "Report on Central Arizona Project." Project Planning Report No. 3-8b-4-2, December.

———. 1935a. "President Roosevelt Dedicates Boulder Dam, September 30, 1935. Text of Dedicatory Address." *RE* 25(10):193–4.

———. 1935b "Honorable Harold L. Ickes, Secretary of the Interior Delivers Address at Dedication of Boulder Dam." *RE* 25(11):209–10.

———. 1914."The Irrigation Farmer's Creed." *RE* 5(3):140.

U.S. Congress. 1977a. Senate Report 95-301. "Public Works for Water and

Power Development and Energy Research: Report to Accompany Appropriations Bill, 1978." Committee on Appropriations, 95th Congress, 1st session.

———. 1977b. House Report 95-379. "Public Works for Water and Power
Development and Energy Research: Report to Accompany Appropriations
Bill, 1978: Report together with Additional and Minority Views to Accom-
pany HR 7553." 95th Congress, 1st session.

———. 1977c. House of Representatives. Hearings, Subcommittee on Public
Works, Committee on Appropriations. 95th Congress, 1st session, part 7.

———. 1969. House Report 91-378. "Council on Environmental Quality."
91st Congress, 1st session, 2–3.

———. 1951. House of Representatives. Hearings, Committee on Interior
and Insular Affairs. "Central Arizona Project." 82nd Congress, 1st session.

———. 1947. Senate. Hearings before a Subcommittee of the Committee on
Public Lands. S. 1175, "Bridge Canyon Project." 80th Congress, 1st session.

U.S. Department of Interior. 1873–1906. *Annual Report of the Commissioner of
Indian Affairs.*

U.S. General Accounting Office. 1981. "Federal Charges for Irrigation Projects Reviewed Do Not Cover Costs." Report No. PAD-81-07, March 13,
p. 36.

Statutes:
Colorado River Basin Project Act of 1968, Pub. L. No.90-537, 82 Stat. 885.
National Environmental Policy Act of 1969, 102 U.S.C. 4332 (1970).

Secondary Sources

Adams, John A., Jr. 1990. *Damming the Colorado: The Rise of the Colorado River
Authority, 1933–1939.* College Station: Texas A&M University Press.

American Public Works Association. 1976. *History of Public Works in the
United States, 1776–1976,* edited by Ellis L. Armstrong, Michael C.
Robinson, and Suellen M. Hoy. Chicago: American Public Works Associa-
tion.

Anderson, Frederick R. 1973. *NEPA in the Courts: A Legal Analysis of the National Environmental Policy Act.* Baltimore: Johns Hopkins Press.

Andrews, Richard N. L. 1976. *Environmental Analysis and Administrative
Change.* Lexington, MA: Lexington.

Apt Associates (Stephen J. Fitzsimmons, Lorrie I. Stuart, and Peter C.
Wolff). *Social Assessment Manual.* Boulder, CO: Westview Press.

Babb, Sarah. 1996. "A True American System of Finance: Frame Resonance
in the U.S. Labor Movement, 1866–1886." *American Sociological Review*
61(6):1033–52.

Baram, Michael S. 1980. "Coping with Technology through the Legal Process." Paper presented at Atomic Industrial Forum Conference on U.S.
Energy, January 10, 1977.

Becker, Gary. 1976. *The Economic Approach to Human Behavior.* Chicago: University of Chicago Press.

Beetham, David. [1974] 1985. *Max Weber and the Theory of Modern Politics.* Cambridge, England: Polity Press.

Beisel, Nicola. 1997. *Imperiled Innocents: Anthony Comstock and Family Reproduction in Victorian America.* Princeton: Princeton University Press.

Bourdieu, Pierre. 1985. "The Social Space and Genesis of Groups." *Theory and Society* 14:723–44.

Bourke, John G. 1891. *On the Border with Crook.* New York: Scribners.

Brinkerhoff, Sidney B. 1964. "Camp Date Creek, Arizona Territory." *Smoke Signal* 10:1–20.

Bronson, Leisa. 1980. "The Long Walk of the Yavapai." *Wassaja: The Indian Historian* 13(1):36–43.

Brown, Curtis A. 1984. "The Central Arizona Water Control Study: A Case for Multiobjective Planning and Public Involvement." *Water Resources Bulletin* 20(3):331–37.

Brubaker, Rogers. 1984. *The Limits of Rationality: An Essay on the Social and Moral Thought of Max Weber.* London: Allen & Unwin.

Brunsson, Nils. 1985. *The Irrational Organization: Irrationality as a Basis for Organizational Action and Change.* New York: Wiley.

Buechler, Steven M. 1995. "New Social Movement Theories." *Sociological Quarterly* 36(3):441–64.

Butler, Carolina. 1978. "Fort McDowell and Orme Dam." In *The Yavapai of Fort McDowell,* edited by Sigrid Khera. Fort McDowell, AZ: Fort McDowell Indian Community.

Caldwell, Lynton K. 1982. *Science and the National Environmental Policy Act: Redirecting Policy through Procedural Reform.* University: University of Alabama Press.

Calhoun, Craig. 1993. "New Social Movements of the Early Nineteenth Century," *Social Science History* 17(3):385–427.

Chamberlain, Abbey A. 1975. "The Fort McDowell Indian Reservation: Water Rights and Indian Removal, 1910–1930." *Journal of the West* 14(4):27–34.

Champagne, Duane. 1996. "Bureau of Indian Affairs." In *Native America in the Twentieth Century: An Encyclopedia,* edited by Mary B. Davis. New York: Garland.

Chong, Dennis. 1996. "Values versus Interests in the Explanation of Social Contract." *University of Pennsylvania Law Review* 144 (5):2079–2134.

Clark, Burton R. 1956. *Adult Education in Transition.* Berkeley: University of California Press.

Clemens, Elisabeth. 1997. *The People's Lobby: Organizational Innovation and the Rise of Interest Group Politics in the United States, 1890–1925.* Chicago: University of Chicago Press.

———. 1996. "Organizational Form as Frame: Collective Identity and Political Strategy in the American Labor Movement." In *Comparative Perspectives on Social Movements,* edited by Doug McAdam, John McCarthy, and Mayer Zald. New York: Cambridge University Press.

———. 1993. "Organizational Repertoires and Institutional Change: Women's Groups and the Transformation of U.S. Politics, 1890–1920." *American Journal of Sociology* 98:755–98.

Clifford, James. 1988. *The Predicament of Culture*. Cambridge, MA: Harvard University Press.

Coffeen, William R. 1972. "The Effects of the Central Arizona Project on the Fort McDowell Indian Community." *Ethnohistory* 19(4):345–77.

Coleman, James. 1990. *Foundations of Social Theory*. Cambridge, MA: Harvard University Press.

Comaroff, Jean, and John Comaroff. 1991. *Of Revelation and Revolution: Christianity, Colonialism, and Consciousness in South Africa*. Chicago: University of Chicago Press.

———. 1988. "The Colonialization of Consciousness in South Africa." *Economy and Society* 18:267–95.

Corbusier, William F. 1886a. "The Apache-Yumas and Apache-Mohaves," *American Antiquarian* 8(6):325–39.

———. 1886b. "The Apache-Yumas and Apache-Mohaves," *American Antiquarian* 8(5):276–84.

Cornell, Stephen. 1988. *The Return of the Native*. New York: Oxford University Press.

Cyert, Richard, and James G. March. 1963. *A Behavioral Theory of the Firm*. Englewood Cliffs, NJ: Prentice-Hall.

Darnell, Alfred. 1990. "Creating Political and Cultural Order: State Policies and Ethnic Responses in Alaska." Ph.D. diss., Department of Sociology, University of Chicago, Chicago, IL.

DiMaggio, Paul J., and Walter W. Powell. 1991. Introduction to *The New Institutionalism in Organizational Analysis*, edited by Walter W. Powell and Paul DiMaggio. Chicago: University of Chicago Press.

———. 1983. "The Iron Cage Revisited: Institutional Isomorphism and Collective Rationality in Organizational Fields." *American Sociological Review* 48:147–60.

Dobbin, Frank R. 1994. *States and Industrial Cultures: Britain, France, and the United States in the Railway Age*. New York: Cambridge University Press.

Elster, Jon. 1989. *Nuts and Bolts for the Social Sciences*. New York: Cambridge University Press.

———. 1983. *Sour Grapes: Studies in the Subversion of Rationality*. Cambridge: Cambridge University Press.

———. 1979. *Ulysses and the Sirens*. New York: Cambridge University Press.

Espeland, Wendy. 1994. "Legally Mediated Identities: The National Environmental Policy Act and the Bureaucratic Construction of Interests." *Law and Society Review* 28(5):1149–79.

———. 1992. "Contested Rationalities: Commensuration and the Representation of Value in Public Choice." Ph.D. diss., Department of Sociology, University of Chicago, Chicago, IL.

———. 1998. "Legal Structure in Colonial Encounters: Bureaucratizing Culture, Environment, and Identity in the American Southwest." *Law and Social Inquiry* 20.

Espeland, Wendy Nelson, and Terence Halliday. 1994. "Resurrecting the

Dead: Commemoration and the Ritual Reconstruction of Professional Identity among Chicago Lawyers," Working Paper, Center for Urban Affairs and Policy Research, Northwestern University, Evanston, IL.

Feldman, Martha, and James G. March. 1981. "Information in Organizations as Signal and Symbol." *Administrative Sciences Quarterly* 26:171–86.

Felstiner, William L. F., and Austin Sarat. 1992. "Enactments of Power: Negotiating Reality and Responsibility in Lawyer-Client Interactions." *Cornell Law Review* 7:1447–98.

Ferejohn, John A. 1974. *Pork Barrel Politics: Rivers and Harbors Legislation, 1947–1968.* Palo Alto: Stanford University Press.

Finn, Terence T. 1973. "Conflict and Compromise: Congress Makes a Law— The Passage of the National Environmental Policy Act." Ph.D. diss., Department of Political Science, Georgetown University, Washington, DC.

Fradkin, Philip L. 1981. *A River No More: The Colorado River and the West.* New York: Knopf.

Friedman, Debra, and Carol Diem. 1993. "Feminism and the Pro (Rational-) Choice Movement: Rational Choice Theory, Feminist Critiques, and Gender Inequality." In *Theory on Gender/Feminism on Theory,* edited by Paula England. New York: Aldine de Gruyter.

Gadamer, Hans-Georg. 1985. *Truth and Method.* New York: Crossroad.

Gifford, Edward W. 1936. "The Northeastern and Western Yavapai." *University of California Publications in American Archaeology and Ethnology* 34(4): 247–354.

———. 1932. "The Southeastern Yavapai." *University of California Publications in American Archaeology and Ethnology* 29(3):177–252.

Goldberg-Ambrose, Carol. 1994. "Of Native Americans and Tribal Members: The Impact of Law on Indian Group Life." *Law and Society Review* 28(5): 1123–48.

Golze, Alfred R. 1961. *Reclamation in the United States.* Calwell, ID: Caxton Printers.

Gooding, Susan Staiger. 1994. "Place, Race, and Names: Layered Identities in the *United States v Oregon,* Confederated Tribes of the Colville Reservation, Plaintiff-Intervener." *Law and Society Review* 38 (5):1181–229.

Gottlieb, Robert. 1993. *Forcing the Spring.* Washington, DC: Island.

———. 1988. *A Life of Its Own: The Politics and Power of Water.* New York: Harcourt Brace Jovanovich.

Gouldner, Alvin. 1950. "The Iron Law of Bureaucracy: Michels' Challenge to the Left." *Modern Review* (January).

Gray, Kenneth E. 1979. "NEPA: Waiting for the Other Shoe to Drop." *Chicago-Kent Law Review* 55 (2):361–82.

Green, Donald and Ian Shapiro. 1994. *Pathologies of Rational Choice.* New Haven, CT: Yale University Press.

Gressley, Gene M., ed. 1966. *The American West: A Reorientation.* Laramie: University of Wyoming Publications.

Gusfield, Joseph. 1955. "Social Structure and Moral Reform: A Study of the Women's Christian Temperance Union." *American Journal of Sociology* 61: 221–32.

Habermas, Jürgen. 1975. *Legitimation Crisis*, translated by Thomas McCarthy. Boston: Beacon Press.

———. 1973. "Reason and Decision: On Theory and Practice in Our Scientific Civilization." In *Theory and Practice*, translated by John Viertal. Boston: Beacon.

———. 1972 "Technology and Science as Ideology." In *From a Rational Society*, translated by Jeremy Shapiro. Boston: Beacon.

Hall, Stuart. 1992. "New Ethnicities." In *Race, Culture and Difference*, edited by J. Donald and A. Rattansi. London: Sage.

———. 1988. "The Toad in the Garden: Thatcherism among the Theorists." In *Marxism and the Interpretation of Culture*, edited by C. Nelson and L. Grossberg. Urbana: University of Illinois Press.

Hansen, Art, and Anthony Oliver-Smith, eds. 1982. *Involuntary Migration and Resettlement: The Problems and Responses of Dislocated People*. Boulder, CO: Westview Press.

Hays, Samuel P. 1980. *Conservation and the Gospel of Efficiency: The Progressive Conservation Movement, 1880–1920*. New York: Athenaeum.

Hechter, Michael. 1990. "Reading Denzin." *Rationality and Society* 2:501–2.

Hochschild, Arlie. 1983. *The Managed Heart: Commercialization of Human Feeling*. Berkeley: University of California Press.

Hopper, Joseph. 1993. "Oppositional Identities and Rhetoric in Divorce." *Qualitative Sociology* 16:133–56.

Horkheimer, Max. [1967] 1977. *Critique of Instrumental Reason*. New York: Continuum.

———. [1947] 1974. *Eclipse of Reason*. New York: Continuum.

Horkheimer, Max, and Theodore Adorno. [1944] 1972. *Dialectic of Enlightenment*, translated by John Cumming. New York: Seabury Press.

Hundley, Norris, Jr. 1986. "The West against Itself: The Colorado River—An Institutional History." In *New Courses for the Colorado River: Major Issues for the Next Century*, edited by Gary Weatherford and F. Lee Brown. Albuquerque: University of New Mexico Press.

———. 1975. *Water and the West: The Colorado River Compact and the Politics of Water in the American West*. Berkeley: University of California Press.

Hurley, S. L. 1989. *Natural Reasons*. New York: Cambridge University Press.

Ingram, Helen. 1990. *Water Politics: Continuity and Change*. Albuquerque: University of New Mexico Press.

Iverson, Peter. 1982. *Carlos Montezuma and the Changing World of American Indians*. Albuquerque: University of New Mexico Press.

Jaffe, Louis, 1968. *Administrative Law*. Boston: Little, Brown.

Jay, Martin. 1973. *The Dialectical Imagination: A History of the Frankfurt School and the Institute of Social Research, 1923–1950*. Boston: Little, Brown and Co.

Johnson, James. 1989. "Rational Choice and Culture: Skeptical Remarks on the 'Renaissance of Political Culture.'" Unpublished paper, Dept. of Political Science, Rochester University, Rochester, NY.

Johnson, Rich. 1977. *The Central Arizona Project, 1918–1968*. Tucson: University of Arizona Press.

Khera, Sigrid, ed. 1978. *The Yavapai of Fort McDowell.* Fort McDowell, AZ: Fort McDowell Indian Community.

Khera, Sigrid, and Patricia S. Mariella. 1982. "The Fort McDowell Yavapai: A Case of Long-Term Resistance to Relocation." In *Involuntary Migration and Resettlement: The Problems and Responses of Dislocated People,* edited by Art Hansen and Anthony Oliver-Smith. Boulder, CO: Westview Press.

Lamont, Michele. 1992. *Money, Morals, and Manners.* Chicago: University of Chicago Press.

Lawson, Michael L. 1994. *Dammed Indians: The Pick-Sloan Plan and the Missouri River Sioux, 1944–1980.* Norman: University of Oklahoma Press.

Layton, Edwin T. 1971. *The Revolt of the Engineers.* Cleveland: Case Western Reserve University Press.

Lazarus-Black, Mindie. 1994. *Legitimate Acts and Illegal Encounters.* Washington, DC: Smithsonian Institution.

Lear, Linda J. 1985. "Boulder Dam: A Crossroads in Natural Resource Policy." *Journal of the West* 24(4):82–93.

Leidner, Robin. 1993. *Fast Food, Fast Talk: Service Work and the Routinization of Everyday Life.* Berkeley: University of California Press.

Leveen, E. Philip. 1978. "Reclamation Policy at a Crossroads." *Public Affairs Report* 19: 1.

Levine, Donald. 1971. Introduction to *Georg Simmel: On Individuality and Social Forms,* edited by Donald N. Levine. Chicago: University of Chicago Press.

Levine, Noga Morag. 1994. "Between Choice and Sacrifice: Constructions of Community Consent in Reactive Air Pollution Regulation." *Law and Society Review* 28(5): 1035–77.

Lilly, William II, and Lewis L. Gould. 1966. "The Western Irrigation Movement, 1872–1902: A Reappraisal." In *The American West: A Reorientation,* edited by Gene M. Gressley. Laramie: University of Wyoming Publications.

Liroff, Richard A. 1976. *A National Policy for the Environment: NEPA and Its Aftermath.* Bloomington: Indiana University Press.

Lowi, Theodore. 1979. *The End of Liberalism.* New York: Norton.

Lukàcs, Georg. 1968. *History and Class Consciousness,* translated by Rodney Livingstone. Cambridge: MIT Press.

Mann, Dean E. 1963. *The Politics of Water in Arizona.* Tucson: University of Arizona Press.

March, James G. 1994. *A Primer on Decision Making.* New York: Free Press.

March, James G., and Johan Olsen. 1976. *Ambiguity and Choice in Organizations.* Bergen: Universssitetsforlayet.

March, James G., and Herbert A. Simon. 1958. *Organizations.* New York: Wiley.

Mariella, Patricia. 1983. "The Political Economy of Federal Resettlement Communities: The Fort McDowell Yavapai Case." Ph.D. diss., Department of Anthropology, Arizona State University, Tempe, AZ.

Mariella, Patricia and Violet Mitchell-Enos. 1996. "Yavapai." In *Native*

America in the Twentieth Century: An Encyclopedia, edited by Mary B. Davis. New York: Garland.

Marx, Karl. 1978. "Economic and Philosophical Manuscripts of 1844." In *The Marx-Engels Reader,* edited by Robert C. Tucker. New York: Norton.

———. 1977. *Capital.* Volume One. New York: Vintage Books.

McConnell, Grant. 1971. "The Environmental Movement: Ambiguities and Meanings." *Natural Resources Journal* 11(3):427–35.

———. 1966. *Private Power and American Democracy.* New York: Vintage Books.

McCool, Daniel. 1987. *Command of the Waters: Iron Triangles, Federal Water Development, and Indian Water.* Berkeley: University of California Press.

McPhee, John. 1970. *Encounters with the Archdruid.* New York: Farrar, Straus, and Giroux.

Mertz, Elizabeth. 1994. "Legal Loci and Places in the Heart: Community and Identity in Sociolegal Studies." *Law and Society Review* 28(5):971–92.

Messinger, Sheldon L. 1955. "Organizational Transformation: A Case Study of a Declining Social Movement." *American Sociological Review* 20 (Feb.): 3–10.

Meyer, John W. 1986. "Social Environments and Organizational Accounting." *Accounting, Organizations, and Society* 11:345–56.

Meyer, John W., and Brian Rowan. 1977. "Institutionalized Organizations: Formal Structure as Myth and Ceremony," *American Journal of Sociology* 83:340–63.

Michels, Robert. [1915] 1949. *Political Parties: A Sociological Study of the Oligarchical Tendencies of Modern Democracy.* Glencoe, IL: Free Press.

Minnow, Marthow. 1990. *Making All the Difference.* Ithaca: Cornell University Press.

Moore, Kelly. 1996. "Organizing Integrity: American Science and the Creation of Public Interest Organizations, 1955–1975." *American Journal of Sociology* 101(6):1592–627.

Morris, Aldon D. 1992. "Political Consciousness and Collective Action." In *Frontiers in Social Movement Theory,* edited by Aldon Morris and Carol McClurg Mueller. New Haven: Yale University Press.

Moss, Frank E. 1967. *The Water Crisis.* New York: Praeger.

Mukerji, Chandra. 1994. "The Political Mobilization of Nature in Seventeenth-Century French Formal Gardens." *Theory and Society* 23:651–77.

Nelson, Samuel B. 1963. "Snake-Colorado Project: A Plan to Transport Surplus Columbia River Basin Water to the Arid Pacific Southwest." City of Los Angeles, Department of Water and Power, October.

Nussbaum, Martha C. 1986. *The Fragility of Goodness: Luck and Ethics in Greek Tragedy and Philosophy.* New York: Cambridge University Press.

———. 1984. "Plato on Commensurability and Desire." *Proceedings of the Aristotelian Society* 58(Supp. Vol.):55–80.

Offe, Claus. 1985. "The Divergent Rationalities of Administrative Action." In *Disorganized Capitalism,* edited by John Keane. Cambridge, MA: MIT Press.

———. 1984. *The Contradictions of the Welfare State.* Cambridge, MA: MIT Press.

O'Sullivan, Michael J. 1982. "The Psychological Impact of the Threat of Relocation on the Fort McDowell Indian Community." Ph.D. diss., Department of Psychology, St. Louis University, St. Louis, MO.

Padgett, John. 1986. "Rationally Inaccessible Rationality." *Contemporary Sociology* 15:26–28.

Perrow, Charles. 1963. "Goals and Power Structures." In *The Hospital in Modern Society*, edited by Eliot Greidson. New York: Free Press.

———. 1961. "The Analysis of Goals in Complex Organizations." *American Sociological Review* 26:854–66.

Porter, Theodore. 1995. *Trust in Numbers: The Pursuit of Objectivity in Science and Public Life*. Princeton: Princeton University Press.

Portney, Paul R. 1994. "The Contingent Valuation Debate: Why Economists Should Care." *Journal of Economic Perspectives* 8(4):3–17.

Posner, Richard. 1992. *Sex and Reason*. Cambridge: Harvard University Press.

Rawls, John. 1971. *A Theory of Justice*. Oxford: Oxford University Press.

Raz, Joseph. 1986. *The Morality of Freedom*. Oxford University Press.

Reisner, Marc. 1986. *Cadillac Desert: The American West and Its Disappearing Water*. New York: Viking.

Robinson, Michael. 1979. *Water for the West*. Chicago: Public Works Historical Society.

Rodgers, William H., Jr. 1977. *Handbook on Environmental Law*. (2d ed.: 1994.) St. Paul, MN: West.

Roosevelt, Theodore. 1919. *Theodore Roosevelt: An Autobiography*. New York: Macmillan.

Rucker, Randal R., and Price Fishback. 1983. "The Federal Reclamation Program." In *Water Rights*, edited by Terry L. Anderson. Cambridge, MA: Ballinger.

Sahlins, Marshall. 1981. *Historical Metaphors and Mythical Realities: Structure in the Early History of the Sandwich Islands Kingdom*. Ann Arbor: University of Michigan Press.

Sarton, May. 1948. *The Lion and the Rose*. New York: Rinehart.

Schelling, Thomas C. 1986. "The Mind as a Consuming Organ." In *The Multiple Self*, edited by Jon Elster. New York: Cambridge University Press.

Schnaiberg, Allan. 1986. *The Environment: From Surplus to Scarcity*. Oxford: Oxford University Press.

Schnaiberg, Allan, and Kenneth Alan Gould. 1994. *Environment and Society: The Enduring Conflict*. New York: St. Martin's.

Schroeder, Albert. 1974. *Yavapai Indians*. New York: Garland.

Selznick, Philip. [1949] 1984. *TVA and the Grass Roots: A Study of Politics and Organization*. Berkeley: University of California Press.

———. 1957. *Leadership in Administration: A Sociological Interpretation*. Berkeley: University of California Press.

Sen, Amartya. 1990. "Rational Fools: A Critique of the Behavioral Foundations of Economic Theory." In *Beyond Self-Interest*, edited by Jane Mansbridge. Chicago: University of Chicago Press.

———. 1982. *Choice, Welfare, and Measurement*. Cambridge: MIT Press.

Shanks, Bernard. 1974. "The American Indian and Missouri River Water Developments," *Water Resources Bulletin* 10(3):573–59.

Sica, Alan. 1988. *Weber, Irrationality, and Social Order.* Berkeley: University of California Press.

Simmel, Georg. 1971. "The Problem of Sociology." In *Georg Simmel: On Individuality and Social Forms,* edited by Donald Levine. Chicago: University of Chicago Press.

Simon, Herbert. 1955. "A Behavioral Model of Rational Choice," *Quarterly Journal of Economics* 69:99–116.

———. 1945. *Administrative Behavior.* New York: Free Press.

Smart, J. J. C., and Bernard Williams. 1973. *Utilitarianism: For and Against.* New York: Cambridge University Press.

Smith, Dorothy E. (1982) "Textually Mediated Social Organization." *International Social Science Journal* 99:1–24.

Smythe, William. 1905. *The Conquest of Arid America.* Norwood, MA: Norwood Press.

Snow, David A., and Robert D. Benford. 1992. "Master Frames and Cycles of Protest." In *Frontiers in Social Movement Theory,* edited by Aldon Morris and Carol McClurg Mueller. New Haven: Yale University Press.

Snow, David A., E. Burke Rochford, Jr., Steven K. Worden, and Robert D. Benford. 1986. "Frame Alignment Processes, Micromobilization, and Movement Participation." *American Sociological Review* 51:464–81.

Spicer, Edward H. 1962. *Cycles of Conquest.* Tucson: University of Arizona Press.

Stegner, Wallace. 1954. *Beyond the Hundredth Meridian: John Wesley Powell and the Second Opening of the West.* Boston: Houghton Mifflin.

Steinbrunner, John D. 1974. *The Cybernetic Theory of Decision.* Princeton: Princeton University Press.

Stevens, Joseph E. 1988. *Hoover Dam: An American Adventure.* Norman: University of Oklahoma Press.

Stigler, George J., and Gary S. Becker. "De Gustibus Non Est Disputandum." *American Economic Review* 67(2):76–90.

Stinchcombe, Arthur L. 1990. "Comment." *Rationality and Society* 2(2):214–23.

———. 1978. *Theoretical Methods in Social History.* New York: Academic Press.

Stokey, E., and R. Zeckhauser. 1978. *A Primer for Policy Analysis.* New York: Norton.

Sunstein, Cass R. "Incommensurability and Valuation in Law." *Michigan Law Review* 92(4):779–861.

Swidler, Anne. 1986. "Culture in Action: Symbols and Strategies." *American Sociological Review* 51:273–86.

Taylor, Serge. 1984. *Making Bureaucracies Think.* Palo Alto: Stanford University Press.

Terrell, John Upton. 1965. *War for the Colorado River: The California-Arizona Controversy.* Glendale, CA: Arthur H. Clark.

Thompson, James D. 1967. *Organizations in Action.* New York: McGraw-Hill.

Thrapp, Dan L. 1967. *The Conquest of Apacheria.* Norman: University of Oklahoma Press.

———. 1964. *Al Sieber: Chief of Scouts.* Norman: University of Oklahoma Press.

Todorov, Tzvetan. 1982. *The Conquest of America,* translated by Richard Howard. New York: Harper & Row.

Tyler, Tom R. 1990. *Why People Obey the Law.* New Haven: Yale University Press.

———. 1988. "What Is Procedural Justice? Criteria Used by Citizens to Assess the Fairness of Legal Procedures." *Law and Society Review* 22: 301–55.

Vaughan, Diane. 1996. *The Challenger Launch Decision: Risky Technology, Culture, and Deviance at NASA.* Chicago: University of Chicago Press.

Ventresca, Marc. 1995. "When States Count: Institutional and Political Dynamics in Modern Census Establishments, 1800–1990." Ph.D. diss., Department of Sociology, Stanford University, Palo Alto, CA.

von Neumann, John, and Oscar Morgenstern. 1947. *Theory of Games and Economic Behavior.* Princeton: Princeton University Press.

Walton, John. 1992. "Making the Theoretical Case." In *What Is a Case? Exploring the Foundations of Social Inquiry,* edited by Charles Ragin and Howard S. Becker. New York: Cambridge University Press.

———. 1991. *Western Times and Water Wars: State, Culture and Rebellion in California.* Berkeley: University of California Press.

Warne, William E. 1973. *The Bureau of Reclamation.* New York: Praeger.

Waters, Frank. 1946. *The Colorado.* New York: Reinhart.

Weber, Max. 1988. *The Agrarian Sociology of Ancient Civilizations,* translated by R. I. Frank. London: Verso.

———. 1982. *General Economic History,* translated by Frank Y. Knight. New Brunswick, NJ: Transaction Books.

———. 1978. *Economy and Society,* edited by Guenther Roth and Claus Wittich. Berkeley: University of California Press.

———. 1976. *The Protestant Ethic and the Spirit of Capitalism,* translated by R. I. Frank. London: Verso.

———. 1946. *From Max Weber,* edited by H. H. Gerth and C. Wright Mills. New York: Oxford University Press.

Welsh, Frank. 1985. *How to Create a Water Crisis.* Boulder, CO: Johnson.

Williams, Bernard. 1985. *Ethics and the Limits of Philosophy.* Cambridge, MA: Harvard University Press.

Williamson, Oliver. 1975. *Markets and Hierarchies.* New York: Free Press.

Winchell, Dick Glenn. 1982. "Space and Place of the Yavapai." Ph.D. diss., Department of Geography, Arizona State University, Tempe, AZ.

Wittfogal, Karl. 1957. *Oriental Despotism: A Comparative Study of Total Power.* New Haven: Yale University Press.

Worster, Donald. 1992. "Hoover Dam: A Study in Domination." In *Under Western Skies: Nature and History in the American West.* New York: Oxford University Press.

———. 1985. *Rivers of Empire: Water, Aridity, and the Growth of the American West.* New York: Pantheon.

Zald, Mayer N., and Roberta Ash. 1966. "Social Movement Organizations: Growth, Decay, and Change." *Social Forces* 44(March):327–40.

Zald, Mayer N., and Patricia Denton. 1963. "From Evangelism to General

Service: The Transformation of the YMCA." *Administrative Science Quarterly* 8(September):214–34.

Zelizer, Viviana. 1994. *The Social Meaning of Money.* New York: Basic.

———. 1989. "The Social Meaning of Money: 'Special Monies.' " *American Journal of Sociology* 95(2):342–77.

———. 1985. *Pricing the Priceless Child.* New York: Basic.

Index